THE NEW FACE
OF GOVERNMENT

How Public Managers Are Forging
a New Approach to Governance

*Advancing excellence
in public service . . .*

American Society for Public Administration
Book Series on Public Administration & Public Policy

Evan M. Berman, Ph.D.
Editor-in-Chief

The Facilitative Leader in City Hall:
Reexamining the Scope and Contributions
by James H. Svara

Mission: Throughout its history, ASPA has sought to be true to its founding principles of promoting scholarship and professionalism within the public service. The ASPA Book Series on Public Administration and Public Policy publishes books that increase national and international interest for public administration and which discuss practical or cutting edge topics in engaging ways of interest to practitioners, policy-makers, and those concerned with bringing scholarship to the practice of public administration.

THE NEW FACE OF GOVERNMENT

How Public Managers Are Forging a New Approach to Governance

DAVID E. MCNABB

American Society for Public Administration
Series in Public Administration and Public Policy

CRC Press
Taylor & Francis Group
Boca Raton   London   New York

CRC Press is an imprint of the
Taylor & Francis Group, an **informa** business

CRC Press
Taylor & Francis Group
6000 Broken Sound Parkway NW, Suite 300
Boca Raton, FL 33487-2742

© 2009 by Taylor & Francis Group, LLC
CRC Press is an imprint of Taylor & Francis Group, an Informa business

International Standard Book Number-13: 978-1-4200-9387-2 (Hardcover)

Library of Congress Cataloging-in-Publication Data

McNabb, David E.
    The new face of government : how public managers are forging a new approach to governance / David E. McNabb.
        p. cm. -- (American Society for Public Administration series on Public administration and public policy)
    Includes bibliographical references and index.
    ISBN 978-1-4200-9387-2
    1. Public administration--Management. 2. Nonprofit organizations--Management. I. Tit¹ ² ³ ....

JF1351.M256 2009
351--dc22

Visit the Taylor & Francis Web site at
http://www.taylorandfrancis.com

and the CRC Press Web site at
http://www.crcpress.com

This book is dedicated to the thousands of public servants who every day demonstrate by example their dedication to the principles of good public management and commitment to the concept of true public service.

Contents

Preface

> The point is that usually we look at change but we do not see it. We speak of change, but we do not think about it. We say that change exists, that everything changes, that change is the very law of things. Yes, we say it and we repeat it; but those are only words, and we reason and philosophize as though change did not exist. In order to think about change and see it, there is a whole veil of prejudices to brush aside, some of them artificial, created by philosophical speculation, the others natural to common sense.

Henri Bergson (1946)*

This book is about the changes that elected and appointed leaders are making to the art and practice of governing, governance, and government. It is about how public managers are shaping and guiding governments' responses to a fundamental movement for change that began in the last decades of the twentieth century. The changes taking place over the last two decades in all levels of government have been, in a word, transformational; the administrative model of governance that guided public administrators for more than a century has been turned on its head, to be replaced by a new type of governing by new kinds of public managers (Rhodes 1997).

Actions to change the way government functions are global in scale and national, regional, and local in scope (Painter 2005). For example, more than 5,000 participants attended the 2005 Global Forum on Reinventing Government at Seoul, Korea (Kim et al. 2005). Although reforming governance became the primary theme of the forum, other major themes of the forum included:

- Sharing of other nations' experiences in reinventing government
- Promoting cooperation between government, business and industry, and nonprofit organizations in efforts to improve the quality of governance

---

* This reference and later references to William James (Chapter 5) and Ilya Prigogine (Chapter 9) are from Tsoukas and Chia (2002).

- Reviewing issues that pertain to achieving United Nations millennium development goals
- Identifying possible north-south and south-south cooperation and collaboration in national efforts to improve nations' capacity for participatory and transparent government
- Beginning groundwork for developing a global network for reinvention that includes representatives from all sectors and players in governance

In the new model of governance that emerged from the forum, government was just one of the many participants involved in governance. Depending on the level of government, other actors include the private sector; local, regional, and global social service organizations and other nongovernmental and faith-based organizations; and private citizens, working alone and in groups. The new model of governance envisioned at the forum is governance based on networks of individuals and organizations. Thus, in its new form, governance is defined as "the process of policy making through active and cohesive discussion among policy makers who are interconnected through a broad range of networks" (Kim et al. 2005).

The participants went beyond just identifying the new governance paradigm; they made *good* governance a central focus of the forum and a core concept of the new governance paradigm. Elements of good governance that were a part of the forum included: government reform and innovation, strengthening local government and regionalism, transparency in government, citizen participation and public–private partnerships, and responding to poverty and development through social integration.

Forging the New Model of Governance

The great change movement underway in government has made it possible for public managers to forge a new model of governance, one in which the exercise of authority is no longer top-down but across levels and sectors in coordinated, collaborative systems or networks of public, private, and nonprofit organizations, and for which authority is centralized (Bingham, Nabatchi, and O'Leary 2005; Kahler and Lake 2004; Nye and Donahue 2000; Sholz and Wang 2006). From this trend, the key point of research in public management is no longer the institution; it is, instead, the network. In addition to efficiency and effectiveness, the core concepts in this new model of governance have become coordination, collaboration, cooperation, and competition, with the salient concept being collaboration (Callahan 2007; Greasley and Stoker 2008; Feiock 2004; Heinrich, Hill, and Lynn 2004; Kamensky and Burlin 2005; Kettl 2002).

Some of the changes being made are the product of innovations in governance that have been created by members of the profession of governing. Much, but certainly not all, of that innovation is technological in nature. Other changes are organic; they deal with the new structural systems that governments are designing and organizing to increase their ability to respond to the needs of citizens while doing so with declining financial and human resources. And still other changes are being made in the nature of the work processes used by the men and women we entrust to deliver the government services we desire.

Some of these efforts to change the face of government are reactions to fundamental changes in the internal and external environment. But more are proactive, highly creative approaches to solving old problems while forging new solutions to new problems. Of course, there are a number of reasons why some of these innovations and transformational changes have failed and others will fail in the future. Sometimes there are few viable substitutes for existing ways of providing public services, e.g., air traffic control.

As reasons for these failures, the old charges of bureaucratic incompetence and resistance to change of any kind by a "bloated bureaucracy" are still aired by critics within and outside of government. However, much of that criticism can no longer be supported, as the examples shown in this book—and the hundreds of similar success stories that cannot be included because of limited space—will attest.

That does not mean that all the problems of governing have been solved, that all the ambiguities in policy making and administration have been resolved, or that the resistance and resentments of those who fear change of any kind have been dealt with. But it does mean that there is much hope for the future. The successes and failures shown here should illustrate this promise while also serving as guideposts for those public managers who find themselves faced with similar problems and new challenges.

This book describes some of the building blocks of this new face of government and the way it is reshaping the way managers govern. Yet, even as the pressures for reform in governance—or, to recall its earlier label, government reinvention—continue to grow, public managers are advised to heed the faint voice of caution:

> … improved performance is not the only measure of government effectiveness. Conformity with long-established rules of administration, the views of politically influential officials and groups, and expectations created by previous programs matter as well. Government is less a matter of invention or reinvention than of evolution and compromise (Lendowsky and Perry 2000, 306).

Acknowledgments

This and other books and papers could not have been written without the support and encouragement of my present and past, talented and knowledgeable management and administration colleagues at Pacific Lutheran University, at the Evergreen State College, and at the University of Maryland's University College overseas graduate programs, as well as the many fine leaders, managers, and administrators I have known in legislative bodies and government agencies. Throughout the research and writing process, those dedicated professionals gave freely of their time and encouragement and support to these efforts. They will always have my gratitude for the knowledge they have shared over the years. I also owe a large debt of gratitude to the many researchers and authors whose work I have referred to and adapted for this story of the big changes taking place in the face of government.

I am particularly indebted to Dr. Evan Berman, senior editor of *Public Performance and Management Review* and editor-in-chief of the ASPA Book Series in Public Administration and Public Policy for his unflagging encouragement during the preparation of the book. I wish to also thank Dr. Michael Novak, U.S. government senior research specialist and president of the federal government knowledge management working group, for his review and recommendations of an earlier version of the manuscript. I am grateful for the help and support of Taylor & Francis Group Senior Editor Ray O'Connell, who passed away before he could see the fruit of our labor. And I thank Jay Margolis and Sophie Kirkwood for their efforts at Taylor & Francis.

Much credit is also due to the editors and anonymous reviewers who helped make the book possible, and to the many authors whose work I have referenced in these pages. Finally, I wish to also extend special recognition to my recently retired friend and organizational studies colleague of more than 25 years, Professor Emeritus F. Thomas Sepic. It was his work in organizational studies that got me started in this exciting field.

The Author

After a career in business and government that has included positions as director of economic development for the City of Fullerton, California, and communications director for the majority caucus of the Washington State House of Representatives, David E. McNabb entered a second career in academia. He advanced to the rank of professor on the faculty at Pacific Lutheran University. He has a BA from California State College at Fullerton, an MA from the University of Washington, and a PhD from Oregon State University. He has taught a variety of public and private administration and management courses both in the United States and abroad, including college and university programs in Latvia, Bulgaria, Germany, the United Kingdom, Italy, France, and Belgium. He is the author of nearly 80 peer-reviewed conference papers and articles. This is his seventh book.

He has continued his service to the community, serving at different times as a member of the Seattle, Washington, Citizens' Advisory Committee on Solid Waste Management; the Kirkland, Washington, Central Business District Advisory Committee; and the Port of Tacoma, Washington, International Trade Association, among others. He has been a member of the Propeller Club and Rotary. He was a thesis advisor for the Evergreen State College MPA program, and remains a visiting faculty member. He is also a visiting professor at the Stockholm School of Economics-Riga. He continues to write and teach graduate and undergraduate courses in business and public administration.

List of Boxes

List of Figures

List of Tables

Chapter 1

Creating a New Face for Government

The challenge facing government administrators in the twenty-first century is that they can do their jobs by the book and still not get the job done. They can issue regulations as required by Congress and discover that the problems they were seeking to prevent occur nonetheless. They can audit taxes only to discover that they upset taxpayers when they get it right and enrage members of Congress when they get it wrong. They can produce programs that work better and cost less only to discover more demands that they work even harder and spend even less.... The challenge is to rewrite the book to get the job done.

Donald F. Kettl (2002)

Important changes taking place in the operating environment of government organizations have forced leaders in many nations to reshape the way they carry out their assigned tasks. Public administrators are developing new ways of managing their organizations and delivering their services to citizens; in the process, they are changing the face of government. And, these changes are occurring around the globe (Batley and Larbi 2004).

Government managers must now deliver services under a set of environmental conditions dramatically different from what they knew only a few years earlier. Among the pressures facing government managers are:

- Learning to cope after several decades of pressures to downsize, reorganize, reinvent themselves, and do more with less

1

- Delivering new and expanding services with declining resources for mainte-nance, repair, and replacement of decaying infrastructure
- Seamlessly integrating new technologies alongside aging systems and stove-pipe management architectures
- Dealing with discrepancies between personnel needs and available staff while capturing and disseminating knowledge being lost because of retiring workers
- Finding ways to form and structure new organizations—such as virtual orga-nizations and private–public-sector collaborative units

The Process of Change

The transformational change process in government organizations begins with recognition by senior agency or unit managers of an organizational or delivery problem that cannot be resolved with minor modifications to the existing system. Instead, a complete overhaul of the operating system, the organization's structure, and services delivery methods is called for.

The change process accelerates when an organization's leaders identify a need for a critical transformational change in order to cope with a crisis facing the orga-nization. Need recognition must occur for follow-on change initiatives to stand a chance of succeeding. The crisis must be powerful enough to shake the agency to its very roots.

A Federal Crisis Example

An example of such a crisis situation is the breakdown in management and coor-dination—and hence, effectiveness—when the Federal Emergency Management Agency (FEMA) was unable to cope as expected with the aftermath of devastation brought on by Hurricane Katrina (GAO 2007b). A 2007 review of the plan by the Department of Homeland Security (DHS) to ensure that emergency response workers can communicate with one another during an emergency revealed that agencies have been working on the problem of the lack of interoperability at least since 1983. Yet, as of 2007, not one federal standard had been adopted. Many stud-ies have sought to identify the cause for the administrative breakdowns in the gov-ernment's response to Katrina, but they all revolve around what Saundra Schneider (2005) called "cloudy mission and lack of focus."

There has been, however, no shortage of studies on nearly every aspect of the hurricane, the failure of the levies and subsequent flooding, and the successes and failures of federal, state, and local government administrators and agencies, and the many nonprofit agencies that became involved in the aftermath of the disaster (see Cigler 2007; Choi and Kim 2007; Col 2007; Comfort 2007; Derthick 2007; Donohue and O'Keefe 2007; Eikenberry, Arroyave, and Cooper 2007; Farazmand 2007; Garnett and Kouzmin 2007; Haeuser 2007; Jurkiewicz 2007; Lester and

Krejci 2007; Morris, Morris, and Jones 2007; Stivers 2007; O'Keefe 2007; Simo and Bies 2007; Von Heerden 2007; Waugh 2007).

The Government Accountability Office (GAO) reported that DHS is still urging local public safety agencies to purchase more-expensive radios that still may not be able to communicate with other systems. Further examples of transformation-driving crises include declining or accelerating demand for the agency's services, declining worker morale or discontent and disruption in the workplace, and the important force of legislative mandates for action. The radio interoperability program is one of two disaster management communications initiatives managed by the Department of Homeland Security: DisasterHelp.gov and SAFECOM (OMB 2007).

Once an alternative is selected, leadership must get everyone in the organization onboard the transformation train. This may be the most problematic of the entire process because of the need to initiate often far-reaching changes in the organizational culture. Implementation includes a variety of management tools for transforming an organization. These include team building, employee empowerment, cross training, reengineering or reorganizing, devolution, and other actions. The final step is full implementation of the desired changes.

An Emerging Crisis at the State and Local Levels

State tax and expenditure limitations in the face of rising wages and salaries of state and local workers, pension contributions, and huge investment in sorely needed infrastructure renewals are common woes heard in the halls of state and local governments. Compounding these difficulties is the fact that, if current trends continue, by 2020 the expenditures of state and local governments will exceed their ability to pay (GAO 2007e). As a result, state and local governments must soon make the tough choices in taxing and spending policy that the GAO called for.

As it is for the federal government, the growth in the costs of healthcare is the primary driver of the fiscal challenges facing state and local governments. Rising medical costs are having greatest impact in two service areas: Medicaid expenditures for needy citizens, and the rising cost of health insurance for state and local employees and retirees.

The Global Change Movement

Transformational change in government is a global movement that has been underway since the 1980s (Deming 1986). Common goals of this movement to transform government have been to bring about reductions in the cost and size of government—while at the same time improving the content and the delivery of government services. Professor Donald Kettl (2005) has identified six common characteristics in the movement:

1. Improving productivity in the public sector by reducing the number of government workers while providing additional services
2. Privatizing some services and implementing greater collaboration across agencies and levels of government to allow the market to bring about greater efficiencies
3. Focusing on improving customer services and agency responsiveness by making it easier for citizens to connect with government by expanding the number and variety of services delivered via the Internet and other e-government approaches
4. Decentralizing government by greater power sharing across levels of government and by giving front-line managers more decision-making power and responsibility
5. Restructuring the policy-making role of government by separating procurement of services from the delivery of services
6. Improving government accountability by initiating performance measurement, thereby placing greater emphasis on outputs rather than processes

These efforts to reshape government are not entirely new. Governments have been trying to find ways to transform their operations for years. A survey of ten years of the successes and failures of the reforms now underway in the United States, the United Kingdom, Australia, and New Zealand suggested that one reason for some of the failures might be because governments have placed too much emphasis on results and relatively little on managerial flexibility, or because they have adopted some elements of the New Public Management (NPM), but not all (Moynihan 2006).

The reform movement that has produced NPM and other new approaches to governance can be traced to the activities that began during the Progressive Era at the close of the nineteenth century. Those efforts were greatly expanded during the administration of President Franklin Roosevelt (Smith and Licari 2006). President Harry Truman established the Hoover Commission under former President Herbert Hoover, charging the members with the task of finding ways to improve the effectiveness and efficiency in the executive branch.

President Ronald Reagan established the Grace Commission, headed by businessman J. Peter Grace, for a similar purpose. Under President Bill Clinton and headed by Vice President Al Gore, the National Performance Review was established for the purposes of *reinventing* government by making it more businesslike (Beckett 2000).

President George W. Bush built on the Clinton-Gore effort with three broad management reform initiatives, not all of which were adopted: (a) the President's Management Agenda (PMA) in 2002; (b) a set of freedom-to-manage legislative proposals (the Freedom to Manage Act of 2001 and the Managerial Flexibility Act of 2001); and (c) the Program Assessment Rating Tool (PART), a 25-item questionnaire for measuring progress on program purpose and design, strategic planning, program management, and program results (Breul 2007). The purpose of these and related initiatives was to facilitate the transformation of government, improving its cost-effectiveness by implementation of management tools developed in the business sector.

There never will be a time when all the good work on a topic is done. Rather, changes and new advances are constantly occurring. During the writing of this book, for example, an administration change took place in the United Kingdom as Gordon Brown became prime minister, and the election to succeed George W. Bush was under way with Barack Obama becoming president. There is no guarantee that any successors would follow their predecessors in adopting the transformation initiatives discussed in this book, but the successes and failures still merit airing for others to follow or deny.

New Goals, New Strategies

According to political science professor Donald F. Kettl, the models of public administration that worked in the nineteenth and twentieth centuries can no longer meet the challenges of governing society in the twenty-first century. The environment of globalization and devolution of responsibilities within which governance must function has changed public administration such that new ways of governing must be found. The new model of governance has government located at the center of a complex, collaborative structure of private, public, nonprofit, foreign, and domestic organizations functioning together to do what government once attempted to accomplish on its own. Administration today focuses on coordination and cooperation amidst what Kettl calls "a hyperpluralistic background." Thus, the art and science of governance is undergoing a fundamental transformation.

Professor Kettl (2005) identified ten fundamental constructs that must be addressed when forging the strategies that will build the bridges needed to span the gap between the public administration that was and the public administration of the new century. Paraphrased, the ten strategic considerations or principles are:

1. The traditional concepts of a bureaucratic hierarchy and authority cannot be entirely replaced; rather, they must be recast to better reflect the requirements of the new model of governance.
2. Traditional hierarchical government agencies are increasingly surmounted by layers of complex networks of nongovernment organizations, thereby requiring the use of new ways of managing government functions.
3. Public administrators must develop and use more interpersonal skills along with, or sometimes in place of, their traditional authoritarian skills.
4. For this age, *information* is without question the fundamental component for implementing the transformation of governance.

5. Performance measurement, accountability, and performance-based management that transcend cross-organizational boundaries must be substituted for traditional organization-chart management structures.

6. Trust and confidence in government are possible only when government is transparent and available to all citizens; e-government is finally making this a reality.

7. Investing in human capital—providing existing workers with the new skills they need and hiring new people with the right skills for the complex and technical jobs of tomorrow—means reshaping civil service systems to reflect the realities of the transformed government workplace.

8. New strategies and tactics that engage public participation at ever-increasing levels must be devised and implemented.

9. The private and public collaborators and partners of government must be encouraged to accept greater civic responsibility—adopting the same ethos of public service that has characterized the best in public managers for centuries.

10. Because the transformation of governance is bringing new issues to old traditions and processes, new constitutional strategies must be devised for dealing with conflict between levels and constituencies.

Themes of Government in Transformation

Governments in the early years of the twenty-first century face many of the same challenges of operating in a vastly different world than existed just a few short decades or so ago. Public administrators must govern in a flatter, more globalized world (Friedman 2006); constituents expect better, more responsive performance while also demanding greater value for their tax dollars. Internally, Congress and the executive office are exerting pressure to reduce the cost of support functions and redirection of cost savings to the delivery of services (Kettl 2002). Government managers must learn to "think outside the box" and transform themselves in ways that make them better fitted to deliver high-quality services while managing operations in ways that make it possible to use scarce resources with the highest possible efficiency and effectiveness (EDS 2006). Four broad policy themes have come together to guide public managers in their efforts to reshape government at all levels (Berg 2006). Although many changes are occurring in the field of government management, these four broad policy themes are elements of a far-reaching, global movement calling for a complete transformation of government.

First, administrators are being required to transform the traditional maintenance model of public administration to a business-driven, *public management* approach to the governance of agencies and departments. The underlying goal of this movement is the transformation of all government organizations into high-performing learning operations. Second, governments must replace their legacy information technology (IT) systems (the *stovepipe, legacy,* or *silo* systems that were designed for a single use 20 or more years earlier) with next-generation systems that enable cross-functional and cross-agency collaboration across all government levels. Third, threatened with mass departures of baby boom–age government workers through retirement, governments are adopting strategic human resources plans and implementing comprehensive knowledge-management systems. Finally, increasing attention is being brought to the critical need to change the way governments deliver the services expected of them. An example of this recognition is the warning by the comptroller general of the United States, David M. Walker, that the U.S. federal government today is sitting on what he refers to (GAO 2000, 2007b) as a "burning platform" that will soon be a problem larger than the country can cope with.

These closely related themes are forcing elected and appointed public administrators across all government levels to formulate and implement change policies. Change in this instance means shifting from the traditional bureaucratic maintenance model of governance to a business-centered, customer-driven system that delivers public services in an increasingly efficient and effective manner. These services are increasingly being outsourced to private organizations under contract with government bodies at the federal, state, and local government levels. In short, government is becoming more collaborative than it has ever been in the past.

One little-researched facet of the trend toward greater collaboration is the role of special districts (Bowler and Donovan 2004). These special-purpose organizations are formed by state legislatures to provide a specific purpose, often services that at one time were provided by larger "full service" municipal governments (schools and libraries are examples). Because they have powers to tax, charge fees, issue debt, and appropriate land for public use, special districts can be a major contributor to successful collaborations.

Theme 1: The "New" Public Management

Governments and their sister organizations in the nonprofit sector are being pushed to move away from Industrial Age bureaucratic thinking and become more like the businesses they are supposed to serve, regulate, and/or augment. This process is the New Public Management (NPM), and it is facilitating a shift in public-sector focus from administering policy to managing resources (Osborne and Plastrik 1991). NPM, which has been transforming governance processes around the globe for more than two decades, has found its greatest acceptance in the English-speaking nations of New Zealand, Australia, Canada, the United Kingdom, and the United States. Such private-sector-developed processes as strategic planning, performance measurements, and program assessment are part of this approach.

Transparency is a key feature of the public management approach. To support this policy, President G. W. Bush signed the Federal Funding Accountability and Transparency Act on September 26, 2006. That act requires the Office of Management and Budget (OMB) to oversee the development of Web sites that the public can use to access information about grants and contracts with federal agencies (OMB 2007).

The government of New Zealand, among the first to adopt NPM approaches, had by 2007 taken the privatization process farther than other countries. Not everyone has considered NPM a welcome development, however. Because NPM focuses on greater effectiveness and efficiency, it has been accused of erasing the traditional "commitment to public service" aspect from careers in government. Also, some critics of the movement are saying that, like most management fads, NPM has run its course or will do so shortly. Disagreeing with the supposition that NPM is fading with the election of new officials and appointments of new administrators, Ewan Ferlie (2002) has argued that NPM will not simply fade away. Rather, it is a reflection of what he described as a "deeply rooted shift towards both a more management and market-like orientation ... within the public sector. As a result, there is a convergence with private-sector models of organization and management in some specific ways."

Guiding Change in the United States

The transformation policies implemented in government centers in the first decade of the twenty-first century have been guided by the broadly based management agenda program of enterprise transformation included in the G. W. Bush administration's 2002 President's Management Agenda (PMA). The objectives of the PMA were to make government more transparent, efficient, accountable, and accessible. The transformation process promoted by the PMA is being facilitated through five governmentwide initiatives, and the Office of Management and Budget (OMB) has been charged with managing the implementation of the initiatives in all agencies and departments of the federal government. In addition, many state and local governments have followed the federal government's lead in adopting similar transformation programs.

The PMA focuses on five governmentwide line-of-business areas, all of which impact management in government. The five governmentwide areas are: (a) strategic management of human capital, (b) competitive sourcing, (c) improved financial performance, (d) expanded electronic government, and (e) budget and performance integration (Figure 1.1).

One of the concerns of advocates of these private-sector-based changes is the question of whether the processes in the management agenda will continue under Presidenet Barack Obama.

Theme 2: Next-Generation Technology

The second theme shaping change policy is the drive to replace older legacy information and communications technology (IT) systems with next-generation systems

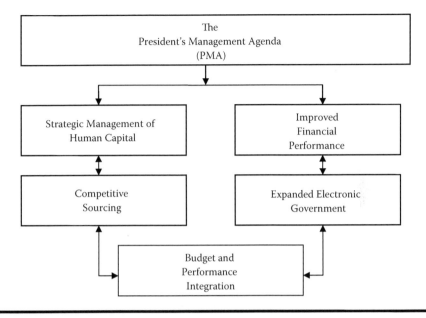

Figure 1.1   Management agenda initiatives. (*Source:* White House 2002.)

that enable cross-functional cooperation, collaboration, and access across all internal and external boundaries for the acquisition and sharing of information.

These older systems are referred to as *stovepipe* or *silo* systems; this name refers to the fact that they function independently, and only a limited number of users within the organization can access the database. They were originally installed as functional systems, designed to assist a single agency manage data for a single purpose. As such, other users cannot access the information and were forced to create their own single-purpose systems. Often, the systems were custom designed by in-house or contract suppliers using software languages they were familiar with, with no regard to standardization.

The problems associated with stovepipe systems exist across the full spectrum of federal, state, and local government agencies. As the terrorist attacks of September 11, 2001, and the aftermath of Hurricane Katrina revealed (GAO 2007b), this inability to communicate across databases and systems is of particular importance for emergency services. To facilitate better value for its IT investments—budgeted at $62.5 billion in 2007—government is requiring agencies to complete an enterprise architecture analysis before proceeding with the acquisition of replacement or new IT systems (Pulliam 2007). This amount represents a total increase of 7.1 percent over the 2005 budget and an 11 percent increase over the fiscal year (FY) 2004 budget.

Local government administrators are generally eager to adopt new technologies when they promise to improve public service and reduce department operating costs. The published evidence indicates that the process of adopting innovative information and communications technologies (ICT) are alive and well in state and local government, albeit perhaps not to the degree that they are accepted in the private sector.

Governments typically face fewer opportunities for implementing innovations in ICT than is the case for private-sector organizations. Governments provide intangible services that are typically produced as they are provided. This tends to restrict the number of innovative ways to supply the service. Moreover, governments must depend upon tax revenues and appropriations that have no direct connection to the labor expended or the perceived value of the service. They must also compete with other agencies for portions of an appropriations pie that is either finite or, more commonly, shrinking. As a result, much of the innovation in government has focused on introducing relatively minor, low-cost, and low-risk adjustments or gradual upgrades to existing services or processes (Altshuler and Behn 1997). Efforts to implement next-generation transformation of the nation's air transportation system are noted in Box 1.1.

Administrators have been less able to turn their attention to a policy of researching, planning, and implementing innovation at the more far-reaching, jurisdiction-wide, strategic level. Holley, Dufner, and Reed (2002), for example, found that only two of the 50 states—Utah and Washington—had begun statewide ICT-need evaluation and strategic information systems planning.

Box 1.1 Implementing Next-Generation Technology into the National Airspace System

The existing aviation system cannot be expanded to meet the problems caused by the increasingly overcrowded skies over the United States—more than 740 million passengers in FY 2006. Recognizing the need for transformation of the system, in 2003 Congress adopted public policy aimed at preventing the problems a failure of the system would create when it authorized establishment of the Joint Planning and Development Office (JPDO). JPDO is required to work with multiple federal agencies, including the departments of Transportation, Commerce, Defense, and Homeland Security; the Federal Aviation Administrations (FAA); the National Aeronautics and Space Administration (NASA); and the White House Office of Science and Technology to plan the transformation of the Next Generation Air Transportation System (NextGen). As of March 2007, JPDO and partners were finalizing key plans for operations and enterprise architecture.

Source: **Fleming (2007)**

Theme 3: A Focus on Human Capital and Knowledge Management

The third theme seen in this movement to shape the new face of government is a heightened focus on attracting, retaining, and empowering workers to replace the expected increases in the retirements of thousands of baby boom–generation government employees. Programs to retain, distribute, share, and archive the knowledge held by those departing workers is an important supplement to these activities. Together, these efforts are sometimes gathered under a strategic management emphasis that includes personnel issues and knowledge-management programs under the umbrella sobriquet "human capital." Thus, many federal, state, and local governments are developing and implementing strategic human-capital plans and programs with comprehensive knowledge-management systems in their efforts to ensure that the right numbers and skill mix of workers are on hand to carry out their critical missions. Not surprisingly, the success of these programs depends in large part upon the application of ICT capabilities.

This theme of human capital and knowledge management in public management is often addressed in efforts to bring about a "transformation of public service." Furthermore, the emphasis on implementing changes in the way public servants provide public services is not restricted to just the United States; governments around the globe are working to develop plans and programs to meet the challenges they face in the new century (see, for example, Abramson 1996; Skweyiya 1997; Alford 2002; Department of Finance Canada 2005).

Theme 4: Enterprise Transformation Policy

Theme four—transformational change of government—is the overarching process that makes all other changes possible. The GAO's objective of this drive is "to create a more positive future by maximizing value and mitigating risk within current and expected resources levels" (Walker 2007b). Fundamentally, this means getting control of the government's huge budget deficits and making every dollar spent return the highest possible value.

The government faces huge challenges as it seeks to find a way to change its fiscal policy. It must also change a foreign policy that seems to have focused more on making enemies than friends. Government also faces sustainability challenges in education, social security, healthcare, energy, the environment, immigration, and the war on terrorism. Thus, all branches of government are being pushed to transform their practices and processes to enable greater transparency, accountability, and citizen accessibility in all government activities. Transformation is not only making government more accessible and accountable, it is changing the very nature of work in government agencies.

The GAO has identified five ways in which the federal government must change; these same change principles apply to state and local government agencies as well. For government to achieve the changes it must make, agencies must:

1. Become less hierarchical, process-oriented, "stovepiped," and inwardly focused
2. Become more partnership-focused, results-oriented, integrated, and attentive to their citizen customers
3. Achieve a better balance between a focus on results, on customers, and employees
4. Collaborate with other government organizations, nongovernment organizations, and private-sector organizations, both at home and internationally
5. Focus on maximizing value, managing risk, and enhancing responsiveness within its current and expected resource levels

If the transformation of government practices, procedures, and methods is to occur as desired, both the legislative and executive branches must adopt a policy that embraces the idea that change is not only welcome, it is absolutely necessary. John P. Kotter, a leading proponent of change in organizations, spelled out the requirement for organizations to learn to cope with change in his book, *Leading Change* (1996). He noted that the amount of "significant, often traumatic change in organizations has grown tremendously" during the 1980s and 1990s, and that it was not only likely to continue, but to grow in intensity and scope.

Kotter was also quick to recognize that there is a downside to change; not everyone in organizations undergoing change will benefit from the process, and pain is inevitable. However, the change process can be less painful if the leadership of an agency considering a change follows a few simple steps, the first of which is recognizing that the organization is, in some way, in deep trouble—facing a crisis—and must undergo a fundamental change in order to survive.

The crisis must be recognized by all senior administrators and be great enough to send a message that a change is absolutely necessary. Interested parties then come together to formulate a policy of transformation and to hammer out a strategy for implementing the policy. In government, the parties include the legislative and executive branches, appropriate agency leadership, and representatives from relevant constituencies. If they agree on a policy, they can then formalize it by putting it into law. Once it becomes the law of the land, the policy can then be turned over to the professional administrative staff for implementation.

Summary

This chapter began with a review of some of the changes in the operating climate of governments and the actions that public managers are making in response to those environmental pressures. There are several environmental trends shaping the new face of government. In response to these trends, governments are changing to:

- Better cope after several decades of pressure to downsize, reorganize, reinvent themselves, and do more with less
- Deliver new and expanding services with declining resources and, in many cases, decaying infrastructure
- Integrate new technologies and management structures and architectures
- Adjust to discrepancies between personnel needs and available staff
- Capture and disseminate knowledge that would otherwise be lost because of an aging and shrinking workforce

To meet these challenges, public managers are finding ways to form and structure a new governance model, one that includes cooperative arrangements and networks, virtual organizations, and public-public, public and nonprofit, and public–private-sector collaborative networks.

The chapter also introduced some of the key elements that are driving the accelerated pace of changes now taking place in governments. It also discussed four closely related trends in government transformation: changes in the way government is structured and functions; an emphasis on performance analysis and reporting; improvements in the delivery of services; and greater collaboration among same-level and across-level agencies.

Chapter 2

The Shape and Scope of Changes in Government

> In order for government to fulfill its role, it must continually transform itself within the boundaries of the Constitution to deliver on its mission within an environment that is more and more uncertain.
>
> **NASCIO (2007a)**

Pity our poor public servants. They are being bombarded from all corners with calls to change what they do, change the way they work, stop wasting the taxpayers' money, and do a better job of providing citizens all the services they want, when and where they want them. On the one hand, they hear talk about the "bloated bureaucracy"; on the other, they are told they must hire more people to replace the thousands of government workers who are ready to retire.

Demand for reform of public management has become a call with which public managers at all levels of government are very familiar. They are besieged with calls by elected officials, candidates for public office, senior executive branch officials, members of public and private organizations lobbying for their interests, and by private citizens who see that changing the way governments operate is the solution to a host of public ills. On the one hand, the manager is told that wasting the taxpayers' dollars must stop; on the other hand, the public manager is told to do more with less. A cry heard around the globe is that government must change. In the jargon of the day, this change has become *transformation*, and the process through which the changes occur has been formalized as *enterprise transformation*. It is changing the face of government at the federal, state, and local levels. Figure 2.1 is a model of some of the forces involved in shaping the organizational transformation

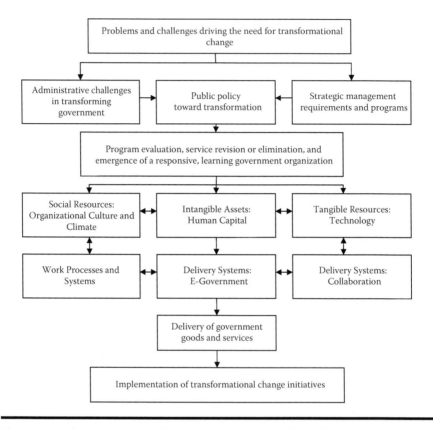

Figure 2.1   Elements involved in the process of transformation.

process. This chapter describes three approaches to implementing a transformation: the Sandia National Laboratories approach, a four-level transformation model that focuses on identifying a transformation trigger, and an eight-factor public management model.

A Need for Transformation

Testifying before the congressional subcommittee on the federal workforce and agency organization in 2006, U.S. comptroller general David M. Walker warned that if changes were not made soon in the way the U.S. federal government acquires and uses its resources, government revenues would be able to do little more than meet interest payments on the national debt.

Walker identified a list of issue areas that needed to be addressed: homeland security threats, increasing global interdependence, the shifting economy, increasing diversity and aging of the population, rapid scientific and technological change, growing concern for the quality of life, and an evolving structure of government (GAO 2005b). These are among the salient forces in the environment of government that are forcing administrators onto the path of transformation.

Globally, the transformation of the U.S. federal government has been quietly underway for more than 20 years. The first widespread public sign of the drive to transform government in the United States began in the early 1990s. In 1990, 14 federal programs were placed on a "high-risk" list issued by the federal Government Accountability Office (GAO). Since that first report, 33 additional programs have been added; 18 have been removed; 2 have been combined; and 3 were added in 2007 (GAO 2007a).

Initially, high-risk operations were identified because of their susceptibility to fraud, waste, abuse, and mismanagement. Thus, leading the 1990 list were such areas as the Medicare Program, Defense Department supply chain management, weapon systems acquisition, and contract management. Additional Defense Department programs were added in 1992, 1997, and 2005. As the GAO program expanded, the basis for a high-risk designation was expanded to include areas where transformations were needed to achieve greater economy, efficiency, effectiveness, accountability, and sustainability of key government programs. Current designations are directed by GAO guidelines issued in 2000. Before a program can be added to the high-risk list and be targeted for transformation, GAO must determine that at least $1 billion is at risk. This can be in such areas as impaired assets; failure to realize expected revenue; major assets lost, stolen, damaged, wasted, or underutilized; improper payments; or other similar liabilities.

An executive-branch plan for facilitating faster movement on these needed transformations—the President's Management Agenda (PMA)—was established in 2002. Like the Reinventing Government plan introduced during the Clinton-Gore administration a decade earlier, the PMA called for dramatic and immediate steps to be taken for transforming the way that government is structured and operates. The Executive Office report detailing the PMA began with the following call to action (OMB 2002):

> The need for reform is urgent. The General Accounting Office (GAO) "high risk" list identifies areas throughout the federal government that are most vulnerable to fraud, waste, and abuse. Ten years ago, the GAO found eight such areas. Today, it lists 22. Perhaps as significant, government programs too often deliver inadequate service at excessive cost.... New programs are frequently created with little review or assessment of the already-existing programs to address the same perceived problems. Over time, numerous programs with overlapping missions and competing agendas grow up along side [*sic*] one another—wasting money and baffling citizens.

Change at the Sandia National Laboratories

In a study to establish the applicability of private-sector experience with enterprise transformation for the nation's Nuclear Weapons Complex (NWC), researchers at Sandia National Laboratories conducted a survey of concepts and processes involved in enterprise transformation in government agencies and private industry (Slavin and Woodard 2006). The researchers found significant commonality between the NWC and private industry in most of the key concepts in transformation. They determined that the NWC, like a business enterprise, has customers and other key stakeholders. Because these customers have their own transactions with the NWC for products, policies, and procedures, they have different expectations and values that the NWC must address. Moreover, they are able to influence federal funding for the NWC.

Slavin and Woodard (2006) saw the following common premise underlying transformations in both sectors: "For organizations facing a significant crisis, successful transformations can be characterized by an effective leader and a supporting coalition:

- Convincing their organization that success depends on changing the way it does business,
- Conceiving a new organizational paradigm to bring about this change,
- Leading the organization down the path to the new paradigm, and utilizing metrics to guide the necessary change."

The following conclusion from the Sandia National Laboratory study on enterprise transformation serves to bring the dangers that managers and administrators face when attempting to impose a transformational change into their organizations (Slavin and Woodard 2006, 23):

> We close with a caution and a challenge. Transformation has many elements, and the failure of any one can doom the entire process. Research shows that most transformations fall short of their desired goals, with many failing outright. Thus, if confronted with the need to transform, the organization and its leadership must be steeled for an arduous process that has bested many capable people and worthy organizations. As such, successfully transforming, and thereby maintaining relevance and securing continued existence, is one of the highest challenges to which an organization and its leadership can aspire.

Five Important Change Success Factors

From their extensive review of the transformation literature, case analyses, and interviews with private-sector managers, the Sandia team found that success of the transformation process is constructed around five key factors:

1. Effective, fully committed leadership that extends beyond just the top leaders
2. Organizationwide acceptance of the idea that a crisis looms for the organization and an agreed-upon sense of urgency for resolution of the crisis before it destroys the organization
3. A common vision of what the transformed organization will be like in the near- to long-term future (five to ten years) and development of the strategic plans that will guide the organization to achieving the goal
4. The resources and will to make the tough choices necessary for successful implementation (execution) of the actions and activities spelled out in the strategic transformation plan
5. Identifying and applying the appropriate goal-achievement measurements (metrics), including progress measurements from the first common description of the crisis at hand, through agreeing upon the ultimate vision and the plans needed to move the organization along the path of transformation, and ultimately to implementation of the planned transformational changes.

It is important to recognize that this is not the end of the process. Organizations are constantly in flux; changes will occur and must be allowed to occur. Each of the core success factors are discussed in greater detail in the following subsections.

Factor One: The Need for Leadership

Slavin and Woodard (2006) are adamant in their opinions on the critical need for effective leadership and go so far to conclude that, without it, the remaining elements of the transformation effort will fail. This means that the transformation program must never be delegated to an outside consultant; doing so almost always leads to failure. This does not mean that consultants should not be involved. Rather, it means that they should not be in charge. They can be of inestimable help in such activities as surveying attitudes and opinions. Consultants recommend actions based on their interpretation of events; they have neither the power nor the authority to make the hard choices, allocate or withhold the appropriate resources, or break down the barriers that result from vested interests in the status quo.

It is impossible, of course, for a strong, capable leader guiding the change initiative to carry out all the tasks necessary to achieve transformation of an organization; he or she must have the support of a strong, fully committed coalition of middle and upper managers. This usually begins with a small core team at the initial phases of the transformation process, but often expands to many committed supporters as the process moves forward. Moreover, these champions must be managers of the line functions of the organization, not just the support staff. Eventually, the support team may also include members from other internal and external stakeholder groups. Brenda Cammarano (2004, 9) of IBM had this to say about the importance of leadership in the management team:

Initiating and managing an Enterprise Transformation project is by no means for the faint of heart. Rather, this is effort requiring dedication, discipline, and a cohesive Enterprise Transformation team. The team must be willing to pioneer through the ... [crisis identification and planning] phases to establish the state of the enterprise and map out a strategy for its transformation. Once these phases are complete, the team can then enter the [implementation] phases, where the plan is executed and finally transitioned into ... operations.

Factor Two: Recognition of a Crisis and Its Urgency

Disequilibrium in an organization does not occur without some justification; there is always a reason for the real or impending crisis. Leadership's role is to thoroughly identify the cause so that everyone in the organization understands what factors are behind the crisis—and the penalty of inaction. These causes or drivers can occur from inside or outside of the organization, or both. They provide two possible internal drives of the disequilibrium: relevance and viability. Relevance refers to the degree to which the organization's business model matches the values desired by its client or customer base and is, at the same time, distinguishable from other services and other providers. Viability suggests a measure of the sustainability of the business model and of the strengths and weaknesses of the organization, its structure, leadership, resources, and skills as well as management's acceptance of risk and uncertainty.

Disequilibrium in an organization's culture is often a driver of a crisis (Greif and Laitin 2004). Changes in an organization must have an external origin; no one in the organization has an incentive to deviate from the normal or approved behavior. The unwillingness of managers or staff to accept change is often rooted in a culture of inertia and bureaucratic thinking. Failure or inability of an agency's management or staff to adapt to changed conditions can also bring on a crisis. Agencies often discover that they are in need of a transformation simply because the way they operated in the past—regardless of how successfully—is no longer effective. However, because of those past successes, they are loath to change. The old saw, "If it ain't broke, don't fix it," has been the cause of too many crises in organizations. It should be replaced with, "If it ain't broke, fix it anyway!" The desired transformation is not going to happen unless the organization's workers believe that the problem is real and that the proposed solution strategy will be effective. Only then can they integrate the new way of operating into the organization's culture.

External causes of an organizational crisis can spring from any of the uncontrollable factors that result in threats to or constraints of the organization's operations. For example, a crisis in a government organization can be sparked by the threat of an across-the-board reduction in the federal budget, failure by the legislative arm to provide promised appropriations, real or threatened reductions in staffing levels for any reason, shift of political leadership with a commensurate shift in public-policy direction, war, natural disasters, recession, and any number of similar uncontrollable factors.

Factor Three: Developing a "Must Be" Vision

Gaining staff agreement on a "must be" vision statement is an integral early step in all strategic management programs. The "must be" vision is senior leadership's view of how and what the organization will be at some unspecified time in the future, and it often includes a statement of what the organization values (such as honesty, superior customer service, fastest possible response time, etc.). However, the vision in the transformation process is not the same as the vision in the strategic plan, although they are similar in many ways. An organization's transformational vision begins with a description of what the organization must accomplish in order to deal effectively with the crisis. The goal is a target that everyone in the agency can support, and the transformation strategy consists of a specific plan of action to achieve that goal. The strategic plan must begin with a clearly identified understanding of what events or threats led to the crisis and then state what needs to be done—often with a timeline—in order to bring about the organization's desired new, or transformed, state.

Factor Four: Applying the Necessary Resources and Will to Succeed

The actions spelled out in a transformation initiative will not happen unless they are *made* to happen by management and staff. Everyone has heard the saying that every journey begins with a first step. The same is true for a transformation journey. People in the organization must feel a sense of urgency and agree that change is absolutely necessary for the organization to survive. Simply mandating tasks and activities from the top levels of the organization seldom results in staff commitment to the cause. Slavin and Woodard (2006, 16) refer to this as instilling in everyone acceptance of a "change or die!" attitude, adding that:

> Leadership must link crisis urgency to hope provided by the vision. Researchers have observed that a crisis environment can create fear and panic, which, by themselves, drive out the optimism necessary for successful transformation. To combat this, as leadership beats the drum of crisis, it must also highlight its vision as the means for tackling the crisis.

Senior management begins by working with team leaders to identify appropriate objectives and performance measurements. Allocating resources, assigning responsibilities and authority, identifying progress goals and objectives, and establishing performance appraisals are integral to this phase. Individuals, teams, groups, and operational units must be the ones to determine how the transformation strategy—which is just a description of what is going to be done to resolve the crisis—will be implemented.

Transformation actions should be limited, with key elements selected for implementation first, and follow-on steps held until the earlier actions are integrated into the organization's culture. The Sandia Laboratories management team, for example, warned that a transformation initiative should not demand more than the people in the organization could accomplish. That is, the initiative should not force the people responsible for implementing the transformation to bite off more than they can chew.

Factor Five: Selecting Appropriate Performance Metrics

Experienced agency administrators know that no single measurement can provide the information they need to determine the progress of each of the various processes involved in a transformation. Just as the punishment must fit the crime, the measurement must fit the people, place, and time. Metrics are application specific, and they must make sense to the people for whom they are applied.

Slavin and Woodard suggest using a number of different measurements rather than a single metric. They recommend such tools as the Kaplan and Norton "balanced scorecard" (1992) and "strategy map" (2000) in both the transformation-strategy development and the performance-measurement phases of a transformation. The balance scorecard identifies the metrics needed to develop a transformation strategy. It also offers a way of measuring the organization's activities in relation to the vision and strategies developed earlier in the transformation process.

The key to the balance-scorecard process is that it does not simply focus on financial outcomes. Rather, it also considers the human issues that enable those outcomes. These human activities are often referred to as the "drivers of success." Thus, organizational leadership is able to focus on the future and take actions that affect the future of the organization by adopting the financial side of the organization's activities as well as client/customer, process, and staff activities.

The balanced-scorecard approach includes a number of tools for designing and implementing strategies, among which are a strategic map, measurements that relate specifically to the change strategies, and initiatives that focus on achieving the planned strategic objective. The strategic map places strategic objectives in one of four balance perspectives: financial, client/customer, internal business processes, and learning and growth (Inamdar et al. 2000). In public and nonprofit organizations, mission-oriented objectives are substituted for financial objectives, and the client/customer (e.g., citizen, beneficiary) perspective becomes the highest level of outcome measurement. Using a balance between short- and long-term objectives, performance metrics are designed to monitor progress in each of these perspectives. It is important to remember, however, that most partnerships between public and nonprofit services tend to be highly informal. The partnerships are often led by government agencies, with the nonprofits providing only weak collaboration, little shared authority, and marginal support (Gazley 2008; Teisman and Klijn 2002). Among the reasons why nonprofits provide only weak support for partnerships with government agencies is the complexity of the tax systems as well as the extensive and often-confusing government regulations under which they must operate (Berry 2005).

Changing the Face of Government

In the last years of the first decade of the twenty-first century, the United States faces a range of sustainability challenges that need urgent attention. In its triennial updating of its strategic plan, GAO identified seven key sustainability challenges (Table 2.1). These challenges occur in such diverse areas as government financing, homeland security, defense and the war in Iraq, immigration, education, energy, foreign policy, the environment, healthcare, and the nation's aging infrastructure (GAO 2007c).

In transmitting the updated plan to Congress, Comptroller General David M. Walker warned that to deal with these and other challenges, the government and the country at large will need to reexamine what it does in the world, how it does business, and with whom it does business. Moreover, the task will require partnering with all levels of government, the private sector, and nonprofit organizations. Addressing this issue of transformation, Walker (GAO 2007c, 3) added:

> If our nation is to be prepared for the challenges and changes that are coming, government transformation is essential. Nothing less than a top-to-bottom review of federal programs and policies is needed to determine if they are meeting their objectives.... Such a transformation requires leadership by elected and public officials that is dedicated, courageous, creative, committed, constructive, cooperative, and stewardship oriented.... Appointed and career officials at every federal agency and program need to give careful thought to their missions and operations in light of current trends and future realities.

Walker also addressed the public-policy formulation process, calling for a redesign of the policy process to better support policy makers as they reexamine federal programs, update budget priorities, and review commitments and entitlements. Congress and the president must determine which policies and programs are to remain priorities, and which can be overhauled or removed.

Table 2.1 Challenges, Themes, and Issues Facing the U.S. Government

Themes	Challenges and Issues
Threats to national security	Terrorism; growing instability, rogue nations, failed states, and nuclear proliferation; border and port security; transnational and violent crime; natural disasters; infectious diseases and public health
Sustainability concerns	Fiscal deficits and debt burdens; healthcare quality, access, and costs; defense and homeland security strategies; social security commitments; tax gaps; energy, environment, and resource protection; food and water resources
Economic growth and competitiveness	Education, skills, and knowledge; immigration; tax policy; regulatory policy; saving and investment; innovation and change management
Recognizing global interdependency	Trade; capital markets; information; transportation
Adapting to demographic and social changes	Aging and life spans; dependency ratios; demographic diversity; income distribution gaps; changes in social behaviors
Maintaining citizens' quality of life	Retirement security; employment; work and family; urbanization and sprawl; housing
Managing advances in science and technology	Productivity and economic growth; information and communications technology; cybersecurity and personal privacy; data quality and reliability; space exploration; humanity and ethics; elections and citizens' involvement

Source: GAO (2007c).

Four Levels in the Transformation Process

There are four levels in the transformation process:

1. A crisis triggers recognition of a needed change. An example is a state of *disequilibrium* in an organization that triggers a need for transformation. (A survey instrument to help in diagnosing disequilibrium in organizations

is included in Appendix A, together with a report on its application in a public-safety organization.)

2. Agency managers must select a transformation strategy to alleviate the disequilibrium.
3. The agency leadership must adopt a distinctive perspective to follow in the transformation process.
4. The leadership must focus the transformation action on the appropriate level of agency work outcome.

These levels and their respective processes are illustrated in Figure 2.2.

Level I: Identifying and Assessing a Transformation Trigger

Many forces for change confront contemporary administrators in government organizations and agencies. Forces for change are rooted in today's distinctly altered economic, administrative, and social environments. Included are such factors as the new model for economic activity, including e-government, deregulation, and privatization of once-public services and functions. For public agencies, some of the factors that are exerting pressure for change include leaner departmental budgets

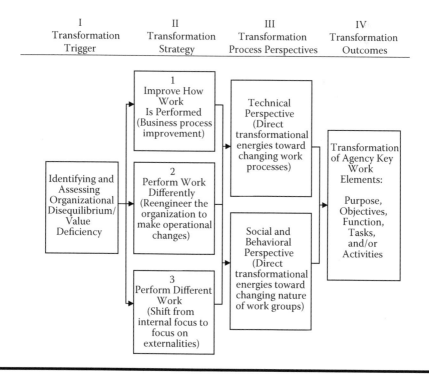

Figure 2.2   Levels of enterprise transformation.

caused by competition for shares of diminishing tax revenues, scarcity of skilled workers, and heightened demands for environmental accountability.

Public-safety agencies have not been protected from these pressures. If anything, the threats of terrorist activity and the additional services mandated by Congress, together with increasing needs to cope with environmental disasters, have made the problem even greater for local public-safety agencies. A growing gap exists between rising demand for police services and limited resources in many departments. This, in turn is resulting in higher turnover, difficulty in recruiting new candidates, and job-related stress. The hardest-hit departments have suffered from a condition called "general service default," where government can no longer deliver the services that enhance or protect the life of its citizens (Levine 1988).

Another force for change includes increasing diversity among constituents, with its commensurate change in new client and customer expectations, needs, and wants. This diversity springs from the dramatic shifts that have occurred in the demographic makeup in the nation's workplace and, indeed, in society at large. The compelling need for organizational transformation has created a simultaneous requirement for shifts in the way strategy—and policy—is implemented in the organization. The once-stable economic and social environments that fostered old but tried-and-true ways of doing things have been rendered inadequate by this new paradigm (Cappelli et al. 1997).

Level II: Evaluating and Improving Work Processes

The second level involves identifying areas in the agency or work processes in critical need of reform (transformation). These represent the points of disequilibrium or *value discrepancy* in an organization's operations. For example, in 2004, the U.S. government identified 12 operational areas in critical need of transformation. Once identified, an in-depth analysis of the area and its antecedents is required. GAO proposed five broad classes of investigation and sample questions for analysis in each of the 12 operational areas.

A transformation process can be directed at four different work-activity constructs in the targeted organizational area: The first involves strategies aimed at *improving* the way work is done in the organization. These are called *business process improvement* strategies. Although they may, indeed, improve efficiency, these strategies are least likely to bring about a lasting transformation in the agency or department.

The second body of transformation strategies involves changing the flow of work through an organization. These *organization reengineering* strategies are designed to implement dramatic operational changes. Without extensive and lasting changes in the way the organization does its work, these strategies may generate a transformation, but one that is typically far less than the transformation generated by the next group of strategies.

The third group of transformational strategies includes those designed to completely change the work that the organization performs. These are *organizational culture strategies*; they are designed to transform agencies from traditional, internally focused bureaucratic organizations to client/customer-focused, high-performance, and cost-effective organizations.

The fourth level of transformation strategies refers to the specific characteristics of the agency's work that are engaged in the transformation process. Five such characteristics have been identified: purposes, objectives, function, tasks, and activities (Champy 1995; Rouse and Baba 2006).

It is widely recognized that every organization has its own distinctive *culture*. This is true for organizations in the public as well as the private sector. *Organizational culture* refers to the patterns of learned beliefs, values, and behavior that are distinctive in each individual organization. *Culture* has also been defined as a system of shared values that are exhibited through the organization's different cultural artifacts (Peters and Waterman 1982). Schein (1985) and Wilson (1989) define culture as the shared beliefs, values, and assumptions of the members of a specific group or organization.

Culture may, of course, be a positive force for transformation in an organization, or it may be a negative force that contributes to greater and greater disintegration of the organization. Good or bad, the culture of an organization is what binds it together. It is also what differentiates it from other groups either in time or in space. Cultures are not the same thing as organizational structures; rather, they are real systems of thought that express the belief system of the people within the organization (Vasu, Stewart, and Garson 1998).

One of the reasons why transformation can be so problematic is that organizational change involves altering these behavior patterns and belief systems. Organizational transformation cannot take place without organizationwide concurrence that the organization is floundering, and that change of some kind is needed if the organization is to survive. This sense of the organization's floundering, of its failure to attain desirable goals, can be described as a state of *organizational disequilibrium*.

Disequilibrium is evidenced by such symptoms as deteriorating staff morale, supervisors and managers questioning whether the organization can survive under existing strategies, and by increasing demands for autonomy by highly skilled, technical staff members. These symptoms do not identify the underlying cause. Only diagnostic assessments can ferret out the root cause of such problems. Unfortunately, assessments alone cannot bring about a transformation of the organization. They are only a means for identifying problem areas and for planning subsequent transformation actions.

The literature of organizational change clearly reveals that transformation initiatives are not always successful. When administrators fail to involve the entire organization in the process of acknowledgment, diagnoses, and transformation, little long-term gain is achieved. Without a total commitment to change, the transformation attempt may either reinforce disequilibrium in the organization or result only in cosmetic change or short-term gains. A study on changes in the nature of work and work organization sponsored by the National Planning Association (Cappelli et al. 1997, 53–54) contained this caveat:

> [Transformation] actions taken singly, research studies suggest, tend to achieve few enduring gains. In the absence of a broader plan [for example] downsizing the workforce may generate short-term cost savings, but often at the expense of long-term cost increases.... Introduction of [TQM] or reforming into strategic business units without a host of associated changes may yield little enduring gain. Studies of the introduction of new information technologies, lean manufacturing methods, and employee stock ownership plans, for example, reveal that alterations in each of these areas without parallel changes in the culture, compensation, and reporting structure of the company tend to leave the intended effects largely stillborn.

Level III: Embracing Appropriate Transformation Perspectives

The third level in enterprise transformation is selecting the appropriate transformation perspectives. These are the philosophical underpinnings of change initiatives, and they serve as approaches to framing the planned change to fit into the technical and human aspects of the change.

The Social and Behavioral Perspective in Transformation

This perspective centers on changing the nature of work. A large body of literature has been published on work and work process. Of the two perspectives—technical and human—the least understood is the human side (Duck 2001).

Few, if any, public organizations can comfortably function in the old bureaucratic model of the past. Administrators and managers have found that the culture and climate that led to their success in the past renders them ill-equipped to launch transformation efforts that are needed today. Public administrators find themselves forced to refocus their goals, design new strategies, and embrace organizational transformation as a means to improve productivity, quality, and stakeholder satisfaction. This new way of functioning has rekindled interest in employee commitment and organizational identification. A transformation, a *revitalization* of spirit, and a renewed shared belief in the future are emerging in these organizations.

Acknowledging a need for transformation is, by itself, no guarantee of success. Successful transformation is likely to occur only when key conditions of organizational health are present (Beer, Eisenstat, and Spector 1990; Jick 1991). Public managers must keep in mind the point that organizational transformation will not eliminate diversity, nor will it automatically result in a coming together of beliefs or values. The change desired may not occur in the organization, and things may never be the same (Belbin 1996, 76):

> Cultures can be changed, not in the first place by training or education, nor by the exercise of force, but by bringing about an organizational transformation. The appropriate organization will in time create a culture of its own. It will be a culture where behavior develops predictable patterns, which does not mean that the employees all share the same personal values. In a cosmopolitan society personal values will [continue to] vary immensely. But how those values are expressed in terms of behavior will depend on the shape of the organization.

To achieve the desired transformational change in the organization—to create new ways for coping with altered conditions and for managing resources astutely—organizations must capitalize on deep, widespread internal commitment (Beckhard and Harris 1987). Whether employees are willing to adopt this commitment depends upon whether the *culture* and operating *climate* of a public organization fosters this behavior.

Level IV: Achieving Desired Change Outcomes

The broad set of values held in common by managers in public organizations is exemplified in their shared feeling of purpose, goals, and objectives, and by the way they carry out their functions, tasks, and related activities. Improving and reinforcing these values and work processes are typical desired transformation outcomes. These common values have been summarized into a number of points, among which are the following list of shared values that may be considered to represent a culture of public service (Vasu et al. 1998, 268):

1. Public administrators manage for the general will.
2. Government is a public trust to be used for the common good and not for special interests.
3. Government administrators are servants of the public, not the other way around.
4. Public officials should embody all the public virtues; they are hard working, honest, wise, sincere, etc.
5. Public administrators are loyal to their superiors and their organization; they subordinate their own interests to those of the group. If they disagree with the mission, they should leave office.
6. Public administrators perform their duties efficiently and economically, with the greater good of the public always in mind.
7. Merit alone should be the basis for appointment to public office, not privilege.
8. Public officials are subject to the law, just as are all other citizens.

These and other common values manifest themselves in different ways, depending on the function and mission of each organization and the leadership styles of senior managers. These different manifestations are what we see and measure as *organizational culture*. Organizational disequilibrium occurs when the personal values, attitudes, and opinions of members of the public organization are no longer in harmony with the culture of public service.

Improving the Probability of Organizational Change

Not many public managers will disagree with the statement that achieving a successful transformational change in an organization, especially a large government agency, is an extremely difficulty endeavor and one that can take years. It is possible, however, to improve the odds of achieving that success. It requires paying attention to fundamentals and building the right kind of foundation. Fernandez and Rainey (2006) looked at this issue and concluded that many change initiatives fail because managers did not do their homework. They often overlooked, ignored, or underestimated a short list of factors that, if given proper attention, may have dramatically increased their odds of success and made the tasks far easier in the process. The eight factors that Fernandez and Rainey urged public managers involved in a change activity to monitor are:

1. Ensure a need for change exists, and be sure that need is communicated to everyone involved in the agency and its stakeholders.
2. Do not begin without a specific plan of action that identifies the strategies to be followed, the measurements of success, and contingency plans to fall back on when events require alterations to the original plan.
3. Build internal support for the change by engaging staff in the planning and implementation of the program. Ensuring that personnel know that a crisis looms will often overcome resistance to changes.
4. It has long been a truism that without top-management support and commitment, changes in an organization cannot be achieved. Just one senior manager who drags his or her feet or actively denigrates the effort or denies the need can sour the entire effort.
5. External support is just as important as internal support. That is, partners, clients, recipients of services, legislators, and oversight bodies must be enlisted in the effort. Bringing these external stakeholders on board and keeping them informed before the inevitable problems occur is the same thing as enlisting your allies in the battle before the invasion begins.
6. Before beginning, make sure the needed resources are located and determined to be available. There is nothing more disheartening to a staff involved in a transformation change than to find they must stop because there is not enough money or people to complete the task.

7. Institutionalizing change means working with employees to develop an organizational culture that embraces the idea and act of change. Workers must know that they will be rewarded for taking risks and for innovating to improve operations, eliminate waste, and provide better service. The other side of this coin is that they must also know they will not suffer if the innovation fails to achieve the success it was thought to bring about. A change initiative requires innovative behavior everywhere and for every step of the change effort.

8. The final factor often missed by change agents is failure to include all aspects of the organization in the planned change. Changing one element of an organization will inevitably affect all other aspects of the agency. Thus, for a behavior change to take place, the public managers leading the change must make changes to the subsystems of the organization so that the whole organization reflects the changed state. Small changes may seem easier to achieve than broad, comprehensive changes, but this approach often results in failure to achieve the desired transformational change.

Summary

The transformation of the public sector that has been underway since the 1980s will most likely continue well into the future. Moreover, there does not seem to be any large-scale organized criticism agitating for a return to the old bureaucratic, top-down maintenance model of public-sector governance. Although it may be too early to term enterprise resource planning a failure, it has turned out to be fraught with problems, highly prone to overcharges in installation, and unable to bring about much of the benefit for which it has been touted.

This chapter focused on two central themes. The first dealt with the questions of why governments feel they must change. The second discussed three approaches to describing the process of change in organizations: the Sandia Laboratories' team model, a compendium four-level transformation process model, and an eight-factor public management model proposed by Fernandez and Rainey.

The chapter closed with a review of a number of important factors that public managers often overlook, ignore, or underestimate during the course of a change initiative. Even if these factors are addressed, they do not guarantee success; they can only improve the odds of a successful change effort. If they are ignored, however, the probability of failure is increased significantly.

Chapter 3

Forces Driving Changes in Government

> Government performance is important to citizens and public managers alike. Citizens expect the law to be enforced, the environment to be protected, labor and health safety laws obeyed, and a plethora of goals to be accomplished. Against the background of growing citizen expectations, and the widespread belief that a performance deficit exists at all levels of government, public managers have continued to develop new ways to meet public objectives.

Richard C. Kearney and Evan M. Berman (1999)

Professor Sheila Kennedy (2006), writing on the outsourcing of government services, described the government institution as "an association having universal compulsory jurisdiction within territorial boundaries." Although this description helps to clarify what it is we mean when we are talking about government, the description is not complete. Everyone working in government knows that public organizations exist to perform certain specific tasks and that it is impossible to define the organization without including a description of the people the organization serves and their particular needs. A description of the style and substance of a public organization is not complete unless it also includes the people who receive and are affected by its services. Thus, public organizations and the people with whom they have contact are bound together in a common context of needs, wants, and services. When the needs of the people or the environment in which the government renders its services change, the organization must also change. The outsourcing of government services mentioned by Professor Kennedy is an example of governments' reactions to changes in the environment.

Other forces are also at play in forcing change upon government managers. For example, an important task of government administrators when planning an organizational change is to ensure that the recipients are involved in designing and implementing the change.

The mission of an agency is to perform its assigned tasks effectively and efficiently. In fulfilling its mission, the agency must interact with many other stakeholder groups that are more or less affected by those operations. Agency managers must ensure that the agency does what it is supposed to do, and where and when it is supposed to do it, without adversely affecting others. The managers of government agencies are increasingly being held responsible for making sure this happens.

This introduction leads to four conclusions that can be made about government organizations, all of which are addressed in this chapter:

1. They are a collection of people who are brought together for a common purpose.
2. The people within the organizations are organized in such a way as to employ a particular set of coordinated systems and processes.
3. The people in the group have a common stake in accomplishing a common social goal.
4. The common goal has to do with responding to the people they serve by delivering services that are best provided by government.

As they deal with each of these realities, public managers must do so within the framework of a spate of dramatic changes taking place in their operating environment (Figure 3.1).

Environmental Forces Shaping the Face of Government

Managers in public and private enterprises around the globe are increasingly constrained in their range of decision alternatives by a body of related environmental forces that are functioning as drivers of change in government. To cope with the challenges of these and other environmental forces of change, public managers find that they must design and implement new ways to carry out their functions. The following subsections describe six environmental forces driving dramatic changes in the ways that governments function and government work is accomplished.

Declining Citizens' Trust in Government

The first of the forces driving the effort to reshape government is a crisis of trust that appears to permeate nearly every sector of society. This loss of trust and faith in

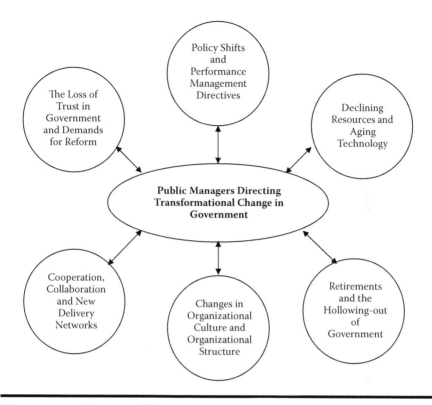

Figure 3.1   Environmental factors shaping the new face of government.

our civil society are particularly pervasive in their power to influence the attitudes of people toward their government and those who work in government (Yang and Holzer 2006).

As in the private sector, public agencies depend upon the good will of the public to accomplish their goals. As a result, most if not all government organizations go to considerable lengths to influence public opinion. But, it seems not to be working. Rather than improving, the public's trust in their government is continuing to decline, and it is a global phenomenon. People simply do not trust their government to do the right thing. This results in taxpayer revolts, motions for recall or impeachment, initiatives by the people to their legislatures, and, in extreme cases, mass demonstrations and bloody riots.

Trust is a central requirement for the functioning of all spheres of government. Most elected and appointed leaders clearly seek to be seen as trustworthy public servants, and to have their agencies recognized as organizations worthy of the public's trust in everything they do. Of course, it does not always happen that way. Public servants can be as venal as the most avaricious private businessperson. When ethical lapses by public servants become public, citizens' trust in government tumbles (Kampen, Van de Walle, and Bouckaert 2006). Public service had become so clouded with the thick air of cynicism that, in 2007, new congressional leaders placed ethical reform at the top of their list of first-term objectives.

Government, industry, organized religion, nonprofit organizations, and other sectors of the economy are all suffering through this apparent breakdown in ethics. This breakdown has, in turn, seriously eroded the level of trust that citizens hold toward their leaders in government, business, and society in general. For example, a 2006 poll by Harris Interactive found that only one in ten Americans strongly believes charities are "honest and ethical" in their use of contributed funds. Moreover, nearly one in three respondents agreed that nonprofit organizations have moved away from their primary mission (Hoffman 2006).

These and other examples of dissatisfaction with leadership have brought about what many now describe as a *crisis of trust* (Hoffman 2006; Hasen 2005; Young 2004; Millstone and Zwanenberg 2000; Cohen 1996). That crisis of trust exists in politics and government, business and industry, the church and the media, science and health services, education and voluntary nonprofit organizations, and all types of institutions around the globe. The ethos of social responsibility that makes it possible for society to function is being severely strained.

New Policy Concerns and Performance Management

Shift in Policy Priorities

The first element in this changing environmental force is the great shift in policy priorities occurring in all levels of government as a result of global-warming-related disasters and terrorist activity such as that which occurred in the United States on September 11, 2001, and elsewhere thereafter. These changes in policy direction have a dramatic effect on the missions of government agencies, and often result in dramatic changes in agency appropriations.

Such rapid changes in legislative priorities often occur as a result of some catastrophic event, such as an energy crisis; wide-area blackouts; a stock market crash; hurricanes, tornadoes, and other natural disasters; disclosures of bribes or payments in cash or kind for preferential treatment; terrorist actions, and similar catastrophic events. Legislators often react to such events with mandates for new or improved public-service programs. When this happens, administrators must develop programs to carry out the goals inherent in new or changed policy—and do so while continuing their existing services. Some believe that an effect of global warming will be more severe and a greater occurrence of natural disasters, including hurricanes, rain storms, droughts, and related problems.

The changes in public policies—supportive or controlling—seldom if ever remain permanent, however; they are always subject to change. It is easier to soil a reputation than it is to repair one. Airing of an account of an unethical or irresponsible business decision can result in immediate control-and-prevention legislation, as can charges of malfeasance or incompetence. On the other hand, a published report of a positive action or policy may be welcomed, but be less likely to reverse an ingrained unfavorable attitude. Today, public agencies recognize that their responsibilities go beyond traditional public service; they must be ready to adjust to new needs, new demands, and new technologies. Moreover, they know that they must work at being "good citizens" in all that they do, and with all the stakeholders with whom they interact.

Becoming better prepared to react to natural and human-made disasters has required public managers to adopt strategic planning as a defensive measure. The first step in strategic planning is in-depth analysis of the environmental factors that are expected to have an impact on an organization's operations.

Administrative Reforms

The second element in this trend is a shifting paradigm of public administration that calls for greater emphasis on public-sector effectiveness *with* greater efficiency. These administrative reforms are implemented in response to calls for government performance to cost less, but not at the expense of effectiveness. Some critics loudly proclaim that the benefits of the administrative reforms come at the perceived expense of traditional public-service values. Greater efficiency—and therefore, administrative reform in general—is one of the key concepts underlying the New Public Management (NPM) movement in public administration.

Two related philosophical approaches are among the forces shaping transformation in government agencies. One of these is the introduction of free-market values into the ethos of government administration. These values are the rationale behind the global NPM concept that has entered academic discourse on public-administration issues. NPM, believed by some observers to be an evolutionary phenomenon rather than a revolution in thinking and action, was founded upon an effort to move the public-administration discipline from its traditional focus on bureaucracy to one that more closely follows a free-enterprise model (Adams 2000; Barzelay 2001; Christensen and Lægreid 2002, 2007; Ferlie et al. 1996; Lane 2000).

A related process of NPM is a global drive to reshape government so that it more closely reflects the best practices found in the private sector. *Enterprise transformation* is a process used to bring about the desired transformation. Together, the concepts of public management and enterprise transformation are blurring the distinction between the public and private sectors. The evolutionary changes taking place have been described by Christensen and Lægreid (2002):

> Since the 1980s, the international tendency in administrative reform has been a neo-liberal one, encompassing managerial thinking and a market mentality. The private sector has become the role model, and public administration has come to be seen as a provider of services to citizens who were redefined as clients and consumers.... These new administrative doctrines came to be known collectively as New Public Management.

Declining Resources and Aging Technology

A third environmental issue affecting government managers is the emerging need for government organizations at all levels to meet growing demands for more and improved services with declining resources and an aging infrastructure. Testifying before Congress in November 2006 on the business transformation plan of the Department of Defense, the Comptroller General of the United States, David M. Walker, laid out the challenge facing government: "It is important that DoD get the most from every dollar it invests. Out nation is not only threatened by external security threats, but also from within by growing fiscal imbalances due primarily to our aging population and rising health care costs."

Walker also said that the trends are being "compounded by the near-term deficits arising from new discretionary and mandatory spending as well as lower revenues as a share of the economy. If left unchecked, these fiscal imbalances will ultimately impede economic growth, have an adverse effect on our future standard of living, and in due course affect our ability to address key national and homeland security needs. These factors create the need to make choices that will only become more difficult and potentially disruptive the longer they are postponed" (GAO 2006).

Environmental Changes Hit Michigan Child Support

Michigan, once a long-time leader in child-support-enforcement performance, spent ten years trying to meet federal certification standards for its automated child-support system. Over the decade of the 1990s, the state was only able to implement the mandated system in 73 of the state's 83 counties. However, the ten counties in which the state was unable to implement the program contributed more than half of the statewide caseload. When an October 1, 2000, federal deadline passed without full compliance, Michigan was slapped with an escalating series of financial penalties. From 1998 through 2001, the federal government levied penalties of $68.6 million, with another $112 threatened for 2002 and 2003. Clearly, something had to be done; the state had to implement a transformation in the Department of Human Services and the state Department of Information Technology.

The transformation began with the forming of a project governance model with strong executive support and leadership. This was followed by establishment of a Project Control Office which set standards, performance measurements, and processes for operations. In addition to the child-support-enforcement program, the new procedure was also applied to five highly visible projects that included (a) development of a Medicaid management information system, (b) a traffic accident reporting system, (c) a system of bridge transfer assistance for new applicants, (d) an information technology system for unemployment insurance, and (e) a project to reengineer the drivers license and vehicle registration processes. By 2005, the system had been transformed into what some called the "Michigan Miracle," saving the state $147 million in unlevied penalties for 2001–2003 and a return of $35 million of penalties paid earlier. Moreover, although the total cost reached nearly $814 million to implement, the state estimates that the total accumulated benefits from the project would exceed $1.7 billion by 2007.

Michigan was the recipient of the 2006 NASCIO Outstanding Achievement Award for Outstanding IT Project and Portfolio Management. The following statement (NASCIO 2006b) described the award:

> Michigan's child support system…is an excellent case study of how a large failing project can be transformed to a successful one with the aggressive application of project management processes. Further, it illustrates how one success can be grown into an enterprise solution with the backing of both the information technology management team and the critical business stakeholders.

Technology and Change

Technology, including advances in information and communications technologies, is one of the principle drivers of transformation in all organizations. The coordinative effort to develop and implement enterprise architecture has become, therefore, a major strategic direction in modern government (Ross, Weill, and Robertson 2006). Enterprise transformation is the government's drive to use management principles to coordinate the way government puts to use such resources as people, processes, and technology to perform its many missions in ways that are more cost-effective and performance-enhanced. Government agencies at all levels are saddled with aging, stovepiped systems that severely hinder their ability to perform their core missions. Box 3.1 describes a technology-based transformation initiative implemented in Great Britain under the leadership of Prime Minister Tony Blair.

Box 3.1   Transformational Government and Technology

Transformational Government, published in November 2005, describes a vision for ambitious changes in the delivery of public services in the United Kingdom. The transformation in the way government works is enabled by the judicious application of technology. For the vision to occur, three important transformations must take place.

1. *Transformation of public services*: Government services made possible by technology must be designed around the needs of citizens and/or businesses for which they apply, rather than the needs of the agency or department providing the service. Moreover, delivery must occur through modern, coordinated channels. The underlying objective is to gain better policy outcomes, eliminate unnecessary paperwork, and improve efficiency by eliminating duplication and routine processing. The goal is to use technology to leverage capacity and streamline processes.
2. *Transformation of corporate services and government organization infrastructure*: Government must move to a culture of shared services at every level and position possible, thus supporting greater standardization and cross-agency collaboration and sharing of resources.
3. *Transformation of the way work is done in government organizations*: The third transformation entails expanding and deepening the level of professionalism among administrators and managers. This professionalism pertains to the planning, delivery, management, skill levels, and governance of information and communications technologies (ICT). The objective is to reduce or eliminate costly program duplications or delivery failures while increasing citizen confidence in technology-delivered services.

Source: **HMSO (2005)**

Retirements and the Hollowing Out of Government

A fourth related environmental factor is that government is on the brink of a crisis in agency staffing levels. This, in turn, is resulting in a loss of critical knowledge. These deep reductions in staffing levels are occurring because of the accelerating rate of retirements of aging baby boomer–generation government workers.

These retirements are hollowing-out government at all levels (Agranoff and McGuire 1998). Federal, state, and local governments in the United States face a number of personnel problems that promise to impact nearly everything that government touches. Among the problems are the huge number of retirements, the need to find cash to pay pensions, and a structural transformation in the pay, classification, and performance-management systems of government workers. A brain drain—the departure of as much as 40 percent of the federal work force from 2005 to 2015—is truly hollowing out the federal labor force.

The "brain drain" phenomenon has been defined as "a departure of intellectually or technically skilled personnel from government employment to another environment" (PPS 2005). When this happens, untold years of experience and knowledge are lost—often forever. It is one of the driving forces behind government's intense interest and investment in means to collect, archive, and share knowledge before it is lost. The loss of many top-level employees at the Federal Emergency Management Agency (FEMA) is often cited as one of the reasons why the agency had so much difficulty in responding to Hurricane Katrina.

The Explosion in Government Retirements

Although the average age of the American worker has increased over the past decade, the federal civil service has twice as many workers over 45 years of age (61 percent) as the private sector (31 percent). As of October 2004, the federal Office of Personnel Management estimated that 58 percent of all fulltime supervisory personnel and 42 percent of nonsupervisory workers will be eligible to retire by the end of fiscal year 2010. Another 200,000 federal workers are expected to resign over the same period, resulting in the potential loss of nearly 900,000 federal employees. For example, fully 40 percent of managers at the Department of Homeland Security will be eligible to retire by 2009; 42 percent of all the federal government's senior executive service is expected to retire by 2010; and 87 percent of Social Security Administration claims assistants and examiners and 94 percent of the agency's administrative law judges will retire by 2010.

The brain drain threat is already having an impact on federal, state, and local government. Work rules negotiated through years of labor negotiations stipulate that, in many positions, employees can retire after a set number of years, usually 25 or 30, or upon reaching age 55. These work rules are common in education, utilities, and public safety, among others. Beverly Goldberg (2005), writing for the public-policy research organization The Century Foundation, reported that teacher shortages are becoming endemic in the United States, with school districts expected to need as many as 2.7 million new teachers by 2008. Where these new teachers will come from is anyone's guess; certainly, there are not that many preparing in college and university teacher-education programs.

Of course, finding replacements for the retiring workers is not the only problem facing federal, state, and local governments. What may be even more problematic is finding the cash to pay the pensions promised decades ago. Shifting cash into retirement payments is likely to have a big impact on many other programs that are already straining to make do with tight budgets (Goldberg 2005).

Changes in Organizational Culture and Structure

In addition to the problems associated with departures due to retirements and the need to find the cash to pay the huge pension bill, government is also in the midst of a thoroughgoing change in the structure of the traditional civil service system (Thompson 2006; Perry, Mesch, and Paarlberg 2006). As a result, the General Accountability Office listed strategic human capital management first on its 2007 list of high-risk government programs (GAO 2007a). Human capital was first added to the high-risk list in 2001. At that time, the chief reason for adding this area to the high-risk list was the anticipated problems arising from transformations being made in the civil service system, which in turn are creating hugh cracks in the culture of public service agencies.

Those transformations were bringing government-side changes to workers' pay, classification, and performance-management and -motivation systems. GAO recommended that Congress make pay and performance-management reform the first step in any governmentwide human-resource reform strategy. Moreover, GAO urged the Office of Personnel Management (OPM) to apply the lessons it learned while implementing a performance-based pay system for senior executives to future human-capital reforms.

Classifying Government Organizations

The work of governments is carried out by groups of people with special skills who are brought together and provided the resources necessary to accomplish the goals and objectives of the society they serve. The role of public managers is to organize these individuals together in such a way that they are able to effectively and efficiently perform their specific purposes. Thus, to understand how governments function, it is necessary to understand organizations.

Max Weber, one of the pioneers in the study of organizations and one of the first to look upon them as *systems*, saw the organization as "a system of continuous purposive activity of a specified kind" (1947). He then defined a *corporate organization* as "an associative social relationship characterized by an administrative staff devoted to such continuous purposive activity." Nadler, Hackman and Lawler (1979), writing more than 30 years later, defined the *organization* as a social system operating within larger environments, thereby continuing this tradition of looking upon organizations as systems.

It is possible from these definitions to agree on a definition that considers the organization to be *a group of people, processes and goals organized in a system and working to achieve a common goal or goals*. A fundamental purpose of transformation is to make it possible for the organization to do a better job at what it was organized to do. A difficulty in achieving the best possible performance of an organization is that different managers have different ways of organizing their people and resources for carrying out their tasks.

Features of Public Organizations

As noted, public organizations are groups of people brought together perform certain specific tasks as desired by the citizens they serve and which the larger body politic agrees should be performed.

Professor Sheila Kennedy (2006), writing on the outsourcing government services, defined the State as "an association having universal compulsory jurisdiction within territorial boundaries." This means that public organizations are responsible for the provision of their agency services in their specific social and political jurisdictions. The task of public managers is to ensure that their agencies do what they are supposed to do, where and when it is supposed to happen; they are increasingly being held responsible for making sure that this happens.

From this brief introduction, it is possible to arrive at four conclusions about public organizations: First, they are a collection of people who are brought together for a common purpose. Second, the people are organized in such a way as to employ a particular set of coordinated systems and processes. Third, the people in the group have a common stake with the public whom they serve in accomplishing a common goal. And, fourth, the common goal has to do with delivery of services that the public believes in—or was—best provided by government. How they are organized to perform their missions will have a large impact on the effectiveness of their actions.

Forms of Government Organizations

Government organizations can be categorized in many different ways. The system used in the following discussion is based on Max Weber's early work in the theory of social and political organizations. He categorized organizations into three classifications: bureaucratic, collegial, and entrepreneurial.

Bureaucratic Organizations

It is probably a safe assumption that most citizens incorrectly view government agencies as *bureaucratic organizations.* Bureaucratic organizations tend to have a rigid hierarchy of supervisors and managers, routine procedures, and excessive red tape. For most of the twentieth century, most government organizations were designed to be bureaucracies. When the bureaucratic approach was first adopted in the nineteenth century, this seemed to be a good way to function because it provided tight controls over people and expenses, and this approach was soon adopted in many profit and not-for-profit organizations as well as government operations. It is still a relevant model for large organizations in stable markets with products or services requiring little technological innovation.

The administrative goals of bureaucratic organizations are stability and order. Managers are expected to rely on stable policies and practices that have changed in the past only because of some dramatic shift in public policy or political administration. Examples include the federal government's shift to become the *regulator* of business after the public's demand for trust busting and product safety in the early 1900s. That trend only ended after a turnaround demand for deregulation of business occurred in the 1970s and 1980s.

Collegial Organizational Culture

Collegial organizations are those in which decision making by consensus is the prevalent management practice. This is the type of organization that many observers ascribe to large Japanese and Korean enterprises. Sticking one's neck out—taking chances—runs counter to the cultural foundations of this type of organization, where each member of the group may have the power to veto others' decisions. This power may be formal or informal. However, the type of collegial organization found most often is one where the veto is not an issue. Rather, members consciously consult with other members of the group before a decision is made. Progress occurs, but slowly. When a conflict of interest arises, the conflict is worked out through negotiation, with adjustments made by compromise. Weber (1947, 398–399) was less convinced of the effectiveness of the collegial model, noting:

> Except in the case of the monocratic type of collegiality where there is mutual veto, collegiality almost inevitably involves obstacles to precise, clear, and above all, rapid decision.... Collegiality favours greater thoroughness in the weighing of administrative decisions ... it divides personal responsibility, indeed in larger bodies this disappears almost entirely. Large-scale tasks which require quick and consistent solutions tend in general, for good technical reasons, to fall into the hands of monocratic "dictators," in whom all responsibility is concentrated.

Much of the present financial difficulties through which many firms and governments are suffering can be attributed to an inability or unwillingness of top administrators or managers to make needed hard choices. This is typical of the negative outcomes of the collegial organization model.

Entrepreneurial Organizations

Entrepreneurial organizations are possibly the most innovative of all types of organizations (Carnall 1995). This is also the model that most transformational managers in government are trying to emulate. Entrepreneurial organizations are characterized by the greatest amount of flexibility—and often the greatest willingness to accept transformational change. The entrepreneurial administrator may, for example, decide—with little or no formality—to shift from an ineffective delivery method to a new one, to hire or fire a specialist or other assistant, or to borrow from a successful program seen in another agency or in the private sector. In a word, such a manager is willing to learn from others; his or her organization is more likely to also be a learning organization.

The entrepreneurial organization is not without its problems, however. The power to make major decisions in entrepreneurial organizations often remains in the hands of the entrepreneur or entrepreneurial manager, thus limiting any sense of major accomplishment among some innovative employees. These key leaders also do much of the work in entrepreneurial organizations, a fact that can be problematic when it becomes time for the leader to move on and be succeeded by another.

The important thing to remember about these three types of organizations is that few, if any, government organizations can be said to fall exclusively into any one of the Weberian categories. Rather, most government organizations contain elements of two or more categories. The goal of the enterprise-transformation movement is to facilitate the transformation of organizations from bureaucratic and collegial organizations into entrepreneurial organizations in which change and innovation is celebrated. Gaining an understanding of how this process works in government and nonprofit organizations is the focus of this book.

Cooperation and Collaboration for New Delivery Systems

Another factor affecting public management is the ever-present threat that public-sector managers must be ready to react at any time to legislative mandates to improve the efficiency and cost-effectiveness of government programs. One particularly powerful force for change in this area is the federal, state, and local expenditures on homeland security programs. Others include improving government procurement methods and implementing wide-ranging e-government and e-learning programs.

Government organizations are finding it increasingly difficult to function today without interacting with and gaining the cooperation of other organizations and institutions. In the past, this interaction was sometimes forced: Compliance by lower-level agencies was dictated by law or by the power of the purse at the federal level. This coercive operating model has been shown to be less effective than a collaborative approach (Bozeman and Straussman 1991).

Organizational cooperation can be attained in several different ways: by competition, by collusion, by overlapping fields of operations, and by dependence on the expertise available only in other organizations' area of specialization. In the arena of local government management and governance, this cooperative model is only now achieving common acceptance. Traditionally, management of municipal public services operated under a top-down or donor-recipient governance model. Both models emphasized upper-level control over a subordinate's actions as well as the enforcement of laws, regulations, standards, and guidelines.

Summary

This chapter has introduced some of the most important and interrelated management efforts taking place to deal with the challenges brought on by dramatic changes in the way governments function and government work is accomplished. Six environmental forces were introduced:

1. The crisis of trust
2. Performance-based management of government functions
3. Meeting demographic-driven demands for more and improved services with declining resources and aging technology
4. The hollowing-out of government caused by retirements of baby boom–generation workers
5. The shift from traditional bureaucratic organizational structure
6. Mandates for greater cooperation and collaboration within and across agencies

Chapter 4

Preparing an Organization to Accept Change

> Since efforts to improve performance always contain an element of uncertainty, management is sensitive to these risks, and in government, where service stability is essential, such risk taking might appear foolish. The stereotypical passive, change-resistant bureaucrat could perhaps be understood as simply a wise administrator wary of the nonlinear dynamics that change can create. We can see why public managers may be a cautious lot.
>
> **L. Douglas Kiel (1994)**

Implementing transformational change in a government organization begins with a careful and complete analysis of the organization to assess its readiness to accept change. First on this list should be the readiness of managers to invest the considerable time and effort a change can entail. As Professor Kiel (1994) noted, willingness to accept change is not a widespread characteristic among many public managers. Equally important, workers in any government are likely to have very different attitudes toward change than their managers, who are charged with implementing the change.

Before the transformation process can begin, management must identify the root of any disparities between management and employee attitudes toward change. Transformational change cannot begin until the causes of such disparities are identified and a strategy developed to bring everyone's attitudes to a point where change will be accepted.

The causes of such disparities can usually be found in the culture of the organization or its operating climate. Agency leadership must assess these facets of the organization to identify factors affecting commitment to the organization and its current and projected mission. Successful reshaping of the organizational culture and climate can then become the foundation for building increased levels of commitment to the strategy of organizational transformation. Indeed, such transformation requires a change in the culture in which public agencies function (Lau, Kilbourne, and Woodman 2003).

Importance of Organizational Culture

Public administrators are aware of the difficulties associated with attempts to initiate any long-term change in the culture that exists within their organizations. Organizational cultures are self-perpetuating; they preclude major alterations that are, on the surface, intuitively correct (Litwin and Stringer 1968). That is, a particular culture "works" for the members of the organization at the time and in the place that it exists. In the absence of a culture that brings people in the organization together, working to achieve a common goal, the organization ends up spinning its wheels, accomplishing nothing. This fact is emphasized in this definition of the term *organizational culture*:

> Culture is the pattern of basic assumptions ... a group has invented, discovered, or developed in learning how to cope with its problems of external adaptation and internal integration, and that have worked well enough to ... be taught to new members as the correct way to perceive, think and feel in relation to these problems (Schein 1985, 9).

Organizational culture can also be defined as a system of shared values that are exhibited through the organization's different cultural artifacts (Peters and Waterman 1982). Schein (1985) and Wilson (1989) saw culture as the shared beliefs, values, and assumptions of the members of a specific group or organization. When we talk about organizational culture, we are referring to the shared beliefs, values, and patterns of behavior that are distinctive to a specific organization.

Role of Culture and Climate in Organizational Transformation

Change efforts in organizations, more often than not, fail or achieve only partial results (Duck 2001). Most of the change-adoption failures should not be looked upon predominantly as failures of the administrators who oversaw the change effort. Rather, it may be more appropriate to attribute them to a deeper, more critical source: the fundamental, all-pervasive, bureaucratic culture of traditional government organizations and the operating climate that results in inertia. This unwillingness to accept change has long been considered to be a reflection of the bureaucratic thinking that often characterizes bureaucratic organizations. Public managers become victims of that culture, just as change initiatives become victims of poor or sloppy implementation of a change.

An organization's culture and the operating climate it generates have a direct influence on the *state of readiness* required for a renewal or other organizational change to take place. If the organization's culture and climate make it impossible to achieve change, the transformation initiative and other change programs will most likely fail, regardless of the desires and plans of the organization's leadership. Therefore, to improve the odds of success when attempting to introduce any change into an organization, public managers should first conduct a comprehensive examination of the underlying values and beliefs shared by members of the organization (Keeton and Mengistu 1992).

Tackling climate and culture should be the first step in creating and sustaining any change or innovation. This point was, in fact, the first and most frequently mentioned recommendation made by respondents in a 1997 survey of the top 1,000 firms in the United Kingdom by Coopers and Lybrand and Henley Management College (Taffinder 1998).

Changes at the U.S. Postal Service

When change agents talk about changing the culture of an organization, they are really talking about the way the people in the organization think and act. Walters and Thompson (2005, 5) made this point in their white paper on the transformation of the federal Government Accountability Office (GAO):

> Transforming organizations is a complicated, frequently messy proposition. It is so because of an unavoidable truth about organizations: They are run by people. And so any drive to fundamentally change the way a place does business necessarily means that a central component of such change has to involve the people who work there.

Early reports of a successful transformation initiative at the U.S. Postal Service (USPS) are doubly significant in light of the recent huge deficits and the painful future facing the USPS (Siggerud 2007).

The GAO had placed the USPS on its list of "high-risk" agencies in 2001. At that time the USPS had a projected annual deficit of $2 to $3 billion, faced severe cash-flow problems, a debt that approached its statutory borrowing limit, costs growing faster than revenue, and few if any productivity gains. Major liabilities and obligations were estimated at close to $100 billion—much of it in retirement obligations. Restructuring of the workforce was needed because of large numbers of impending retirements, operational changes, and long-standing labor–management relations problems. GAO noted that the USPS had no comprehensive plan to address these financial, operational, and human-capital changes.

The USPS is one of the nation's largest employers, with nearly 800,000 full- and part-time employees in 2007. Managing this workforce with its complex compensation and benefits requirements is one of the largest challenges facing USPS management. The challenge includes ensuring that the workforce is able to respond to changing operational needs. Management concluded that this and similar challenges supported development of a plan for realigning its infrastructure and workforce, including assessing the impacts of facility changes on the workforce and determining whether the USPS has sufficient flexibility to make needed workforce changes.

USPS managers also recognized that its plans to rationalize its facilities, increase automation, improve retail access, and streamline its transportation network would mean a significant realignment of its workforce. Realignment meant a different mix in the number, skills, and deployment of its employees, possible repositioning, retaining, outsourcing, and reducing the size of the workforce. As expected, the required transformation of the USPS has had a significant impact on the operating culture of this large and vital organization. The good news is that the Postal Service and its workforce seem to be succeeding in the transformation effort; GAO removed the Postal Service from its high-risk list in January 2007.

Aggressive action by Congress and USPS managers was singled out by the GAO as the reason for successes in the transformation. Congress enacted the Postal Accountability and Enhancement Act on December 20, 2006. This legislation provided USPS managers the tools they needed to address the key changes that they were facing. The USPS began its needed changes with the development of a comprehensive transformation plan. Subsequent implementation of the actions called for in the plan resulted in billions of dollars in cost savings, improved productivity, made it possible to downsize the workforce, and improved its system for financial reporting.

Committing the Organization to Change

To achieve the change needed in many public organizations—to create new ways for coping with altered conditions and for managing resources astutely—organizations must capitalize on the existing, widespread internal commitment of their staff members (Gouldner 1960; Lee 1971; Hall and Schneider 1972; Mowday, Steers, and Porter 1979; O'Reilly and Chatman 1986; Beckhard and Harris 1987; Balfour and Wechsler 1990, 1996). Commitment to an organization cannot be expected unless the employees have a belief in, and are ready to accept, the organization's goals and the values held in common. They must become eager to work hard for the organization—behavior that is often expressed in terms of wanting to remain an active member (Moon 2000). The good news is that this commitment does exist in varying degrees in most government agencies. Where it has disappeared, bringing it back should be the first goal of those agencies' leaders.

This unwillingness to commit to the organization and a subsequent failure to achieve a transformation initiative was clearly displayed in the inability of the managers of a small unit of the General Services Administration (GSA) to implement a total quality management program (McNabb and Sepic 1995). Although they conducted an assessment of the culture, agency administrators neglected to do the follow-on work necessary to stimulate commitment among the unit's personnel. Senior administrators were not willing to face up to the issues and problems the assessment revealed. As a result, the transformation effort failed before it even began. Similar results were reported in the failure of a local public-safety organization to implement commitment measures (Sepic and McNabb 2004).

Commitment Antecedents

Balfour and Wechsler (1996) identified three antecedents to describe their causal model of commitment:

1. *Identification commitment*, where employees describe their agency as valuable and respected by the public, one that makes important public contributions, and is regarded as capable and effective
2. *Affiliation commitment*, which is perceived by employees when organization members are seen as caring, and who value belonging to a close-knit organization that values the individual and his or her well-being
3. *Exchange commitment*, which employees accept as more than extrinsic rewards, like money, meaning that public organizations recognize employee contributions and then show concern by providing support and encouragement for this commitment (Figure 4.1)

Mazouz and Tremblay (2006) examined the role of organizational commitment to strategies for public management and administrative reform by the government of Canada. Successful government reforms depend upon three factors: citizen satisfaction with the outcomes, the flexibility of the new structures, and the commitment of staff to acceptance of the new management methods that include performance measurement, accountability, efficiency and economy (doing more with less), ethics compliance, and evaluation of outputs.

An important finding of their study revealed that the supervisors who created supportive and productive social relationships motivated commitment more than any of the other variables of participation, political penetration, and opportunities for advancement. Whether administrators can bring about this commitment, therefore, depends in large part upon their understanding of what motivates commitment, and whether they can forge a *culture* in their public organizations that fosters employee commitment and rewards this behavior.

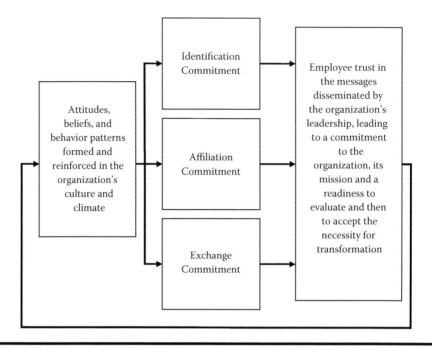

Figure 4.1 Antecedents to organizational commitment.

If administrators at public agencies are to improve their ability to adjust to changes occurring in their operating environments, they must adjust their organizations in ways that will reestablish commitment to public service. Without this commitment, it may not be possible to meet the challenges of this new century. The first step in triggering this change is to reinforce the *service ethos* in the organization. The second is to adjust the operating climate in response to cues from the reactions of employees to the revitalized culture that has been proposed to alleviate negative conditions.

How Cultural Factors Constrain Change Efforts

The forces for change confronting administrators in government organizations are rooted in the distinctly altered economic, administrative, and social environments as well as the organizational cultures that these produce. Among the cultural factors pressing public agency administrators are (Ventriss 2000):

1. An aging worker population
2. Growth in the numbers of minorities and women entering the public workforce

3. Privatization and outsourcing of once-public services and functions with a loss of a culture of service to society
4. A perceived decline in government workers' commitment to quality in service and performance
5. Requirements to establish and function by rigid performance standards
6. Restrictions on government's ability to generate revenue, resulting in income demands by government workers that cannot be met
7. Continued erosion in the public's trust in government

Together, these and other pressures are causing a decline in young workers' commitment to public service, which has resulted in reduced ability to attract and retain skilled employees. Moreover, these changes are diminishing many of the long-term public administration commitments to such service values as equity, stewardship, public spiritedness, and citizenship (Felts and Jos 2000).

Impact on Government Agencies

For public agencies, some of the impacts of these environmental forces have included slashed departmental budgets, competition for shares of the diminishing tax revenues, service delays or breakdowns, scarcity of skilled workers, and heightened demands for environmental accountability (Kiel 1994). These, in turn, have created the public administrator's dilemma of meeting growing demands for service with fewer resources.

Public agencies that once saw themselves as indispensable and above public reproach have not been protected from these external pressures. The growing gap between rising demand for services and limited resources characterizes many departments at all levels of government, resulting in high turnover and job-related stress (McCue and Gianakis 1997). The most severely restricted agencies suffer from a condition called "general service default," where government can no longer deliver the services that enhance or protect the life of its citizens (Levine 1988).

How Increasing Diversity Drives Organizational Change

The increasing diversity of the U.S. population is having a large impact on how public agencies hire, motivate, and retain government workers. A more diverse citizenry has meant new client and customer expectations, needs, and wants for public agencies. This diversity springs from the shifts occurring in the demographic makeup of society at large. Each group demands its "fair share" of the pool of limited resources; their demands are expressed at the ballot box—without recognition or concern for the costs. An environment of resource scarcity, with increasing demands for services and the imposition of strict performance measures (Julnes and Holzer 2001), has resulted in what McCue and Gianakis (1997) referred to as *unfunded mandates*.

The compelling need for organizational transformation has created a simultaneous requirement for shifts in the way human-resources policy and strategy is developed and implemented in public organizations. Time has rendered obsolete and ineffective the stable economic and social environments that once fostered tried-and-true ways of doing things (Andrews, Boyne, and Walker 2006; Cappelli et al. 1997; Goldsmith 1997).

Need for a New Operating Ethos

Many believe that government organizations are badly in need of a new operating ethos, or at least a return to the ethos of unselfish commitment to public service that once characterized many in the government workforce (Kiel 1994). Commitment, however, assumes that those who choose public service have a set of values that prepares them for what is often described as societal disdain for their work and performance.

Pattakos (2004) reminds us that public employees are searching for meaning at work, and although employment security may have been a reason for choosing public service as a career, they truly want to make a genuine difference through their work—or as one employee interviewed explained, "I want to add value to the community, improve the planet, so that when I leave this earth I can say that I made a difference" (Cappelli et al. 1997).

Because of the many changes that have taken place in government over the past decade, the *ethos of service* has lost much of its power to motivate government workers and administrators. Some of the more salient changes include privatization, taxing restrictions, mandated reforms such as the Americans with Disabilities legislation and equal opportunity laws, the imposition of user fees, the introduction of total quality initiatives, unique performance measurements, citizen "interference" in government through active involvement in the initiative process, and other actions.

Three Strategies for Generating a Culture Change

Belbin (1996) identified three different strategies for methods of establishing or changing culture in organizations. The phrase, "Culture is the way we do things around here," represents what Belbin calls *Method One*, in that it refers to reinforcing the good or desired aspects of the existing culture. It occurs internally by appointing trustworthy individuals to promote the existing desired cultural elements.

Method Two occurs when agency managers try to change the values of people in the agency. This is typically a top-down method of instituting a change initiative. This approach fails as often as it succeeds, particularly when the change is mandated from above without first gaining acceptance of the change and commitment to a common goal that includes acceptance of change.

Method Three is the process that happens when employees accept that others do things differently "over there." That is, the members of the group come to recognize that other groups function differently—and that the difference is okay. If this idea is accepted, the group is more likely to accept—without changing—the members of the different culture (Belbin 1996). Method Three is followed when public-sector managers, like their counterparts in for-profit organizations, practice management by walking around (MBWA), thus communicating the point that they share in the values and actions of the organization.

Once one of these strategies is selected, government managers have greater success in their change process if they bring citizens into the process as cocreators of the services the agency will provide, rather than looking on stakeholders as impediments to their work. Pattakos (2004) illustrated this point by describing the experience of a public manager—who often complained of burnout from dealing every day with what he called the *mindless bureaucracy*—who has found a way to revitalize his passion for his work. When his frustration resurfaces, he heads to the "front lines," where he works side by side with the employees who provide the agency's service to citizens. By helping citizens find ways to ameliorate community problems, he is able to recharge his commitment to public service. In doing so, he also reinforces this cultural element among his staff.

The Shifting Character of Administrative Thinking

Critical observers of public administration have often pointed to what they see as the stifling nature of policies and procedures that are perpetuated in the Weberian model of bureaucratic agencies (Kanter, Stein, and Jick 1992; Kiel 1994; Thompson 2000). These critics also point to what they term the "mindless repetition" that characterizes many public service-occupations; the postal service is often cited as an example.

Unfortunately, it is true that work environments that lack challenge, or are driven by directives from above that never ask for feedback or improvement suggestions, can and do curtail change initiatives. Public managers must be alert, therefore, to any change-inhibiting policies that restrain employees from contributing new ideas that would help them meet their job responsibilities. Managers must be alert to the presence of (a) reward systems that benefit a few and ignore the many who contribute to the organization's success and (b) structures that promote routine thinking and decision making.

Public administrators today find themselves forced to refocus their goals, design new strategies, and embrace organizational transformation and commitment to improve productivity, quality, and stakeholder satisfaction. Organizations that have been successful in revitalizing their public-service ethos have done so through a process that entails transforming from a bureaucratic to a learning organizational culture, together with a renewed shared belief in the future. Public administrators and managers have found that the culture and climate that led to their success in the past render them ill-equipped to launch the transformational efforts that are needed today.

Simply acknowledging that a need for transformation exists is, by itself, no guarantee of success. Successful transformation is likely to occur only when key conditions of organizational health are present (Beer, Eisenstat, and Spector 1990; Jick 1991). Of course, organizational transformation will not eliminate diversity, nor will it automatically result in a coming together of beliefs or values.

Changing the Values of the Government Workforce

In addition to their own distinctive culture, all organizations have their own unique operating climate. Climate refers to the valence of values, norms, attitudes, behaviors, and feelings that exist in an organization and that distinguish it from all other organizations. Climate also refers to the level and form of organizational support, openness, supervisory style, conflict, autonomy, and quality of relationships existing in an organization (Lewicki et al. 1988).

Managers in public organizations share a broad common set of values. This ethos holds that public administrators manage for the will of the public, and that government is a public trust to be used for the common good and not for special interests. The shape and strength of these values held in common are a reflection of the degree to which agency members commit to this culture of public service. This ethos of service—the *democratic ethos* of public administration—has been described by Vasu, Stewart, and Garson (1998, 268) as consisting of these key beliefs:

1. Government administrators are servants of the public, not the other way around.
2. Public officials should embody all the public virtues; they are hard working, honest, wise, sincere, etc.
3. Public administrators are loyal to their superiors and their organization; they subordinate their own interests to those of the group. If they disagree with the mission, they should leave office.
4. Public administrators perform their duties efficiently and economically, with the greater good of the public always in mind.
5. Merit alone should be the basis for appointment to public office, not privilege.
6. Public officials are subject to the law, just as are all other citizens.

These and other common values manifest themselves in different ways, depending on the function and mission of each organization and the leadership styles of senior managers. These different manifestations make up what is seen and measured as the *organizational climate* of public agencies.

The attitudes, values, and expectations of people in the organization have a direct influence on the organizational climate. Many climate problems emerge when staff members perceive that a discrepancy exists between what they believe is the cultural norm of the organization—the attitudes, personal values, and expectations—and the way senior managers act.

The term *disequilibrium* can be used to describe this discrepancy in beliefs and norms—what Rouse (2006) referred to as *value deficiencies*. Disequilibrium is exemplified by such symptoms as deteriorating staff morale, supervisors and managers questioning whether the organization can survive under existing strategies, and the increasing demands for autonomy by highly skilled, technical staff members. The operating climate in an organization emerges from an interaction of people functioning within the organization's basic underlying culture. Thus, the active participation of a staff that is committed to the organization's success is a prerequisite for the organizational climate to shift from disequilibrium to equilibrium.

The Need to Involve the Entire Organization in the Change

When administrators fail to involve the entire organization in the process of diagnosing organizational and transformation planning, little long-term gain is achieved. Without a total commitment to change, the transformation attempt may either reinforce disequilibrium in the organization or result only in cosmetic change or short-term gains. A study on changes in the nature of work and work organization sponsored by the National Planning Association (Cappelli et al. 1997, 53–54) contained this caveat:

> [Transformation] actions taken singly, research studies suggest, tend to achieve few enduring gains.... Studies of the introduction of new information technologies, lean production, work force reductions (downsizing) ... for example, reveal that alterations in each of these areas without parallel changes in the culture, compensation, and reporting structure of the (organization) tend to leave the intended effects largely stillborn.

Interaction often obfuscates the deeper, difficult-to-measure, underlying culture. However, climate may serve as a surrogate measure of the organization's culture. An example of the blurred definition of culture and climate may help to underscore the relative importance of both. When moving pictures were first invented, those who began to explore how to turn still pictures into action asked how they could move the still shots quickly enough to give the impression of a lifelike moving picture, or how they could move many still pictures rapidly in front of a lens to give the effect of a moving picture.

There is an enduring need to capture still pictures of where the organization is *right now* in terms of the perceptions of organization members regarding an organization's explicit and implicit values, assumptions, and practices (Ashkanasy, Widerom, and Peterson 2000). This also requires keeping track of the changes that take place over time.

Steven Kelman (2005) described the importance of engaging people in the process of implementing changes in the federal government while also suggesting that the conventional idea that people naturally resist changes is often oversimplified and misleading. However, he agreed that staff discontent—or disequilibrium—in government organizations is frequently a block to successful organizational change initiatives.

A Way of Assessing Staff Attitudes

To understand the deeply rooted, slowly changing culture of an organization, McNabb and Sepic (1998) developed and tested an organizational assessment instrument. This tool, available in Appendix A, had proved to be an effective and efficient method of sampling attitudes of organization members. There is one very important warning that must be considered when measuring attitudes in this way: If employees are asked what they think about their organizational climate, managers and senior administrators must be ready to act on that advice or suggestions. To do nothing after administering the survey is not acceptable—not if agency management wants to engage staff in a transformation process to develop a high-performing government agency.

Steps to Follow in the Change Process

Programs to change an organization typically follow a series of clearly defined steps. The elements or pressure points in the organizational culture and climate must be identified and evaluated. Evaluation includes estimating the power of the problem to influence the ability of the agency to perform its mission and accomplish agency goals and objectives. Embarking on the process, baseline measurements of the key disruptive characteristics are taken, using either a diagnostic survey or participant observation process. The complete six-step process is illustrated in Figure 4.2.

Step 1: Identify Potential Culture-Based Problems

Step 1 involves (a) a detailed description of an organizational climate in which one or more problems exist or (b) an acknowledgment of the presence of a human

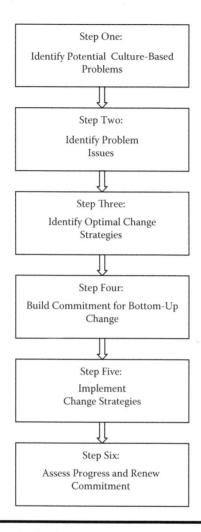

Figure 4.2   Changing organizational culture for a transformation.

barrier to needed change. This move may be prompted by disgruntled employees, unhappy citizens, or from higher administrative levels. A typical change driver is when leaders in top government positions decide that they have to finally act on the numerous voter complaints about government incompetence, malfeasance, or money wasting. Harvey and Brown (2001) mentioned some of the normal causes experienced during an organization's life cycle of this awareness of the need to change, such as rapid organizational growth or precipitous decline in a client population. They also identified problems arising from technology changes or changes in an agency's external environment.

Culture through the Organization Life Cycle

The idea that every organization has a life cycle is appropriate here because too many public-service agencies are accused of having entered the decline stage. Smither, Houston, and McIntire (1996) have suggested that, in the decline stage, many government products and services become obsolete, which in turn causes members of organizations to protect resources and avoid confrontation with vocal clients who demand better services. Unfortunately, unlike private-sector organizations, where customers can find new and better companies who offer a similar service, there are usually no close substitutes for local, state, or federal services; customers are forced to accept outdated service or methods of delivery.

Before resources can be used more effectively, top administrators must have the ability to perceive and react to a real threat. Or, they must experience extreme client or personnel dissatisfaction, or receive a notice that a cut in funding will be forthcoming. A transformation process will not be initiated until the severity of the problem attracts the attention of those with the power to act.

Threat, or perceived need, is only a necessary first step in the process. What is more important is that those in control place the problem in a position of top priority for action to be taken (Greiner 1967). This must be followed by some means that motivates lower-level managers and employees to fully embrace the change as a priority item as well.

Kurt Lewin (1951) described this first part of change as the *unfreezing phase*. This phase requires the introduction of new information or some new experience that may cause those involved to stop and question their values, or to wonder why what they have been doing is now under close scrutiny. Pain need not be the motivator to cause managers to reflect on which values are undermining effectiveness, but something has to signal that a change is needed; without the recognition of disharmony or disequilibrium, no change can begin.

Step 2: Identify Problem Issues

Step 2 is the first action step in the process: the assessment of issues behind the disequilibrium. This step is where people and their attitudes and behaviors come under scrutiny. It has been stressed that assessment cannot be done successfully without trust in the organization. This step involves three phases that begin with an assessment of organizational culture. Estimates have placed the retirement eligibility of senior career government managers at close to 70 percent by 2010 (Ingraham, Selden, and Moynihan 2000), with few individuals seeking public jobs because they have heard too many stories about lazy, dishonest workers, on the take, who have few career opportunities.

The ideology of public service, with divergent attitudinal values (Pattakos 2004) makes the changing of values and behavior problematic. The examination must include:

1. Cultural components, such as the rituals (repetitiveness and the routine nature of most jobs and tasks)
2. The meanings of workplace arrangements and artifacts (the same customer reception area, with sequential numbers creating a long line, similar to a bread line during a depression)
3. The organizational stories that breathe life into the organization

Only then will the manager fully understand what needs to be changed first to start the transformation process.

Another area that must be evaluated is the external environment of the agency. This includes the public agencies and private companies that can provide the same or similar services or substitutes for the services that government agencies provide. This can become a very complex question, due in part to the partnerships that have been created between public agencies and outside organizations who do some, but not all, of the work.

These difficulties are often experienced in public-works departments. For example, private companies who can resurface or repair a road, or install a sewer line, compete for government work—all under the close supervision of public-agency personnel.

Step 3: Identify Optimal Change Strategies

Assessment is needed to identify specific performance and needs of a public-sector agency when evaluating potential appropriate transformation strategies. This involves identifying the barriers to change, building support for a more robust mission statement, and identifying the employees in the agency who will not only participate in the needed decisions, but who can solicit and obtain ideas from their colleagues regarding acceptable change strategies. Most stories of public agencies that have taken the transformation journey emphasize the value of proper evaluation in reducing or overcoming resistance to change as a necessary first step.

Research suggests that potential resistance to change may appear before any official announcement of the changes is forthcoming. Such resistance is often preceded by inaccurate and negative rumors (Smeltzer 1991). Similar to identifying resistance to change, it is also important to try to anticipate which forces in the organization might block the implementation of the transformation program. Example concepts include:

1. Fear of the unknown (not enough information has been provided explaining what will happen, and why)
2. Fear of loss of benefits (will I gain something I need, or lose something of equal importance?)
3. Fear of a threat to one's security and position of power (is there a chance that the power I now have in my current job will diminish, and if so, will I replaced by someone else?)

	Low	High
High	Moderate Resistance/ Moderate Success	High Resistance/ Low Success
Low	Low Resistance/ High Success	Moderate Resistance/ Moderate Success

Figure 4.3 Harvey and Brown change model.

4. Fear of being forced to accept new norms and working with new and different people (will they be people I don't like or who don't like me?)

Harvey and Brown (2001) have created a change model that takes into consideration two variables that occur whenever a change program is considered: The first is the extent of change, and the second is the impact of the change on the culture. Their four-cell matrix displayed in Figure 4.3 illustrates success probabilities and the need for a change manager to consider both variables in terms of their minor and major impact on both variables. For example, if a change is predicted to be major, but the impact on culture is minor, the change manager can expect some employee resistance, with a moderate to high chance of success. Other combinations of resistance and success are displayed in the model.

Fortunately, researchers have provided a number of techniques that managers may employ to lessen anticipated resistance to change initiatives. Kotter and Schlesinger (1979), for example, identified six methods to lessen resistance, together with notes regarding timing and appropriate use, along with the advantages and disadvantages for each of the six methods:

1. Education and communication
2. Participation and involvement
3. Facilitation and support
4. Negotiation and agreement
5. Manipulation and co-optation
6. Explicit and implicit coercion

Harvey and Brown (2001) added five additional methods to the list:

1. Creation of a vision
2. Leadership
3. Reward systems
4. Creation of a climate conducive to communications
5. Power strategies

Nathan (1995, 213) also created a list of grab-bag options for reinvention, including the following:

1. Empower citizens
2. Encourage competitors and government deregulation
3. Use mission-driven leaders who follow a more entrepreneurial approach
4. Encourage some form of quality initiative
5. Decentralize agencies from central administrative decision-making executives
6. Suggest privatization as a way to encourage a budgetary and for-profit mentality
7. Initiate a top-down reform of the civil service

Another important consideration for organizations that are considering a reinvention or transformation program is the target of their efforts: employee empowerment, better control over the budget, reduction in the number of employees, and strategic management initiatives (Durst and Newell 1999).

Step 4: Build Bottom-Up Commitment for Change

When administrators talk about building commitment, they generally mean getting employees to buy into the process of a planned change. Bruhn, Zajac, and Al-Kasemi (2001) supported this premise when they suggested that, if employees were given an active role in structuring the change, they would have a greater commitment to and accountability for the outcomes because they have a practical view of how the organization really works.

Crewson (1997) defined organizational commitment as a combination of three distinct factors: a strong belief and acceptance of the organization's goals and values, eagerness to work hard for the organization, and a desire to remain a member of the organization. Feelings of commitment to organizations are usually due to job experiences or employee perspectives that something important is happening at the workplace; equally important is that they feel respected and capable of doing a challenging job. The process involves encouraging contributions from staff on the question of how to generate a new and better environment in which employees are willing to accept change (Pattakos 2004).

It is necessary to know the causes of resistance before an employee's lack of commitment to the workplace can be changed. Ingraham, Selden, and Moynihan (2000) summarized the need for a reciprocal relationship that will ensure commitment. If employees are given appropriate rewards, adequate incentives, and attractive development opportunities, they will provide the needed skills and expertise to reach higher limits of performance. When these supports are in place, good leaders should expect employees to provide high-quality work or services to community customers.

Remember that the common definition of employee commitment includes a connection between the strength of an employee's identification with the activity of the organization. This reinforces the concept of the value of employee participation in work-related decisions. Others have supported the view that employee participation in planned organization change helps employees attain higher-order needs and decreases resistance to change. Finally, it may be safe to say that employees—in both public- and private-sector jobs—will have higher levels of organizational commitment if they also have a high level of intrinsic motivation. This motivation comes from feelings that their jobs are important and that they are recognized for their achievements (Miller and Monge 1986; Moon 2000).

Step 5: Implement Change Strategies

This step requires the organization to first ask employees to help in the change effort, and then to empower them to not only make improvement suggestions, but to be held accountable for the accomplishment of these suggestions when they are finally adopted. Greiner (1967) calls this step *experimentation and search*. This means that employees are given provisional decision-making authority for some improvement in their department(s), or what is called *trial implementation*. If successful, another department may try an experimental improvement strategy, provided that they are given the power to try this in their department before it is tried elsewhere. If step 4 is done properly, then implementation should be relatively easy.

Public managers can ask for employee "ownership" of the needed changes, but employees will not commit to a transformation process until they believe they have the power to change the nature of their jobs and procedures. A major antecedent here is internalization of the desired behaviors and attitudes. This can only happen if public-service employees are actively involved in all of the change steps. The experience of the FBI in implementing its transformation initiative after 9/11 is an example of the difficulties that government agencies are encountering in their attempts to transform the way they operate and how they are structured (Box 4.1).

Box 4.1   Transforming the FBI after 9/11

The Federal Bureau of Investigation (FBI) has long been considered the nation's chief law enforcement agency. Under J. Edgar

Hoover, its first change agent, the FBI evolved into a highly respected federal agency of 31,000 employees, 56 field offices, and 50 offshore posts. Through the application of masterful public-relations campaigns, the crime-fighting skills and successes of the FBI were brought into every home in America by radio, newspaper, and television. The message was that once the FBI took on a case, a criminal would always be brought to justice. And that reputation was built without the aid of computers. In fact, as late as 2004, most FBI agents did not have email and could not access the Web from their office. Even after all the years of FBI investigations and record keeping, agents could not access an up-to-date computerized database to track and share case information. Most agents did not even have their own office computers. Rather than quick access to digital information, the culture at the FBI emphasized slow, steady investigative progress with detailed paper-based records that documented every aspect of an investigation.

Everything changed after 9/11. The mission of the FBI was shifted from catching criminals after they committed a crime to intelligence gathering and protecting the country and its citizens against terrorist attacks. In its old role, the FBI became a highly compartmentalized and decentralized organization, with the instincts of an independent agent on the scene often taking precedence over long-term strategic plan directions. A former U.S. attorney general described the cultural changes that the FBI would have to undergo as "staggering" and "almost a total transformation of what the bureau does and how it does it." If the transformation was to succeed, old ways of thinking, including the bureau's excessive focus on secrecy, had to be changed; the FBI had to be brought kicking and screaming into the digital age. It began the change with the purchase of 30,000 computers and a new data-management system.

However, the transformation of the FBI is not proving to be an easy task. Its first effort involved a $170 million technology investment—the Virtual Case File (VCF)—that was to make it possible for agents to finally communicate quickly with one another and access records and statistics in real time. This endeavor failed to meet its goals and was scrapped in 2005. The FBI is now replacing VCF with a $425 million system called Sentinel, which is projected to be online in 2009. Meanwhile, agents must still deal with paper-based records and painfully slow exchange of communications. As if that were not enough, the bureau's mandatory retirement age of 57 for agents is resulting in the loss of critical knowledge while also making it nearly impossible to achieve the long-term commitment to cultural change that is necessary for successful organizational transformation.

Source: **Brazil (2007)**

The best path in a transformation such as that attempted by the FBI may be to move slowly, taking incremental steps rather than an immediate upheaval. Administrators must find pockets of support among employees who are eager to try something new. These willing staff members may be new to the organization, or may have received the necessary information through the proper channels to eliminate the gossip and stories that precede actual implementation.

It is also wise to try a test case of the chosen transformation initiative and to remember that, even though jobs may be changed in one area and others outsourced, when the employees themselves do the analysis and contribute to the suggested transformation strategy, the chances of its success are vastly improved. As employees gain confidence in their own successes, they learn a valuable lesson in self-renewal. When they see a successful change that they have helped to implement, they will be open to further change and will help others make the change.

This approach works well until the employees who support change meet with resistance from their colleagues who were not informed why improvement is needed and question what they will gain if they cooperate. There are many change strategies that can make the improvement process work, but it is up to the top managers to employ competent human-resource managers who have the necessary skills to introduce and discuss the needed change strategies, and to enable workers to feel empowered.

Step 6: Assess Progress and Renew Commitment

Regrettably, the assessment step is too often not included in a culture-change or renewal program. However, assessing progress is critical if, once the desired change is underway, the culture *refreezing* process is about to take hold (Lewin 1951). An essential part of this step is the use of rewards and other incentives to perpetuate the new system or to revitalize the government agency. To be meaningful, rewards must be tied to the evaluation of the change program. If change is needed, employees must assess adopted solutions and generate new and possibly different strategies to overcome the drawbacks of an adopted solution. If things have changed in the external community/environment or internally due to an influx of new employees with different values and attitudes, there must be a new commitment for a new problem.

Plan, Do, Check, Act

Tying rewards to change commitment is similar to W. Edwards Deming's "plan, do, check, act" process. Deming suggested that no process can remain static. Rather, all processes should be constantly reevaluated so that, when needed, new processes are ready to meet new customer requirements. Step 6 is all about continuously improving the processes that have already been improved, either because (a) the customers (citizens) have changed, (b) customers have become more attuned to competition in the external market (community), or (c) new budgetary restrictions require belt tightening to keep the organization afloat.

Harvey and Brown (2001) suggested a somewhat different title for step 6, calling it a *continuous improvement* process. This is because they believed that their label more clearly stated the objective of the step, which is more than assessment and commitment. It means never being happy with the current situation, but instead being eager to ask if something could be done differently to improve customer service. High-performing agencies recognize that their clients are partners in the improvement process.

This six-step model presents a process to introduce organizational transformation, or reinvention. This process can make public-service agencies exceptional places to work, providing employees with challenge, ownership of the processes that they believe should be changed, and a desire to remain as active members of the organization because they have made a difference in their world as well as that of the citizens they serve, who now have greater respect for the changed and improved government agency.

Summary

This chapter began with a discussion of the need to assess the organizational culture and climate prior to embarking on a transformation process. The discussion then turned to a model illustrating the antecedents of staff commitment to the organization and the change process in organizations. It then introduced a six-step model of the organizational culture-change process and concluded with a brief description of transformation initiatives underway at the U.S. Department of Homeland Security.

The need for organizational transformation has created a requirement for a change in the way public policy and strategy are developed and implemented in public organizations. The relatively stable economic and social environments that once fostered tried-and-true ways of doing things have been rendered obsolete and ineffective. Government organizations need a new operating paradigm and a revitalized commitment to an ethos of unselfish public service. Commitment, however, assumes that those who choose public service have a set of values that prepares them for what is often described as societal disdain for their work and performance. As the study of two public organizations mentioned in the chapter illustrate, attaining that commitment and its commensurate readiness to accept change is problematic.

Chapter 5

Patterns of Change in Government

> We start with the assumption that to properly understand *organizational change* ... we need to stop giving ... ontological priority to organization, hereby making change an exceptional effect, produced only under specific circumstances by certain people (change agents). We should rather start from the premise that change is pervasive and indivisible; that is, to borrow James' (1909/1996) apt phrase, "the essence of life is its continuously changing character" and *then* see what this premise entails for our understanding of organizations.

> **Haridimos Tsoukas and Robert Chia (2002)**

Understanding the process of transformational change in government begins with understanding the meaning of the term. Most people think of transformation simply as some sort of *change*. However, this definition alone does not sufficiently identify the process of change continuously underway in government. The 2001 edition of the *Microsoft Encarta College Dictionary* defines transformation as "a complete change, usually into something with improved appearance or usefulness." It has also been defined as an act, process, or change in structure or character. Other terms used in defining the word include transmutation, conversion, revolution, makeover, alteration, and renovation. In his chapter on the theory of enterprise transformation, William Rouse (2006, 4) proposed the following definition:

> Enterprise transformation is driven by experienced and/or anticipated value deficiencies that result in significantly redesigned and/or new work

69

> processes as determined by management's decision making abilities, limitations, and inclinations, all in the context of the social networks of management in particular and the enterprise in general.

The important thing to remember about these and similar definitions of transformational change is that it is not accidental, casual, incremental, or evolutionary. Rather, transformation change is complete, planned, and revolutionary and never incremental. It is, in a word, *strategic.* And, it is continuous.

Incremental change, on the other hand, is change that is relatively easy to implement, or it is change that occurs naturally, often over long periods of time, and is not noticeable in the daily life of an organization until it is too late to reverse or react to the change. In organizations, incremental change is considered to be tactical rather than strategic; it is change designed to accomplish modest goals.

The transformational changes taking place in Level I (see Chapter 2) are *always* strategic and disruptive. Its purpose is to achieve "significant, quantum improvements" in the effectiveness of organizations, and it is often designed to produce significant savings in operating costs (Breul 2006a).

Governments are undergoing transformational change because they must. Public administrators and managers are being pressured to implement changes in the structure of government operations and in the strategies needed to meet the challenges they are encountering in the new century. According to Breul (2006a, 7), the new face of government is taking shape because administrators and managers have no alternative:

> Rising public expectations for demonstrable results and enhanced responsiveness will require fundamental *transformation* of government—where roles and even continued existence of some organizations and functions will be at stake.... Government organizations need to pick up the pace to become less hierarchical, process-oriented, stovepiped, and inwardly focused. They will need to become more partnership-based, results-oriented, integrated and externally focused.

Patterns of Change in Government

In 2003, Mark Abramson, Jonathan Breul, and John Kamensky of the IBM Center for the Business of Government, identified four broad categories of changes that government managers are taking in response to these pressures. The authors rewrote their report three years later, adding two more patterns of changes taking place in government, for a total of six. Collectively, the government's response to these and other demands for change is what is involved in the activities included in the practice of *enterprise transformation.* The six patterns of change are:

1. Changes in the rules of government through the way that public work takes place
2. Changes in the management of government operations through implementation of performance-management practices
3. Changes from bureaucratic to market-based governance
4. Changes that enable agencies to provide services on demand
5. Changes from tolerating citizen participation to encouraging and reengaging the electorate
6. Changes in the structure of services delivery to include collaboration, public/private teamwork, networks, partnerships, and coalitions

Changing the Rules of Government

The first of these six patterns of change involves a movement to change the rules of government. This includes revising the formal laws and reacting to the administrative demands with organizational structures to guide the actions of government workers and citizens in the new century. Reform of civil service systems is one of the major components in this trend. Civil service reform has made it possible to use performance and outcome measurements as the basis for hiring, firing, pay, and promotions, rather than continuing to rely on seniority alone. Another key activity in changing government rules is identifying and following the best practices of both private industry and government.

Changing the Rules at the DOE

The actions that governments are taking to reshape the way they work are driving a revolutionary change in the nature of work in the institutions of government. The story of inadequate management at the U.S. Department of Energy (DOE) is an example of why transformation of government operations is so important. After the Department of Defense, the DOE is the largest contracting agency in the federal government; about 90 percent of the department's budget—some $22 billion—is spent on contracts with outside suppliers.

Since 2005, the DOE has engaged in a transformation effort to resolve problems with its contract and project management. Despite those efforts, the Government Accountability Office (GAO 2007a) reported that performance problems still occurred with the department's major projects. For example, the agency continued to experience significant cost and schedule growth in constructing facilities to stabilize and treat 55 million gallons of radioactive waste at Hanford, Washington. The original $4.3-billion contract signed in 2000 to construct the treatment facilities had grown to more than $12 billion by the end of 2006. In addition, eight more years were added to the estimated date for completion; it is now projected that the work will not be completed until 2019.

According to the GAO, these problems are symptomatic of an ongoing series of management process problems at the energy department. The GAO traced many of the reasons for such poor program management to the department's practice of awarding contracts for concurrently designing and constructing one-of-a-kind facilities. This has been exacerbated by poor contractor management and inadequate oversight by DOE.

These problems of oversight at the DOE may occur more often than previously considered. For example, Marvel and Marvel (2007) found that governments tend to monitor the progress of for-profit contractors with a higher level of scrutiny than for internally delivered services. On the other hand, the performance of nonprofit contract partners and other government service providers are monitored much less carefully.

In general, DOE did not ensure that, prior to awarding of contracts for major projects, the contracts included effective performance incentives and penalties for contractors to control project costs and maintain or beat completion schedules. Moreover, GAO found that, prior to developing an action plan to strengthen contract and project management, the energy agency had not conducted a root-cause analysis to fully understand the causes of its contract and project management problems. As a result, the planners did not know what to fix!

While still existing in some agencies, the old public perception of government agencies as inefficient and ineffective hierarchical institutions that focus on maintenance management is being replaced. In its place is the recognition that governments are becoming businesslike, cost-effective, performance-oriented, learning organizations where the ideas of change and innovation are embraced. A core development that has made this transformation possible is recognition that the application of information and communications technologies alone will not make transformation happen. Instead, real transformation focuses on reshaping the way people in organizations think and work.

Changing the Rules at the U.K. Health Service

An example of change in the rules under which work is done in a large government organization was described in a case study of the U.K. national health system. To achieve change that lasts, administrators and managers must develop an organizational working environment in which employees are able to deal with the new circumstances. Pettigrew (1990) termed this as "influencing the conditions that determine the interpretation of situations and the regulation of ideas." It means modifying the organizational culture from a bureaucratic to a learning organization model.

In a case study of transformation at the national level, Ferlie et al. (1996) examined the changes in health and education services that took place from 1990 to 1995. The authors distinguished between several levels or categories of change that were taking place at the same time. Going beyond what they identified as the simple dichotomy between incremental and fundamental change, they saw a more useful classification existing in the differences between large-scale organizational change and organizational transformation.

As noted earlier, the introduction of incremental change in an organization is smaller in scope than that for a strategic change. Implementation of incremental change tends to focus on individual units or small groups within agencies. Strategic change, on the other hand, refers to a major change that affects one or more of the main programs of an organization. Examples include changing a unit's strategy, structure, technology, or control systems. Strategic change is further described by Ferlie as a process of "logical incrementalism, involving both planned and evolutionary processes." Transformational change takes strategic change a step farther, to where it can be described as frame breaking, revolutionary, or involving radical changes to the basic rules in an organization.

Ferlie et al. (1996) also identified a set of organizational indicators that can be used to distinguish between the strategic and transformational levels of change. These indicators can also be used to assess the change process of government from the national to the regional, to the individual organization or agency, or to the units within each level. The first two indicators have greater relevance for large-scale organizational change, whereas the last four apply in larger part to the process of transformational change. The indicators are

1. The range of the more highly changed elements and their interrelations across the unit as a whole
2. Whether new organizational forms are created
3. Development of many layers of change that affect the organization at the unit level
4. Changes created in the services provided by the agency and their delivery methods
5. Shifts in the power relations within the organization—who loses and who gains
6. Extensive alteration or creation of a new organizational culture, ideology, or perceived organizational rationale

Finally, Ferlie et al. (1996) defined transformation as a process of achieving fundamentally different outcomes within an organization. An example of a transformational change is an organization transforming its operating model from providing information technology products to one of helping client organizations find solutions to problems, with the solutions not necessarily involving technology. Ferlie et al. (1996, 89) concluded with a suggested scope for programs to bring about transformational change:

> [S]tart from the premises that transformational change produces more fundamental and pervasive outcomes than strategic change within a large-scale organization or sector. It is suggested that transformational

change, like strategic change, affects a number of the major systems in the organization. In addition, it is a multilayer process affecting different levels of the organization and even the context of the organization's operation, simultaneously. This form of change has much in common with other examples of strategic change in the public and private sectors ... but, it is argued, it also has a number of additive and distinctive characteristics.

Performance-Management Practices

The second important pattern in government is the growing use of performance-management practices to monitor and control operations. Performance management includes tracking progress in achieving goals and objectives, and then adapting programs and services to reinforce strengths and redirect efforts and resources where necessary to eliminate weaknesses.

Administrators are using performance measurements to plan future actions and design new and better responses to operational challenges (Melkers and Willoughby 2005; Moynihan 2005; Yang and Hsieh 2007). Performance government became an important government reform movement with the passage, during the early years of the Clinton administration, of the Government Performance and Results (GPR) Act of 1993 (Wechsler and Clary 2000). The National Performance Review (NPR) task force was established in March of 1993 to administer and monitor the progress of performance-management practices in the federal government. The GPR Act legally obligated government leaders to use performance planning and management practices, and to publicly report on their progress. Under the leadership of Vice President Al Gore, the NPR was re-formed as the National Partnership for Reinventing Government (NPRG) in 1998.

The task force published several advisory documents on implementing systems for managing and measuring performance. It also oversaw a series of employee surveys during the last years of the Clinton administration. One of those documents was a 66-page report on the results of a survey entitled "Balancing Measures: Best Practices in Performance Management." The following bits of advice were summarized from the partners' survey (NPRG 1999):

■ Adapt, don't adopt: make a best practice [used elsewhere] work for you.
■ We aren't so different after all; public or private, federal, state, or local, there are common problems—and common answers.
■ Leadership doesn't stop at the top. It should cascade throughout an organization, creating champions and a team approach to achievement of mission.
■ Listen to your customers and stakeholders.
■ Listen to your employees and unions.

- Partnership among customers, stakeholders, and employees results in success. Telling—rather than asking—these groups what they need does not work.
- The following words of advice were included later in the report and repeated several times: "*There is no such thing as a fixed and truly balanced set of measures*; instead, the *process* of balancing the needs of customers and employees against mission is a constant and living one, flexible and open to change" (emphasis in the original).

The nation's cities and counties, under the leadership of the International City/County Management Association (ICMA), were also quick to adopt performance-management principles and processes. The ICMA, with more than 9,000 members, formed its Center for Performance Measurement (CPM) in 1994, a year after passage of the GPR Act, to help local governments improve the effectiveness and efficiency of their services by collecting, analyzing, and applying performance data in their jurisdictions. CPM provides onsite training and access to best practices and benchmarking resources. Management help is provided in 15 separate government services or operations activities, ranging from code enforcement through human resources and information technology to youth services (ICMA 2005).

Planning, managing, and funding government services based on the measured performance of agencies providing the service is a key component in performance management. The ICMA described the benefits of these practices (Box 5.1):

Box 5.1   Benefits of a Good Performance-Management System

A good performance management system yields the necessary data for assessing service needs and performance. In this sense, a good system helps elected officials in their oversight responsibilities. It also helps them make objective resource-allocation decisions and formulate policy.

Performance management system is a powerful tool for engaging citizens and other stakeholders. By involving citizens in establishing and implementing performance management, local government fosters a broader awareness and sense of ownership of programs on the part of the public. Citizen involvement helps communities clarify their priorities and enables the public to play an active role in holding officials accountable, improving service delivery to the community, and allocating tax dollars.

Source: **ICMA (2005, 5, 7)**

Market-Based Management

The third pattern is a continuing movement toward more market-based operations by government managers. The term *market-based* refers to practices taken from the private sector, and is sometimes referred to as *managerialism*—as seen in the new public management movement. These practices include entrepreneurial activity, competition, choice and incentives in the activities and services of government, as well as managing for continuous improvement in the way that those services are delivered.

Like businesses, governments have also turned to such actions as outsourcing of services for both internal and external applications, public- and private-organization partnerships, and other related activities. One of its most visible and controversial actions is the privatization of many government services, some to businesses and others to nonprofit organizations. Kettl (2005, 17) described the rationale for the acceptance of this movement in Great Britain, New Zealand, and Australia:

> The new public management stemmed from the basic economic argument that government suffered from the defects of monopoly, high transaction costs, and information problems that bred great inefficiencies. By substituting market competition—and market-like incentives—the reformers believed that they could shrink government's size, reduce its costs, and improve its performance.... [A]t its core, the movement sought to transform how government performed its most basic functions.

The privatization of government services is one of the hallmarks of the public management movement. Between March 2000 and December 2003, 75 county-owned nursing facilities in the United States were divested to nonprofit organizations or sold to private enterprise firms (Amirkhanyan 2008). This represented nearly 10 percent of all county-owned nursing homes operating in the country in 2000. Faced with rapidly increasing costs to operate and limited opportunity to increase revenue, county-owned nursing homes are particularly vulnerable to pressures to control costs—a major reason behind the privatization trend. The study indicated that care quality rates did not decline in facilities transferred to nonprofit organizations, but did decline in facilities transferred to the for-profit sector. The declines are somewhat greater in areas where the facilities serve a larger low-income population.

Performance on Demand

The fourth trend identified in the IBM Center's report is identified as performing on demand. This means responding to citizen demands that government be more accessible to their needs—often available "24/7." To make this happen, governments at all levels are embracing the Internet and consolidating services within a single point of access. Four elements are involved in this trend of government agencies.

1. They are embracing *responsiveness* (reacting quickly to need).
2. They *focus* on best practices rather than trying to be all things to all people.
3. They accept *variability* by supporting *changes* in services and activities to meet evolving needs—what is described as being able to provide the right service at the right place and time in the right scale and scope.
4. They have had to become *resilient,* which entails maintaining the ability to perform the mission of the government agency or department regardless of impediment or threat.

E-government is the most visible example of government performing on demand. The E-Government Act of 2002 (H.R. 2458/S. 803), which became effective on April 17, 2003, established an Office of e-Government and authorized appointment of an e-administrator within the U.S. Office of Management and Budget (OMB 2004). A key goal of that legislation was the development of a coordinated cross-government-level policy on the use of information technology in the delivery of government services. Working with state, local, and tribal governments, the general public, and the private and nonprofit sectors, the e-government office is charged with finding innovative ways to: (a) improve the performance of governments in collaborating on the use of information technology to improve the delivery of government information and services; (b) set standards for federal agency Web sites; and (c) create a public directory of government Web sites.

E-government includes government actions to produce and deliver services to citizens, not in the traditional face-to-face manner, but instead through the use of communications technology. Most of these delivery actions now involve the Internet. Thus, e-government uses information and communications technologies (ICT) to ensure that citizens and businesses receive better quality services, mainly through such electronic delivery channels as the Internet, digital TV, mobile phones, and related technology.

In the form established in the President's Management Agenda (PMA), the 2002 e-government initiative was to improve the management and performance of the federal government by focusing on operational areas where deficiencies are most apparent and where the government could begin to deliver concrete, measurable results. PMA included five federal government–wide initiatives and ten program-specific initiatives that apply to a subset of federal agencies. For each initiative, PMA established clear, governmentwide goals (termed *standards for success*) and developed action plans to achieve the goals. The five governmentwide standards for success for e-government included:

■ *Budget and performance integration* (BPI): efforts to ensure that agency or program performance is routinely considered in funding and management decisions, and that programs are monitored to ensure they achieve expected results and continuous improvement

■ *Competitive sourcing* (CS): requires agencies to regularly examine their activities to determine whether it is more efficient for federal employees or the private sector to supply services

■ *Expanded electronic government* (EEG): actions to ensure that the federal $60-billion annual investment in information technology (IT) significantly improves the government's ability to serve citizens, and that those IT systems are secure and delivered on time and on budget

■ *Improved financial performance* (IFP): accounts for taxpayers' money and provides timely and accurate program cost information to improve management decisions and control costs

■ *Strategic management of human capital* (SMHC): processes put in place to ensure that the right person is in the right job, at the right time, and is not only performing, but performing well; associated with government's Human Resources Planning (HRP) initiative

Reengaging Citizens

The fifth change pattern occurring in government is the drive to reengage citizens in their government, whether that be at the local, state, or national level. This trend is referred to as *citizen participation* or *citizen involvement*. A number of important advantages tend to follow greater citizen involvement (Berman 1997; King, Feltey, and Susel 1998; Walters, Aydelotte, and Miller 2000; Yang and Callahan 2005). These include improvements in the agency performance, greater responsiveness by citizens, increased trust in government and belief in the legitimacy of government decisions.

The reengagement of citizens is happening through greater reliance on the delivery of some traditional government services by nongovernmental organizations. Faith-based and traditional nonprofit organizations, with their firsthand awareness of local needs and requirements, are often in the best position to meet local needs (Clerkin and Grønbjerg 2007; Smith and Sosin 2001). These organizations rely heavily upon volunteerism in the conduct of their actions, thus further leveraging their effectiveness. Not everyone supports the idea that faith-based organizations are as effective as their supporters claim. The General Accountability Office reported in 2002 that some faith-based organizations do not have the capacity to collaborate with government or to perform as required because of inadequate information technologies as well as inefficient management structures and financial systems.

Reengagement of citizens into the political arena is a major objective of governments at all levels. The more-proactive communities operate participation academies to help private citizens learn how to be more effective volunteers and participants. One such program operates in Buffalo, New York. Participants in the nine-week program receive detailed explanations of the structure and management of the city, learning about such important city issues as education, public and fire safety, community programs, and community development. Instruction is given by city administrators and department directors. Participants and their families also visit city facilities and attend council and commission hearings (City of Buffalo 2007).

Box 5.2   The Phoenix Municipal Volunteer Program

The City of Phoenix, Arizona, operates a municipal volunteer program, through which more than 20,000 residents each year volunteer in such services as library aids, delivering food to senior citizens, and repairing toys and bicycles for needy children. Other citizens volunteer on the city's village planning committees. These committees have been formed for each of the 15 "villages" into which Phoenix has been divided. Each village comprises several different neighborhoods. The role of the volunteers is to collect the opinions and concerns of all citizens in the neighborhoods in their village and report these to the city planning commission and city council. The city reports that many elected city officials gained their first experience in government as a volunteer on the committees. Still other volunteers serve on citizen advisory committees, groups, boards, or commissions for other departments of the city and other social service functions.

Source: **City of Phoenix (2007)**

Networks, Partnerships, and Coalitions

The sixth pattern of change in government includes the growing use of networks, partnerships, and coalitions to deliver government services. Together, these approaches are referred to as *collaborative management* or *collaborative networks*. They have been defined as "the process of facilitating and operating in multiorganizational arrangements to solve problems that cannot be solved, or solved easily, by single organizations" (Agranoff 2007).

The many challenges facing government administrators is forcing them to transcend the normal ways of thinking and acting in an effort to find new approaches to problem resolution (Agranoff and McGuire 2003; Kicker, Klijn, and Koppenjan 1997; Mandell 2001). The U.S. federal government is leading the way in the change movement that is taking place to meet these and related challenges. The new coalition of agencies that resulted in the formation of the Department of Homeland Security illustrates the scope of changes that are taking place in the federal government.

The Department of Homeland Security (DHS) has been charged with what has been described as "one of the most daunting assignments in the history of the U.S. Government—amalgamating and aligning 22 separate governmental agencies into a single, cohesive, efficient and effective department" (DHS 2007).

One of the most problematic tasks facing DHS leadership has been integration of the often widely diverse cultures of these organizations into one that encompasses the mission and philosophy of a single department. Organizational culture refers to the common relationships, values, beliefs, and processes that create and support the activities of individuals within an organization. It is influenced by the management and leadership styles, motivational processes, and support infrastructures of the organization.

In February 2002, just six months after the September 11, 2001, terrorist attacks on the World Trade Towers and the Pentagon, President George W. Bush signed an executive order establishing a 21-member Homeland Security Advisory Council (PHSAC). The key function of the council was to advise the president on developing and implementing a comprehensive strategy for securing the nation from further terrorist threats. The order also established a number of senior advisory committees (SACs) to advise the PHSAC, chief among which consisted of state and local officials as well as representatives from academia and policy research, the private sector, emergency services, law enforcement, and public health and hospitals. Additional advisory committees and special task forces were added later. One of these task forces was the Homeland Security Advisory Council's Culture Task Force (CTF).

The CTF was charged with producing recommendations to Department Secretary Michael Chertoff with recommendations for forging an "energetic, dedicated, and empowering mission-focused organization: one that leverages, focuses, strengthens and synergizes the multiple capabilities of its components and empowers them to continuously improve the Department's operational capacities and the security of the Nation" (DHS 2007).

Recommendations of the Task Force

The task force issued its recommendations on steps needed to accomplish that mission in January 2007. The report recommended the implementation of six broad steps to strengthen the culture of the organization, with the added caveat that no single homeland security culture is possible or, for that matter, wise. The task force's recommendations included:

1. The DHS headquarters must further define and crystallize its role in the newly organized collection of different operational units.

2. DHS must implement management and leadership models that align the highly diverse and dispersed organization around a common language, common management processes, and common leadership expectations.

3. DHS must establish an "operational leadership position" by establishing a new position of deputy secretary for operations (DSO). The DSO, a professional government administrator with experience in national security operations, would be responsible for departmentwide measures at enhancing integration and alignment of the new department's operational units. In the process, the DSO would provide continuity and reinforce the collective culture necessary for long-term success of the department and its components. Moreover, the DSO would be responsible for developing and enforcing strategic initiatives that are about the security of the homeland, and not about the DHS itself.

4. DHS must create leadership-empowered teamwork and a "blended culture." Given the long history of many of its component organizations, the CTF recognized that developing and enforcing a hierarchically imposed single culture within the department was not possible. However, the CTF believed that a blended culture could be forged. This would be based on common values, goals, and mission focus found in all of the component units. CTF also recommended that a senior employee be assigned the task of developing and sustaining the blended culture across all units.

5. DHS must engage state, local, tribal, and private-sector organizations that are not Washington-focused in the collaborative process necessary to ensure accomplishment of the DHS mission. DHS units should coordinate security actions on a regional basis, taking advantage of existing units' relationships with local agencies and organizations. Those local groups must also be brought into the planning stages of grant funding, thereby improving the transparency and stability of the process.

6. DHS must institutionalize opportunities for innovation at all levels of its units' operations. One role of DHS headquarters should be to manage development of technologies and innovations with a potential for impacting across two or more agencies or units, but without limiting the ability of individual units to develop and implement specific innovations on their own. Moreover, the CTF recommended that all component units adopt a unit similar to that of the included U.S. Coast Guard's Innovation Council to coordinate with a similar position at DHS headquarters.

Factors Resisting the Patterns of Change

Administrators must also be aware of the forces that resist transformational change in government organizations. Transformational change involves instilling a new culture into an existing organization and requiring employees to adopt new ways of thinking and doing new things. Change is a hard sell in most organizations because it means changing the way that people do their jobs. It may also mean creating an entirely different organization out of an old, entrenched bureaucracy. It means starting again at the beginning. Along the way, some people find themselves left behind. That often signals people losing their jobs.

Transformation in organizations means people adopting new values, ideas, and beliefs. It entails a recommitment to the goals and the mission of the organization. David Hurst (1995) referred to it as a *revival* of the beliefs and values, the state of excitement, and the deep personal commitment that employees and managers often feel at the start of an organization. This sense of revival is similar to the workplace atmosphere that has been described as existing in such dynamic private-sector start-ups as Google, Nike, Apple, Starbucks, and Microsoft. It has also been used to describe the climate in revitalized organizations such as General Electric. Because it is something that has to be reintroduced into organizations that are in decline, transformation may also be looked upon as organizational renewal or revitalization.

The Human Factor

The key element in defining and achieving organizational transformation is the human factor. Organizational transformation is a process of altering the activities of *people*, their reactions and interactions, authority structures, and performance standards in such a way as to shift the organization's existing state to some future desired state (Pettigrew 1990). Transformation is not just a change in the way the organization functions; it also involves altering of the *behavior of individuals* in the organization (Vasu, Stewart, and Garson 1998).

Most public managers are aware that successfully introducing a new way of operating or functioning into an organization is not an easy task. It often results in dissatisfied or distressed employees who fail to fully buy into the new way of doing things. Staff resistance to the desired change is often excessive and immediate, a point that has led some researchers to suggest that it may be easier and less costly to start a completely new organization than it is to attempt to renew an existing one (Thompson and Luthans 1990). This, of course, is next to impossible in the public sector, where structures and missions are often mandated and not open to change without hard-to-secure legislative action.

Many believe that a true transformation can only take place after some sort of crisis occurs in the organization or its environment. For example, Kiel (1994) wrote that a "state of chaos" must be introduced into the organization before a transformation or renewal can begin. Hurst (1995) also adopted this crisis theme, using the metaphor of a forest fire to describe the importance of clearing away old ideas and ways of operating and replacing them with a transformed and revitalized organization.

The difficulty of achieving change in an organization is further exemplified by the many organizations that attempted to adopt organizationwide ERP (enterprise resource planning) systems, but failed to do so. Those organizations met with a high rate of inability to achieve the efficiencies promised by ERP providers, or were only partially successful in integrating all of their management systems into the ERP suite. As a result, government organizations are questioning whether ERP is, indeed, right for their operations, despite a slowly growing record of successes in the private sector.

Similar failures can be cited for many other change initiatives. Examples of efforts to institute a transformation in the way government organizations operate include early organizational reengineering, moving to outside sources for services and labor, "delayering" of the organization's structure (downsizing), and public-private joint-venturing. To succeed with any of these change initiatives requires extensive preparation and constant, total-staff commitment; it requires an organizational culture that embraces change, innovation, and invention.

A Choice of Change Strategies

Government managers have the choice of modifying their organizations' culture and climate or changing the existing processes, policies, or technologies to match the dictates of the existing organization's culture and climate. Either way, the process of instituting a major change into an organization needs to be specifically tailored to meet that organization's particular circumstances. Without one or both of these modifications, failure rates will remain high.

However, this should not be unexpected; no one ought to be surprised that organizations resist change. In the past, organizations were supposed to provide employees with a recognized, stable way of dealing with the problems of their environment (Weber 1947; Wilson 1989). In one sense, this defines a classic bureaucracy. In a bureaucratic organization, transformational change is resisted; only gradual changes are permitted to occur, leaving basic processes and structures unaltered. The role of leadership in such classic administrative organizations is to stabilize processes and workers, and to maintain order in an inherently disorderly world (Kiel 1994). Stable operating environments are, however, a thing of the past. Today, private- and public-sector organizations must learn to accommodate transformational change as never before.

Although prior research has produced conflicting results, implementation of change initiatives may become even more difficult when the organization is a public agency, as managers of such agencies are forced to use largely nonmaterial incentives as rewards for adoption (Steinhaus and Perry 1996). Bringing change into such an organization has been shown to be a complex and lengthy process of altering the underlying culture. According to Wollner (1992), such action requires unprecedented technical competence and may take as long as ten years to complete, if at all.

How, then, does a public organization improve its chances of successful transformational change? The one sure way to make it happen has not yet been written.

What works in one agency may result in abject failure in another. The transformation programs included as examples in this book are designed to assist managers in their efforts to revitalize their organizations. To arrive at the best strategy, an understanding of public organizations is essential.

Summary

This chapter looked at some of the important changes now shaping public-sector operations, programs, approaches, and program-delivery systems. Six patterns in administrative change were reviewed:

1. Changing the rules of government
2. Introduction of performance-management practices
3. Market-based operations
4. On-demand service to citizens
5. Enhanced citizen participation
6. Improved delivery through networks, collaboration, and cooperation

However, all the evidence is not in yet; the transformation processes that these patterns of change are producing will require additional monitoring before it can be determined whether these public management approaches and methods are completely relevant to the practice of managing government activities.

To be successful, adoption of new and innovative government activities and programs must reflect what best meets the needs of all stakeholders—administrators, citizens, legislative bodies, the press, and anyone else with a stake in the outcomes of government programs. The services delivered must not be influenced predominantly by the technology available at the time and place of delivery. Rather, government services are becoming increasingly *client-oriented* or *citizen-focused*. To put this phenomenon in private-sector terms, government is becoming more *customer-centered*.

Chapter 6

How Public Managers
Shape and Direct Change

> Effective public administration in the age of results-oriented manage-
> ment requires public agencies to develop a capacity for strategic man-
> agement, the central management process that integrates all major
> activities and functions and directs them toward advancing an organi-
> zation's strategic agenda.

Theodore H. Poister and Gregory D. Streib (1999)

Public managers have available to them a variety of processes and procedures from private enterprise to help them shape and direct change processes.
Adoption of strategic management (SM) processes by government administrators is one example of these private-sector management practices. In their willingness to adopt whatever tools they believe will do the job, these managers are
changing the face of public administration. Managing government agencies
strategically involves putting to work a set of management actions that enable
the coordination of all aspects of an organization's operations. It is a process
that results in identifying and applying the most efficient and effective use of
scarce agency resources.

Strategic management is a way of planning and managing transformational
change. It has been described as the "most effective tool for shaping, defining,
and implementing [transformational] change in public sector" organizations (Cox,
Buck, and Morgan 1994). In all its various forms and adjustments, most versions of
strategic management include some version of these elements (Streib 1992; Bryson
2004; Berman and West 1998):

- Commitment to strategic planning
- Acceptance of a vision for the agency, with statements of what it values and believes
- A mission statement that builds on the vision of the agency leadership
- Statements of broad organizational goals and specific objectives to facilitate achieving the goals
- Environmental analyses to identify key external factors and long-term trends that will shape the agency's future operations
- Analysis of the internal environment to weigh which resource strengths and weaknesses will support or constrain the agency's mission
- Regular reviews of performance progress and, as needed, implementation adjustments to keep the agency headed toward accomplishing its goals and objectives

The Role of Public Managers in Strategic Management

Mark Moore (1995), of Harvard's Kennedy School for Government, described public managers who follow strategic management precepts as "explorers who, with others, seek to discover, define, and produce public value. Instead of simply devising the means for achieving mandated purposes, they become important agents in helping to discover and define what would be valuable to do. Instead of being responsible only for guaranteeing continuity, they become important innovators in *changing what public organizations do and how they do it*. In short,... public managers become strategists rather than technicians" (emphasis added).

The processes in strategic management have a long and successful history of contributing to the transformation of government. The SM process was developed as a tool to help private-sector organizations be more competitive in the global marketplace. However, a growing number of public administrators and elected officials have concluded that strategic management can be as beneficial to government agencies and nonprofit organizations as it is to managers in private enterprise. Many different views have been aired on the use and appropriateness of strategic management in government, and many of those concluded that it could not be done; applying the results-oriented business management tool to the process-dominated world of government was problematic, at best (Streib 1992). However, passage of the Government Performance and Results Act of 1993 has resulted in the requirement for all federal agencies to implement the approach; nearly all state and local governments have also passed similar legislation in which they have adopted most, if not all, strategic management processes. (Poister and Streib 1999).

Although strategic planning—one of the core concepts of strategic management—has enjoyed nearly universal acceptance in all levels of government, state and local government managers were slower in adopting the complete package of management activities (Poister and Streib 2005). This was partly due to the substantial investments in time and resources necessary for all processes, together with a long-term commitment. Managing strategically lays four requirements (Poister and Streib 1999) upon local governments:

■ Managers must continually monitor the fit between the agency and its environment.
■ Managers must identify and track trends in the environment that may affect the jurisdiction.
■ The organization must establish a clear vision of its desired future as well as its values and standards while maintaining a group commitment to the best possible performance of its mission.
■ All other management processes in the organization must be adjusted to support and enhance the overall strategic goals and objectives of the organization.

Three Core Sets of Management Activities

A representation of the activities and processes involved in the strategic management process is displayed in Figure 6.1. As the model illustrates, these activities occur in three separate but closely related sets of management activities:

■ Level one involves internal and external environmental analysis and developing a vision and mission for the agency.
■ Level two involves allocating the core organizational resources and assets that make it possible for an agency to accomplish its mission.
■ Level three is the complex arena of the delivery of agency services. It includes the operational systems that managers and staff employ in the conduct of their activities. Three sets of systems are included in this third level:
  1. Enterprise systems
  2. Systems that enable delivery of programs and services (strategy selection and tactical implementation)
  3. The knowledge system that facilitates feedback, planning, and information distribution as well as knowledge sharing, collection, and archiving for future operations (performance measurement)

Each of these levels is discussed in greater detail in the following subsections.

Level One Activities: Environmental Analysis, Vision, and Mission

Four fundamental processes are included at the first level of strategic management. The first two of these are the foundational processes of analyzing the *environment* in which the agency or department must function. This scanning and analysis of events

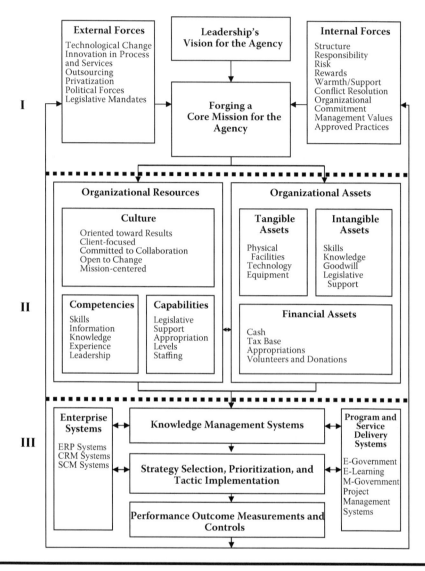

I

External Forces	Leadership's Vision for the Agency	Internal Forces
Technological Change Innovation in Process and Services Outsourcing Privatization Political Forces Legislative Mandates	Forging a Core Mission for the Agency	Structure Responsibility Risk Rewards Warmth/Support Conflict Resolution Organizational Commitment Management Values Approved Practices

II

Organizational Resources

Culture

Oriented toward Results
Client-focused
Committed to Collaboration
Open to Change
Mission-centered

Competencies

Skills
Information
Knowledge
Experience
Leadership

Capabilities

Legislative Support
Appropriation Levels
Staffing

Organizational Assets

Tangible Assets

Physical Facilities
Technology
Equipment

Intangible Assets

Skills
Knowledge
Goodwill
Legislative Support

Financial Assets

Cash
Tax Base
Appropriations
Volunteers and Donations

III

Enterprise Systems

ERP Systems
CRM Systems
SCM Systems

Knowledge Management Systems

Strategy Selection, Prioritization, and Tactic Implementation

Performance Outcome Measurements and Controls

Program and Service Delivery Systems

E-Government
E-Learning
M-Government
Project Management Systems

Figure 6.1 Representation of strategic management processes.

and trends in the environment provides the agency leadership with the background information necessary to construct long-term operational strategies. The next two activities are the initial creative processes of strategic management: constructing a long-term *vision* for the agency or department, and then collaboratively forging a statement that describes the core *mission* of the agency for all relevant stakeholders.

Often referred to as *environmental scanning*, this is one of the core processes of strategic management, and one that managers of government organizations are increasingly using to identify and analyze the salient characteristics and trends that can impact their operational environments. Once carried out only at the beginning of the annual budget cycle, this situational analysis has become an ongoing procedure in nearly all organizations at the federal and state levels, and it is being increasingly applied in municipal governments.

The internal environment includes the culture, capabilities, capacities, and assets of the organization that enable it to carry out its core tasks and evolve into a high-performance organization, a requirement for survival in today's fast-changing world. The external environment includes factors—beyond the control of the agency—that serve both as constraints to its operations and opportunities for innovative change. Together, the internal and external environments shape the progress of the agency in the conduct of its mission.

The *vision* that shapes the global view of a government agency is a reflection of the management philosophy and goals brought to the agency by its senior administrator. The vision statement typically includes the core values of the agency; it is, in other words, a statement of how the administrators, supervisors, and employees of the agency believe the agency should function. In addition, the vision articulates a picture of what the agency will look like in some future attainable time period—often as long as 20 or more years in the future.

The statement of strategic vision is leadership's vision of what the organization stands for, what it values, how it wants to be remembered, and what it wants to be when the transformation is complete. Vision statements are, therefore, typically stated as highly ambitious goals rather than specific, measurable objectives. They are statements that reflect the philosophy that guides the actions of senior administrators.

A vision statement can be as simple as that of the U.S. Government Printing Office (GPO): "To deliver Federal information products and services from a flexible digital platform" (GPO 2004). This is a *transformational visionary statement* because, at the time the statement was published, the GPO did not have a flexible digital platform in effect. Most of what it produced for other government agencies and the public was still printed and delivered in traditional form. It would take many years, millions of dollars, new facilities, new staff, and new technologies to bring this vision to full fruition.

Leadership and Values

Strategic management is, above all, a physical manifestation of good organizational *leadership*. It is a logical and valuable approach for planning and implementing a transformational change in an organization. Achieving the new, planned state for the organization becomes the long-term goal for members of the organization. It also provides an opportunity to set out a set of fundamental values for the organization's personnel. When the objective is a transformational change, it is absolutely essential that it be spelled out in a vision statement that is understandable to all personnel. When it is, the transformational vision statement serves to engage and guide the actions of members of the organization in the way they perform their duties.

The values of the organization are delineated in statements describing how all agency personnel are expected to behave in the performance of their duties. These values are aligned with such concepts as public service, honesty, responsiveness, unbiased treatment of subordinates and colleagues, commitment to the well-being and success of all employees, responsibility to internal and external stakeholders, and the like. There is no hard-and-fast rule of what a vision statement should include in terms of values. Rather, the vision statement reflects the beliefs and values that are important to the people that make it possible for the agency to carry out the transformation in ways that leave everyone proud to be a member of the team.

The U.S. Department of State, for example, includes a list of the values designed to guide department operations so that they align with its mission statement (Box 6.1). The statement includes a conceptual view of what the agency is to look like at some point in the distant future if all things come to pass as planned. In this way, it is both directive and transformational; it tells workers what is important and what they need to do to accomplish the desired change.

Box 6.1   Mission and Values at the U.S. Department of State

Mission:

Create a more secure, democratic, and prosperous world for the benefit of the American people and the international community

Values:

Loyalty: Commitment to the United States and the American people

Character: Maintenance of high ethical standards and integrity

Service:

Excellence in the formulation of policy and management practices with room for creative dissent

Implementation of policy and management practices, regardless of personal views

Accountability: Responsibility for achieving U.S. foreign policy goals while meeting the highest performance standards

Community: Dedication to teamwork, professionalism, and the customer perspective

Source: **DOS (2005)**

The Agency Mission

The mission of the agency is identified in a statement that describes what the agency does now, what it does best, and for whom the agency carries out its core activities—its customer base. The mission statement clearly establishes how the transformational change will be implemented. Because the mission-forging process requires collective agreement on the purpose of the agency, it can become a unifying statement, one that helps ensure that everyone in the agency knows where his or her contribution fits into the larger whole. Because it affects everyone, the mission statement should be a product of collective action. This means that an administrative team must agree on the fundamental rationale for the group's existence, often by restating the original reason for which the organization was formed in light of the current state of reality.

The online strategic planning service mystrategicplan.com (M3 Planning 2006) makes the following point in distinguishing between an agency's mission and its vision:

> A ... mission statement acts as the [agency's] compass. The mission is the path. (The vision is the end point.) The mission directs the [agency] to its vision (dream). With it, anyone in the organization can always judge the direction the [agency] is moving in relation to its stated purpose. With it, one can easily make adjustments to keep ... moving in the direction intended.

Example Statements

Examples of the mission statements of federal, state, and local government organizations are included to illustrate the great diversity found in these important guiding statements. The first example (DOL 2006) is from the U.S. Department of Labor's Office of Veterans' Employment and Training Service (VETS):

> Veterans succeeding in the 21st century workforce: The mission statement for VETS is to provide veterans and transitioning service members with the resources and services to succeed in the 21st century workforce by maximizing their employment opportunities, protecting their employment rights and meeting labor-market demands with qualified veterans today.

The Michigan Department of Labor and Economic Growth (MDLEG) merges its mission and vision statements into one short, two-paragraph declaration. MDLEG first defines its mission as working to: "Grow Michigan by promoting economic and workforce development, stimulating job creation, and enhancing the quality of life in Michigan." MDLEG's mission is further defined to: "Grow Michigan into an economic powerhouse—enriching the lives of its residents by using the creativity and commitment of our staff and partners to develop the tools needed to inspire innovation, attract the best and the brightest, grow entrepreneurs, gain and retain business, protect core industries, enhance our urban and rural communities, nurture diversity, foster inclusion, promote excellence in education, strengthen the workforce and encourage new technology" (DLEG 2006).

Box 6.2   Mission and Vision Statements of the Michigan Townships Association

Mission statement: The Michigan Townships Association promotes the interests of 42 townships by fostering strong, vibrant communities; advocating legislation to meet 21st century challenges; developing knowledgeable, township officials and enthusiastic supporters of township government; and encouraging ethical practices of elected officials who uphold the traditions and unique characteristics of township government and the values of the people of Michigan.

Values statement:

- Build on past traditions and uphold values unique to the township way of life
- Promote the integrity of township government through knowledgeable, ethical, trustworthy, and accountable elected and appointed officials who are dedicated to democratic principles and sound fiscal management
- Embrace integrity as the cornerstone upon which the public's trust is built
- Recognize and celebrate the unique virtues of township government
- Promote an involved citizenry that appreciates and supports townships, and respects those who serve as public officials
- Encourage local leaders to treat citizens with respect, dignity, and fairness
- Enhance access to information and materials to ensure that elected and appointed local officials acquire and apply the necessary knowledge to contribute positively to their townships and society
- Facilitate productive working relationships with the legislative, executive, and judicial branches of government and other organizations with whom our association interacts

- Maintain high standards in the programs and services made available through the association, including endorsed products and third-party relationships
- Encourage officials and citizens to work together for positive change in townships
- Create a future for townships to benefit those generations that will follow

Source: **MTA (2007)**

The mission and vision (values) statements of the Michigan Township Association (MTA) are displayed in Box 6.2. Note that the vision of the association is incorporated into a lengthy statement of values. This is a typical way of presenting these statements to various stakeholder groups. It is effective because it states in one place: This is what we believe in; this is who we are; and this is whom we serve.

The mission statement of the City of Casa Grande, Arizona, is an example of the way local governments use vision and mission statements as part of their strategic management. Casa Grande, an Arizona town of some 30,000 citizens, is a popular wintering home of retirees wishing to spend their summers in the Sun Belt, free from winter snowstorms. The city's mission statement is displayed in Box 6.3.

Box 6.3 Mission Statement of the City of Casa Grande

To provide a safe, pleasant community for all citizens, we will:

Serve Casa Grande through a variety of City Services designed to promote quality of life.
Ensure the safety of the community through aggressive public safety efforts and programs.
Respond to the needs of the community by promoting communications and accessibility.
Value the tax dollar and maintain a fiscal policy that keeps taxes low.
Incorporate safeguards to assure fairness and equitable treatment of all citizens.
Continue to evaluate our services and ourselves to ensure quality.
Endeavor to hire the best people we can find and help them develop their abilities.

In Casa Grande, we are committed to service.

Source: **City of Casa Grande, Arizona (2006)**

Level Two: Managing Resources and Assets

The second level of strategic decisions and activities involves the creative alloca-tion and application of an organization's resources and assets to effectively and efficiently design and deliver programs and services desired by its constituency. Fundamentally, how well organizations accomplish their missions depends upon how well they manage their resources and assets (Rouse 2006; Bryson, Ackerman, and Eden 2007). The resource-based view of the organization—private, public, or nonprofit—may be the most widely used approach in strategy research. There are two key concepts in this approach:

1. Scarce, valuable, and difficult-to-imitate resources are the only assets capable of creating sustained performance differences.
2. Such resources should be predominant in developing organizational strategy.

Three Types of Resources

Organizations have three types of resources and three types of assets. The three resources of an organization are its culture, the distinctive competencies of its peo-ple, and the capabilities that enable it to perform the activities of its mission. The success of any transformational change depends upon how well it meshes with the culture of the organization (Rouse 2006; McNabb and Sepic 1995).

Organizational culture changes slowly, if at all. Often, the culture is not com-patible with the changes that must be made for the transformation to take root. Management must work long and hard to influence the willingness of employees to accept transformational change over less-threatening but often less-effective incre-mental change.

Three Types of Assets

The three types of assets held by all organizations include financial, tangible, and intangible assets. Financial assets refer to the cash available to carry out all its tasks. In government organizations, this typically refers to the budget allocated to the organization by its controlling legislative body. However, a transformation change has moved many agencies from passive, custodial management philosophies to active managers of user-fee-financed services. Public campgrounds of the U.S. Forest Service are an example.

Tangible assets include the physical plant, equipment, and inventory made avail-able by the financial assets. For the Federal Emergency Management Administration (FEMA), tangible assets include all of the emergency equipment, vehicles, and other equipment it needs to provide succor to victims of emergencies and disasters.

Intangible assets include skills, core competencies, knowledge, culture, technologies, and stakeholder loyalties. In the end, all assets function together as a total system that is the enterprise (Smith 1998).

In planning and managing their activities, managers in business and industry have traditionally given more attention to their financial and tangible assets. Governments, on the other hand, often must place more emphasis on their intangible assets. This helps explain why knowledge management is so important in government organizations.

Level Three: Operational Systems

The first two levels of core management activities make it possible for agency leaders to firmly establish what must take place to activate the agency's core competencies and to plan how they will use assets and systems to make it happen. This third level of management activities and decisions involves the operational systems that agency personnel will use to facilitate transformational change and to provide services in ways mandated by the transformation. These include the use of enhanced information- and communications-technology systems to boost the efficiency and effectiveness of all agency operations. During these third-level actions, the administrative team must focus on implementing the programs and policies that constitute the new way of operating. These include three broad classes of technology-enhanced systems:

- Systems that facilitate the management of the enterprise
- Systems that have and are continuing to transform the way that (a) work is done in organizations and programs and (b) services are delivered to constituent groups
- Systems that use these and other human and technical skills and tools to manage the knowledge that is resident within the organization and its people

Identifying and Selecting Strategies

Once transformation objectives are set and prioritized, agency managers must select the strategies they will follow to accomplish the objectives. It is important to note that this is a decision process; typically, many different strategies are possible. Leadership selects the strategies that best fit the environmental conditions, long-term trends, existing and future capabilities, and the costs to complete the strategic actions as well as the costs that will accrue from a failed implementation of the transformation.

Strategy selection always occurs within the physical world, which is where noncontrollable environmental factors form constraints of action. Moreover, strategy is always carried out by people who depend on other people and resources to support their actions. The Strategic and Defense Studies Center at the Australian National University (Frühling 2006, 21) defines strategy as:

> Strategy … can be thought of as the system of causal relationships that underlies the strategic pyramid. Strategy is therefore at work in success and failure alike, and it is usually easy in hindsight to identify the causes for either. Unfortunately, this ease of explanation ex-post stands in stark contrast to the difficulty of "doing" strategy in the here and now, when it is necessary to develop a specific course of action ex-ante that provides a coherent, credible, and realistic way to achieve the political goal with the available means. Because the execution of strategy is inevitably directed at the future, practitioners must forecast the cause–effect relationships that will underlie the strategic effect—a fundamentally different, and much more difficult, problem than identifying them after the fact.

The story of the U.S. Defense Department's land-mine removal program, described in Box 6.4, illustrates how strategies are developed and managed in a major unit of the U.S. Army—the Central Command (CENCOM).

Planning Transformation Tactics

Tactics are short-term actions, often designated in annual functional plans; strategy is long term in scope and is the purview of the strategic plan. Tactical success results from operational success, the third dimension in the strategy pyramid. When operations are successful, strategic success, the fourth dimension, is achieved. It is important to remember that successes on lower levels are necessary, but not sufficient, to ensure success at higher levels. Tactics are another way of describing what it is that people do on the job. Often, tactics are the same year after year, regardless of any planned or proposed change. Like other elements in organizational culture, changing tactics in most organizations is usually an evolutionary process rather than a transformational activity—another factor that can impede transformational change. As a result, administrators must plan tactics with the same amount of care they give to deciding on objectives and strategies.

Performance Outcome Measurements and Controls

Goals and objectives are statements of what the transformation process is to accomplish. As such, they lend themselves handily to metrics for measuring an agency's progress in accomplishing what it sets out to achieve. Goals are very long-term targets that are typically stated in open-ended terms that do not include any specific provision for measurement. As such, they are closely aligned with the agency leadership's vision. The horizons for goals can be 20 or more years in the future, although there is often no established time limit for measuring progress.

Box 6.4   Strategic Management and Humanitarian Aid

The U.S. Central Command (CENTCOM) is one of the five geographically defined unified commands within the Department of Defense. CENTCOM is responsible for planning and conducting all U.S. military activity in a region of 27 countries in Northeast Africa, Southwest and Central Asia, and the Seychelles Islands. Established by the Carter administration in 1983, CENTCOM is responsible for the central area of the globe—the lands located between the U.S. European and Pacific Commands (Hines 2006). One of the command's responsibilities is providing humanitarian assistance, including removal of land mines, within its area of operations.

Based on their experiences with efforts to remove land mines in a number of different locations within the CENTCOM area of operations, Childress and Owen (2000), assigned to CENTCOM, concluded that countries where mines await removal could benefit from adoption of a strategic-management approach to their mine-clearing efforts. In 1999, as many as 100 million abandoned land mines remained in at least 70 countries, and these were responsible for killing or maiming an estimated 500 people each week. They concluded that

Strategic management … expresses a commitment to identifying, prioritizing, and implementing the optimum mix of available mine action resources for a given mine-plagued nation. The key to strategic management, which is a process, is recognizing that the resource equation to address mine problems will most likely differ from one mine-infested geographic or political area to another. That is, mine action resource mixes, not constant, must be tailored to the environment and on evaluation of the Host Nation's ability to sustain a long-term commitment.

The CENTCOM authors saw the strategic-management process as consisting of two distinct phases. The first is achieving an understanding of the host nation's vision, goals, and objectives, together with a mutual understanding of what each donor nation will provide to the de-mining effort. From this beginning, the host nation and lead donor should then develop a strategic plan that includes an optimal mix of resources and objectives. The second phase of the de-mining strategic-management process involves implementing the plan, using a "cyclical process of planning, organizing, resourcing, controlling, and sustaining the mine action program."

Source: Hines (2006); Childress and Owen (2000)

An example of establishing goals without any provision for progress assessment is the seven-goal target that Washington State adopted in 2002. In an effort to align all state agencies with the objectives of enabling sustainability and enhancing the quality of life (State of Washington 2002), the following goals were set for all agencies:

- Institutionalize sustainability as an agency value
- Raise employee awareness of sustainable practices in the workplace
- Minimize energy and water use
- Shift to clean energy for both facilities and vehicles
- Shift to nontoxic, recycled, and remanufactured materials in purchasing and construction
- Expand markets for environmentally preferred products and services
- Reduce or eliminate waste as an inefficient or improper use of resources

These goals are rallying points that could conceivably bring an agency's personnel together to achieve the stated goals. However, in the absence of a relevant metric to measure performance, it is impossible to gauge an agency's level of cooperation in the effort toward transformation. Indeed, with such loosely defined goals, almost any activity could be cited as progress toward the final goal of organizational transformation. Clearly, such vague interim goals are of little value in initiating transformation processes.

Objectives, on the other hand, are specific, measurable, realistic, and achievable targets that an agency plans to achieve within a given time period. Objectives are performance targets and, as such, must be stated in terms of concepts that can be measured. Box 6.5 illustrates how the Wisconsin State Employee Retirement System integrated the three key activities of mission, goals, and objectives into a meaningful whole that provides performance targets for its personnel.

Objectives are specific, measurable statements of what the organization plans to do during the timed period. They are framed by a realistic assessment of what the organization is *capable* of doing with the assets and systems available. These objectives evolve from administrators' analyses of the internal and external environmental factors that establish the constraints within which the transformation of the public agency will take place. Constraints include political mandates and shortfalls in appropriations.

Box 6.5   Mission, Goals, Objectives, and Activities of the WRSB

Mission: The purpose of the [Wisconsin Retirement System Board] is to provide prudent and cost-effective management of funds held in trust by the state. This is achieved with solid investment returns, consistent with the purpose and risk profile of each fund.

Investment of Funds Program Goal: Earn the best rate of investment return, with an appropriate level of risk, for each fund managed.

Objectives: The investment objective for the Wisconsin Retirement System trust funds is to achieve a long-term rate of return that will enable the system to meet pension obligations to current and future beneficiaries. The investment objective for the state investment fund is to exceed its established performance benchmark. The investment objective for the small funds is to meet annual fund cash flow requirements, as established by their governing boards.

Source: **WDOA (2006)**

The strategic plan of Hillsborough County, Florida, included eight broad goals in its 2008 strategic plan, each with its own varying number of specific, measurable objectives. Those goals are listed in Table 6.1, along with one or two representative objectives. The objectives are written so that progress is measurable.

Objectives are developed as a hierarchy, with achievement of lower-level objectives necessary for the accomplishment of higher-level objectives. This concept is illustrated in Figure 6.2. At the highest level are *national* or *global objectives.* These objectives have been defined by the U.S. defense community as "the aims, derived from national goals and interests, toward which a national policy or strategy is directed and efforts and resources of the nation are applied" (DOD Dictionary of Military and Associated Terms 2001).

Objectives at this level may seem more like goals than objectives, but they can be as specific as the writer wishes them to be. An example is the U.K. government's objectives directed at reducing or eliminating tobacco smoking: The long-term objective is to reduce smoking in the U.K. general population from 26 percent in 2002 to 21 percent by 2010 (nosmokingday.org.uk 2006).

In the public sector hierarchy, *branch* objectives refer to executive, legislative, and judicial branch objectives. Each branch will have different responsibilities and play a different role in accomplishing the highest-level objective or goal. For example, Congress passed authorizing legislation to permit the federal and state governments to develop programs to accomplish the national housing objective.

Table 6.1   2008 Strategic Goals and Sample Objectives for Hillsborough County, Florida

	Strategic Goals	Sample Objectives
1	To ensure that Hillsborough County is financially strong enough to influence its destiny by applying efficient and effective policies and practices	Increase the percentage of non-tax general-fund revenue from 15.4% in FY 07 to 16.8% in FY 08
2	To improve the economic well-being of the citizens	Reduce the percentage of county residents living in poverty to the lowest quartile of Florida counties, based on the 2010 Census
3	To work with citizens and neighborhoods to ensure that quality services are delivered in a courteous and responsive manner	Attain by FY 10 a customer satisfaction ratio of 80% on the value of county services compared with their costs
4	To build a high-performance diverse professional organization	Achieve and maintain a human resources rating of at least an A– as determined by the *Governing Magazine* review of 40 counties; improve efficiencies and effectiveness in county services as measured by internal and external benchmarking by FY 08
5	To provide a quality of life to citizens and visitors that emphasizes public safety, arts and entertainment, and sports and recreation—all in a visually pleasing and healthy community	Achieve a customer satisfaction rating of 90% regarding the deputies serving customers' neighborhoods by the end of FY 08; by FY 15, improve the response time of advanced-life-support transport to arrive within 8 min, 71% of the time in the unincorporated county, incrementally improving existing performance by an average of 2% per year
6	To improve transportation in Hillsborough County	Decrease the rate of preventable intersection crashes per million entering vehicles by 5% by FY 10

Table 6.1   2008 Strategic Goals and Sample Objectives for Hillsborough County, Florida (Continued)

	Strategic Goals	*Sample Objectives*
7	To effectively protect and manage our natural resources, including the conservation of the water supply, to create a healthy environment in Hillsborough County	Increase ambient air quality in the county, in partnership with the Environmental Protection Commission, to meet the federal clean air standards by FY 08
8	To make Hillsborough County a desired place to live through managed growth	Improve quality of life for county citizens by establishing and monitoring a set of improvement measures using data from an annual "quality of life" survey

Source: Hillsborough County (2008).

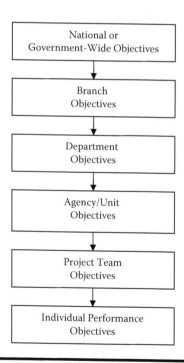

Figure 6.2   Hierarchy of government objectives.

The next level is the department within a branch of government. The U.S. Department of Housing and Urban Development (HUD) is an example. The national objective is "development of viable communities by the provision of decent housing and a suitable living environment and expanding economic opportunities, principally for persons of low- and moderate-income" (HUD 2002). The agency has issued a comprehensive guide for the states in applying for federal Community Development Block Grants (CDBG)—a program that functions at the next level of the hierarchy: agency or unit. The CDBG program ensures that all funded activities meet one of these three national objectives: benefiting low- and moderate-income persons; preventing or eliminating slums or blight; and meeting urgent needs. Also, every grant recipient must spend at least 70 percent of its grant on activities that meet the first of these three objectives.

Summary

In strategic management terms, successful implementation of a transformation initiative requires providing realistic, attainable long-term objectives for every unit in the agency. The organization cannot flourish if staff members rush from fire to fire instead of working together on a set of activities built on the foundations of: a vision of the long-term role of the organization; a clear, concise statement of the agency's mission; and a set of objectives that the agency strives to accomplish. If everyone in the agency is fully cognizant of these three fundamental positions, every member of the organization will be better able to see where his or her tasks fit into the larger mission of the organization.

The strategic management process entails forming both long-term and short-tem objectives, and then identifying and selecting the strategies that hold the greatest promise of achieving those objectives. Administrators use strategic planning to help ensure that all agency activities remain focused on accomplishing their goals and objectives.

This chapter looked at the roles that strategy and strategic management play in facilitating the transformation of government organizations. Strategic management is the set of decisions and activities that administrators and managers use to guide the long-term performance of their agencies. It includes the activities of environmental scanning, establishing objectives, strategy formulation, strategy implementation, progress evaluation, and performance measurement and control. The strategic management process begins with establishing a vision and a mission for the organization, and then uses the agency's competencies, capabilities, and other available resources to develop and implement programs that comply with and enable the carrying out of the organization's mission.

Chapter 7

How Technology Is Shaping the Face of Government

> Technological innovation is transforming our world and New Zealanders expect government to interact with them in new ways. This means using network technologies that people are familiar with in other parts of their lives—social networking websites and tools like blogs, wikis, and folksonomies*—and the full range of digital channels—mobile phones, instant messaging, podcasts and digital TV, as well as Internet pathways.
>
> **State Services Commission of New Zealand (2006)**

Other enabling factors of change in organizations are the organization's tangible and intangible capital assets. Tangible assets are the equipment and facilities that make it possible for agency staff to carry out their assigned tasks. An increasingly important element in an agency's tangible assets is its *information and communications technology*. In fact, some observers consider technology to be the single most important factor in making transformation in government possible (U.K. Cabinet Office 2005). Technology plays a dual role in government: First, technology changes

---

* A *folksonomy* is a collaboratively generated, open-ended labeling system that lets Internet users categorize content such as Web pages, online photographs, and Web links. The labels, called *tags,* help to improve the effectiveness of search engines because content is categorized using a familiar, accessible, and shared vocabulary.

the way that work is done in government. Second, technology makes it possible to implement the change strategies that managers seek in their efforts to gain better control of their information technology infrastructures.

Technology and Transformational Change

Technology has long been touted as a way of boosting productivity in government agencies (Lee and Perry 2002). However, there has been little empirical research to show that, without a doubt, productivity gains do occur with investments in technology. Still, governments continue to annually invest huge sums in purchases of hardware and software.

Managers in public-sector organizations around the globe are looking for ways to get better control of the funds used to purchase technology while, at the same time, eagerly buying advanced technology to replace existing systems that, in many cases, have long been obsolete. The goals of this control movement are connected to mandates to improve financial management, to become more responsive to citizens, and to manage the tacit and explicit knowledge held by agency personnel and in organizational archives. Tacit knowledge is knowledge held in the minds of the men and women who hold, use, and share what they know about things and how to do what they do; explicit knowledge is knowledge that has been or can be written down and contained in documents and other media (Nonaka 1991).

Three Converging Trends

Three converging socioeconomic trends are driving the efforts of public managers to gain better control of their technology acquisitions. The first trend is the accelerated adoption of new technology designed to improve performance and eliminate interagency communications barriers caused by old legacy systems. However, the cost of these technology replacement programs is staggering, and they divert funds from other needed programs. Such diversion of funds for technology is particularly crushing for local governments.

The second trend is the global acceleration in the implementation of e-government services. Agencies at all government levels are increasing the amount and variety of online services available to citizens (Norris and Moon 2005). In 2005, for example, China became the nation with the second-largest number of citizens connected to the World Wide Web—led only by the United States. In what is being called *m-government,* many governments are also providing mobile communications capabilities (e.g., personal handheld devices, smart phones, tablets, and pocket and laptop computers) for their knowledge workers, thus enabling them to communicate in real time as information is gathered.

The third trend is the expected high turnover in knowledge workers as large numbers of the baby-boom generation retire. A number of studies have cited the coming loss of senior project and technical managers as the greatest risk facing the public sector at the start of the new century. This trend is behind the drive to capture, share, and archive critical knowledge that will be lost as a result of the large wave in retirements.

How ICT Affects Government Operations

Information and communications technology (ICT) has had and continues to have a tremendous impact upon all aspects of the strategy and operations of government organizations. Technology helps shape the capabilities and capacities of the organization, and it helps integrate those capabilities into an operational context. Additionally, through its ability to collect, store, and disseminate knowledge and information in real time, technology makes elements of the organizational culture—including its strategies, capabilities, and capacities—available to all personnel at all organizational levels (Hill and Jones 2001).

Passage of the Government Performance Results Act of 1993 (GPRA) required managers in federal agencies to change how they make decisions, implement administrative control of agency operations, achieve higher performance, and reform operations to become more efficient in what they do (Breul 2007; Ho 2007). Similar programs were implemented in state and local governments shortly afterward. To accomplish those goals, public managers were required to make improvements in four key government agency operational areas:

1. Operational and financial efficiency
2. Product, service, and process quality
3. Innovation
4. Client and other stakeholder responsiveness

Although technology is an important facilitator of improvements in the delivery of government services, it is also a unifying force in the government's transformational-change policies and programs. In fact, without the widespread application of technology, high-priority programs such as e-government, e-learning, homeland security, knowledge management, and many others would not be possible. This growing dependence upon technology was highlighted in a White House report (OMB 2005a) on the third anniversary of the E-Government Act:

> The United States Government is one of the largest users and acquirers of data, information and supporting technology systems in the world, currently investing approximately $65 billion annually on Information Technology (IT). The Federal Government should be the world's leader

in managing technology and information to achieve the greatest gains of productivity, service and results.

To summarize, technology greatly affects the ability of an agency to accomplish its operational objectives in each of these areas. This is because one of the key advantages of technology is the *leveraging of knowledge;* technology enables greater sharing and integration of knowledge across organizational functions and units. Knowledge leveraging also helps develop synergies within an agency, thus making it possible to improve delivery of higher-value agency services to clients and customers.

Implementing Changes at HHS

The U.S. Department of Health and Human Services administrator sees the existing state of technology as a radical shift in the department's operating environment. Modern information and communications technology has fundamentally changed the nature of interpersonal communications, whereas technologies simply reduced the time and space limitations between communicators (Figure 7.1). Modern technology has introduced three fundamental changes into the traditional model of communications (Mandersheid 2005):

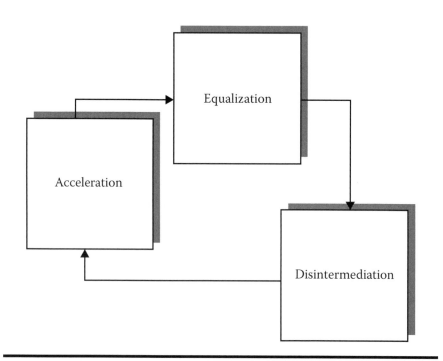

Figure 7.1   A model of forces driving change in communications.

- *Acceleration*: ICT has made instantaneous communication possible with other people anywhere in the world. As a result, it has facilitated far greater networking and interaction in society at any given moment of time.
- *Equalization*: Modern ICT makes it possible for anyone to speak to anyone. It does this through a communications network instead of a hierarchical structure. Traditional barriers of rank, culture, or societies no longer exist. Artificial boundaries between governments and their citizens, government agencies at any and all levels, and between countries can be reduced or even eliminated.
- *Disintermediation*: Possibly the most far-reaching feature of modern ICT is its ability to eliminate the individuals, groups, or organizations that once intervened between communicators. Middlemen or "fixers" can be cut out of the communications loop. In their place direct communications is now possible between end users and providers of goods and services, constituents and appointed or elected officials, student and educator, healthcare consumer and physician, and the like.

Technology also affects an agency manager's ability to innovate and learn, both of which are abilities found in all high-performing organizations. Technology expands the available knowledge, which in turn aids in problem solving and decision making. The expanded knowledge that emerges from knowledge leveraging makes it easier for staff to share the information that is necessary for the agency to engage in collaborative and coordinated services with other agencies and other government levels.

This leveraging of knowledge and information alone will not bring about innovation in agencies. Rather, it is the ability within an agency to creatively use the available knowledge that is the key to promoting innovation and improving performance. It is not simply the absolute level of knowledge within an organization that leads to higher performance; it is the speed with which knowledge circulates within the organization. Effective application of technology improves the flow of knowledge, produces information synergies, and makes it possible to direct knowledge to where it can add the most value (Hill and Jones 2001).

Technology and the Nature of Work

Agencies such as the Department of Defense, Homeland Security, NASA, and FEMA, among others, regularly engage in project-based work that involves the use of cross-functional teams. As projects move forward, the need for various team members varies. Although some members will work on the project from beginning to end, others participate only when their particular knowledge or skill is needed. In these situations, technology gives administrators the ability to monitor project progress and allocate knowledge resources accordingly where needed to optimize project progress.

Technology is also changing organizational structures and promoting innovation inside virtual organizations and collaborative operations. This has taken on greater importance as a result of mandates that government agencies leverage their effectiveness by engaging in greater collaboration in their operations. An important benefit from the use of technology in collaborative activities is the cost savings that can result from the improved flow of information and knowledge between agencies and units. Digital networks make strategic alliances a more desirable option than taking on a new role for the agency or creating a new unit. Also, organizations that use electronic networks not only reduce costs but, because they increase the pool of relevant knowledge, they reduce the risk of mission failure or runaway costs.

Factors Limiting Change

A number of important limiting factors must be considered when designing and integrating new technology into agency operations. Among these are:

1. The high initial cost of technology and its implementation
2. The penalties associated with selecting the wrong technology system
3. Longer-than-anticipated time needed to implement a technology change
4. The high cost of training or hiring new staff to operate the system

These and other costly constraints can severely limit the ability of technology to achieve the improvements in efficiency and innovation promised by its suppliers, as the following statement (Hill and Jones 2001, 16) points out:

> [T]he implications of IT for strategy formulation and implementation are still evolving and will continue to do so as new software and hardware reshape competitive strategy. IT is changing the nature of value chain activities both inside and between organizations, affecting all four building blocks of competitive advantage—efficiency, quality, innovation, and responsiveness to customers.

Technology and Enterprise Architecture Initiatives

Enterprise architecture (EA) is a process for managing information. The goal of EA is to process existing knowledge and use it to discover innovative answers to old and new questions. EA is similar to strategic planning in many ways. It is a method that applies a comprehensive and rigorous process to describe the existing and future structure (and behavior) of an organization's processes, information systems, personnel, and organizational subunits.

Box 7.1 The Federal Enterprise Architecture Program

Federal Enterprise Architecture (FEA): FEA is a business model–based* initiative designed to provide a common framework for improving such areas of federal government operations as budget allocations and budget and performance integration, horizontal and vertical information sharing, performance measurement, cross-agency collaboration, e-government, and component-based architectures, among others. Led by the Office of Management and Budget (OMB), the fundamental purpose of FEA is to identify opportunities to simplify processes and unify work across agencies and within the lines of business of the federal government. A key goal of FEA is to help agencies reflect a more citizen-centered, customer-focused government that maximizes investments to better achieve mission outcomes.

Federal Enterprise Architecture Management System (FEAMS): FEAMS is a Web-based management information repository and analysis system designed to provide agencies with access to initiatives aligned to the FEA and associated reference models. FEAMS was established by the OMB in December 2003 to provide users with an intuitive approach to discover and potentially leverage information technology components, business services, and capabilities across the federal government.

* According to OMB, the business reference model is based on the government's "lines of business" and its services to the citizen, independent of the agencies and offices involved. Thus, one line of business may include two or more traditional agencies.

Source: OMB (2006a)

The final objective is to have the ICT assets of the agency align with the overall core goals and strategic direction of the organization. Box 7.1 describes the federal government's enterprise architecture program. Technology is a key factor in achieving success in this task. Information and communications technology collectively is one of the three chief building blocks of knowledge management (KM). The other two are the people who use knowledge and the processes that enable and enhance knowledge capture and sharing.

Technology has helped KM to evolve into what it has become today—a key management tool used by agencies and institutions to function and flourish in today's knowledge economy. The world has entered a postindustrial economy characterized by globalization, increasingly sophisticated information and communications technology, and a knowledge society (Nonaka and Takenchi 1995; Drucker 1993; Feiock, Moon, and Park 2008). The only certainty in this new economy is that knowledge is the only sustainable source of competitive advantage (Butler et al. 2003).

Technology-enabled or -enhanced transformation is continually shaped by the need for administrators to design and implement organizational change according to mandated enterprise architecture initiatives (EAI). Enterprise architecture applies to the shared ICT services within an agency. Governments are using EAI to gain greater control over technology acquisitions and achieve greater operational efficiencies while implementing more Web-based delivery of services. The emphasis on rationalizing enterprise architecture is a key management objective in U.S. agencies and departments at the federal, state, and local levels as well as in similar programs in other nations.

Enterprise Architecture at the State Level

Although enterprise architecture requirements are close to being widely implemented at the federal level, many of the program's components are also being implemented at the state level. Enterprise architecture is considered by the National Association of State Chief Information Officers (NASCIO) as a management tool that can be used to design and plan government processes and investments in technology as a means of completing its various missions. It serves as a blueprint for change and a guide for organizational structure and workflow. It is formally defined (NASCIO 2007c) as:

> Enterprise Architecture is a management engineering discipline that presents a holistic, comprehensive view of the enterprise including strategic planning, organization, relationships, business process, information, and operations.
> The organization must be viewed as fluid—changing over time as necessary based on the environment and management's response to that environment.

To determine the level of implementation by the states, in August 2005, NASCIO conducted a census to find out how far the individual states have come in adopting enterprise architecture. The results of that survey, published in October 2005, listed results from 37 states and the District of Columbia—a response that represented more than 80 percent of the U.S. population.

The survey found that the states have made significant progress toward adoption of enterprise architecture since 1999, when the previous survey had been done. Key results are that 95 percent of the states had adopted some level of enterprise architecture; 71 percent believed it necessary to have dedicated enterprise architecture staff; and 92 percent believed it necessary to have a defined process for enterprise architecture. However, most of the states' emphasis had only focused on technology architecture, although a minority of states had broadened their architecture to include business architecture, performance management, and process architecture.

Approximately 85 percent of the states responding to the NASCIO survey had adopted technology architecture; nearly 70 percent had adopted program management architecture; and close to 65 percent had adopted architecture program management. A somewhat surprising find is that only about 60 percent of the states have implemented a security architecture. NASCIO found it noteworthy that cyber security is a top priority for state CIOs, although the implementation apparently has fallen behind. The survey also revealed that 70 percent of the states either had or planned to have full-time staff dedicated to managing the enterprise architecture program; 30 percent of the states have no plans to employ full-time staff for their enterprise architecture.

A State Case Example

Washington State is typical of the states now beginning to implement enterprise architecture throughout its operations. The implementation process is under the direction of the State Department of Information Services (DIS). A complete statement of the state's e-government program is spelled out in a planning document published in February 2000 (DIS 2000). Follow-on plans for managing the state's e-government program were released as an initial draft on September 7, 2005, as version 1.0 on September 21, 2005, and as Version 1.1 on November 2, 2005. The plan discussed procedures for managing the state's enterprise architecture program and included items such as program management principles, an architecture life cycle, and program iterations and architecture releases.

To provide overall guidance and oversight, Washington's Information Services Board (ISB) has established an Enterprise Architecture Committee (EAC). The ISB (2006) states that the mission of the EAC is

> to build and maintain an enterprise architecture program that guides and optimizes state resources; enables agencies to meet their strategic goals; facilitates the management of organizational and technological change and complexity; and helps agencies manage the state's IT resources as assets within its portfolio of investments.

In 2006, Washington had standards for one initiative (networking architecture) established and three initiatives underway: Voice over Internet Protocol (VoIP), an integration architecture initiative, and a geographic information technology (GIT) initiative. A charter was written for each initiative, but only the charter for the networking architecture networking standards initiative had been approved by the Enterprise Architecture Committee; charters for the other initiatives were still under development (DIS 2006). These initiatives were to be delivered by June 30,

2006, so that they could be used to make investment decisions for 2007 through 2009.

The purpose of the networking standards initiative is to develop policies, standards, and guidelines for network infrastructure solutions, assets, and services that are common statewide. The initiative seeks to evolve a set of early-adoptions components (Tier One) in the statewide enterprise architecture. The purpose of the VoIP initiative is to provide telephony tools that will assist agencies in making decisions about the deployment of VoIP technologies. These tools focus on:

- Establishing a standard set of measures to assess agencies' technical readiness to implement VoIP
- Establishing standard factors that agencies should consider in making a business case for implementation of VoIP
- Defining standard features of VoIP implementations and establishing potential standard techniques or protocols for implementing those features

The initial usage of these standards, guidelines, and solutions is to support the financial and administrative systems "roadmap" initiative. Information about the roadmap can be found at its Web site: www.ofm.wa.gov/roadmap.

The purpose of the state's integration architecture EA initiative is to simplify implementation of business capabilities and to allow state agencies to benefit from all agency IT capabilities. This initiative's intent is to support the integration of information systems between government agencies without compromise and wherever it is operationally and technically feasible. The infrastructure solutions established by this initiative will be documented within the statewide enterprise architecture's solution architecture. Standards and guidelines will be documented within the technology architecture. The integration architecture initiative also expects to establish information architecture components that are relevant to the integration of information systems. For example, this initiative is expected to develop data modeling conventions and metadata as well as standards for the representation of information as messages between systems.

Finally, a geographic information technology (GIT) initiative is planned to identify a standard approach for integrating all GIT systems in the state. This initiative is jointly sponsored by the ISB committees on enterprise architecture and geographic information technology (DIS 2006).

Enterprise Architecture at the Federal Level

The Office of Management and Budget's office of E-Government and Information Technology, the General Services Administration, and the Federal Chief Information Officers Council have jointly developed a business-driven blueprint for the entire federal government: the Federal Enterprise Architecture (FEA) program. FEA provides all government agencies with a framework to analyze investments in technology, expand interagency collaboration, and ultimately to transform the federal government into a results-oriented, citizen-focused, and market-based organization.

FEA supports six separate models that agencies use to identify duplicative investments and identify opportunities for collaboration within and across agencies. The six models are:

1. A performance reference model (PRM)
2. A business reference model (BRM)
3. Service component model (SCM)
4. Reference model (SRM)
5. Technical reference model (TRM)
6. Data reference model (DRM)

The data reference model is the avenue for transforming the internal thinking of government agencies from an organizational to a functional view. It describes a new view of government as consisting of a number of common business areas instead of from a stovepiped, agency-by-agency view. The BRM is a tool that is used to describe the operations of government agencies in much the same way as a business instead of as a bureaucracy.

The traditional structure of government is referred to in this literature as agencies that are stovepiped, or that function as a collection of independent silos. The term *stovepiped* is used because the agencies functioned independently, with no organized interaction, integration, or collaboration, thereby resulting in much duplication of effort and resources. The business reference model approach is a key facilitator of the overall transformation initiative promoted in the President's Management Agenda. Figure 7.2 illustrates the interrelationships between programs and process, the reference models, and strategic outcomes.

The BRM provides an organized way of describing the day-to-day operations of the government using a functionally driven approach. The lines of business and subfunctions of BRM are different from previous models of the federal government that use old, stovepiped, agency-oriented frameworks. It functions as the basis of the federal enterprise architecture and is the main focus for subsequent data analysis, service components, and technology (White House 2007).

Federal Strategies to Upgrade ICT

Developing strategies for adopting, upgrading, and implementing information and communication systems technologies (ICT) is one of the most pressing concerns of government administrators. At the federal level, analyzing current and future needs and developing long-term plans for ICT purchases is one of the five key

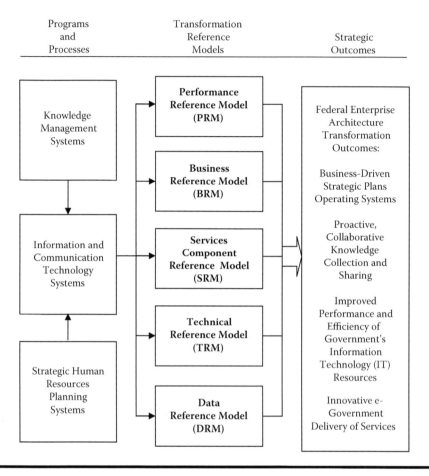

Figure 7.2 Outcomes of technology-enabled government transformation. (*Source:* White House 2007.)

management agendas mandated for all departments. ICT includes computer and communications hardware and software, together with the myriad related technologies and systems that connect people within and outside of an agency. Included are single-purpose database products such as accounting software, word processing software, and spreadsheet software programs.

These systems range from simple personal communications devices to incredibly complex organizationwide systems designed to manage all key functions of an agency. They allow people around the globe to communicate with each other essentially instantaneously using e-mail, voice and video conferencing, the Internet, extranets, intranets, groupware, mobile telephones, satellite-enabled radios, fax machines, personal digital devices, and similar devices and systems (Hill and Jones 2001).

There is no question that planning for purchasing, installing, and upgrading ICTs constitutes a major element in the long-term strategic management strategies of governments at all levels. Government agencies' and organizations' ability to comply with operational mandates is as much affected by their efficient and effective use of ICT as it is by their human resource capabilities. This helps to understand the emphasis placed upon agency compliance with the introduction of strategic management and the development of strategic plans for all enterprise architecture systems before any additional purchases are allowed.

Accelerated Pace of Adoption

The federal government, along with many state and local governments, is in the midst of a major transformation effort to become more results-oriented and accountable to legislative and citizen stakeholders. To achieve these goals, governments began in the 1990s to accelerate their adoption and application of electronic information and communications technology.

Governments are identifying and modeling their decisions on the best practices in business management and information technology. A key objective for these investments is to efficiently and effectively provide timely and accurate information to citizens and government decision makers while ensuring security and privacy. To meet this objective, agency personnel need the latest in information and communications technology.

Technology and Organizational Reengineering

Since the introduction of *Reengineering the Corporation* by Hammer and Champy in 1992, reengineering—the management practice that leads to transformation—has been closely associated with technology: not just any technology, but technology designed to turn the way the organization functions upside down; not simply to improve workflow in government organizations, but to provide citizens the same level of service they have come to expect with the advent of e-commerce.

Technology is one of the fundamental building blocks of organizational transformation. In their revised edition of *Reengineering the Corporation,* Hammer and Champy (2003, 5) explained that technology makes possible the processes that are the very essence of reengineering, adding that

> [technology and reengineering] have a symbiotic relationship: without reengineering,… information technology delivers little payoff; without information technology, little reengineering can be done.

One of the information technology advances with great potential for facilitating large-scale transformation has been enterprise resource planning (ERP). This software system is designed to support the entire organizational process, not just individual functional areas. Implementation of ERP systems has been highly problematic and seldom returned the payoffs promised. One of the reasons for these disappointing results is that organizations have tried to layer an ERP system atop existing processes and technology.

Organizations in both the public and private sectors that have implemented ERP systems without first reengineering their work processes ended up being highly disappointed by the lack of positive changes in bottom-line impact, although most benefited from improvements in information technology operations and lower costs. But things are getting better; ERP providers are learning how to do a better job of helping their clients through the implementation process. Hammer and Champy believe that reengineering efforts in the future will be closely linked with technology that integrates not only operating functions but the entire organization.

Technology-Driven Change at the FAA

For more than 25 years, the Federal Aviation Administration (FAA) has been engaged in a transformation strategy designed to bring about the complete modernization of the nation's air traffic control system. The plan has included the acquisition of new systems and facilities. As of 2007, many new systems had been added and improvements made. However, in many cases those improvements apparently did not keep pace with growth in air traffic. Moreover, many of the FAA's modernization programs suffered from cost overruns, schedule delays, and shortfalls in performance. Table 7.1 displays a number of key operations weaknesses identified by the GAO.

According to the GAO, the cause of these and related problems can be traced to:

1. Immature capabilities for systems acquisitions
2. Lack of an agencywide enterprise architecture
3. Poor cost estimating and accounting practices
4. An incomplete investment management process
5. An organizational culture that bars modernization efforts

For these and other reasons, the FAA has been on the GAO's high-risk list since 1995.

Many improvements have been put into place at the FAA since 1995; indeed, the agency in 2007 was working on 45 improvement projects, including augmenting the Global Positioning System for better control of approaches and landings, improving radar systems, and installing important new color displays for air traffic controllers.

The GAO report on the high-risk status of the FAA closed with the warning that, until these issues are fully dealt with, the agency will continue to face the project management problems, including costs, schedules, and performance, that have affected its ability to acquire systems for improving air traffic control.

Table 7.1   Transformation at the Federal Aviation Administration

Action Area	Status
Establish a framework for improving system management capabilities and addressing weaknesses identified by the GAO on four major air traffic control systems	A framework has been established, but the improved capabilities have not been institutionalized
Develop an enterprise architecture—a blueprint of the agency's current and target operations and infrastructure—including early requirements for the next-generation air transportation system	Development of the enterprise architecture continues; further refinements are expected
Implement key components of a cost accounting system	Implementation complete; further refinements as identified and available
Establish a cost estimating methodology	Established but not yet implemented
Implement basic investment management capabilities	Partially implemented, but the practices are not yet integrated across the agency
Establish an organizational culture that supports sound acquisitions	Still faces many human capital challenges, including obtaining the technical and contract management expertise needed to define, implement, and integrate numerous complex technology programs and systems

Source: GAO (2007a).

Federal Accomplishments in Enterprise Architecture

The federal government has come a long way since 2002 in implementing the federal enterprise architecture, but there is still much work to be done—and even more work is required at the state government level. As part of the PMA's objective to improve federal management, the Office of Management and Budget (OMB) measures the progress of each federal agency and department every quarter. Results are reported on OMB's *balanced score card*. The measurements compare an agency's achievement against where it should be according to approved goals. Results are reported on the scorecard as a stoplight with red, yellow, and green symbols, making it easy to see which agencies are achieving the goals and which are not. A green score indicates the agency is achieving its goals; it is the highest rating possible. A yellow score indicates a need for greater efforts, and a red score signals that the agency is in real danger of not achieving the planned objectives (Weigelt 2006).

Enterprise architecture is obviously of great focus in the federal government, and significant results have already been accomplished. But what about the individual states? Are they working just as hard on implementing technology-enabled transformation?

Summary

The development of the Internet and other information and communications technologies has transformed the way that government functions, delivers its services to stakeholder groups, and collects information and revenue. Citizens and businesses now have 24-hour access to information and services because of a global investment in e-government applications and programs. An additional payoff from this is that government agencies are becoming more responsive, efficient, and accountable (National Research Council 2002).

Enterprise architecture is a management tool that begins with analysis of the environmental conditions in which agencies must operate. It produces a blueprint to ensure the availability of the technology, resources, and processes that are needed to maintain government services. At the same time, it also enables the agency to adapt to change to meet the governmentwide need for a high return on investment and cross-agency interoperability and standardization, among other goals. It occurs in three fundamental steps: identifying and analyzing trends in the environment, assessing the impacts and risks to government from the impact of those changes in the environment, and developing collaborative planned responses to those impacts.

Chapter 8

Technology and Systems Change

> Systems, whether paper or computer-based information systems, which aid in the management of information are critical to organizational success and development.

Peter Flett, Adrienne Curry, and Adam Peat (2007)

Accomplishing a successful transformational change in any of the operating and delivery systems of a government organization results in the need to address changes in all of the organization's other systems. This chapter illustrates this interrelated sequence of changes with a case study of a Department of Defense (DoD) organization: the Defense Logistics Agency (DLA).

For the last 20 or more years, managers who were engaged in changing the work processes of government believed that adding new and more powerful technology was the true driver of organizational transformation. They recognized that computers had changed forever what government workers do and the way that they do their work. Today, however, most public managers recognize that successful transformation requires much more than technology. Rather, technology-based information systems exist to *support work processes*, not the other way around. The conflict that once raged between technology and people no longer exists.

Information and communications systems are now such a large part of the government's operating budgets that, for the last several years, changing the way these systems are purchased and implemented was a primary objective of every new administration. Legislative bodies and chief administrators recognized that getting control over these expenditures was a major objective and one of the first changes they would make. In the United States, this effort to better manage technology expenditures resulted in such overarching programs as the federal government's enterprise architecture (EA) initiative. Under EA controls, before agency managers can purchase new systems, they were required to first complete a comprehensive analysis of their existing information technology (IT) architecture. They then prepared a plan that ensures inter- and cross-agency compatibility for all new IT system installations.

State and local governments are following suit in this effort to make technology purchases more rational and cost-effective. Another goal of this EA coordinating effort has been ensuring that replacement of old, custom-designed (or "legacy") systems was achieved with existing, commercially available hardware and software, that is, the new technology has to be systems available "off the shelf."

Organizational Processes

To carry out their missions, organizations employ various combinations of common and unique processes and procedures. These processes are "the patterns of interaction, coordination, communication, and decision making employees use to transform resources into products and services of greater worth," as described by Christensen and Overdorf (2000). The use of information and communications technologies (ICT) has made it much easier and effective to carry out many of the processes and procedures. These process systems available to government managers include (Tonichia and Tramontano 2004):

- *Management processes.* These are the enterprisewide processes that coordinate and monitor all major processes for the agency. They include programs and actions for improving efficiency and effectiveness as well as programs for becoming more client-centered, learning organizations.
- *Supply-chain processes.* These are routine activities that enable procurement, specification development, receiving, storing, and distributing products within the organization and to its downstream service partners.
- *Service-delivery processes.* These processes are similar to sales in the private sector. They involve assistance for client agencies and final recipients in determining needs, specification of quality requirements, customer relationship database management, and related value-chain activities. These are also referred to as *transaction processes.*
- *Customer/client service processes.* These services are closely related to delivery processes. They involve providing design assistance prior to specification and quotation requests; ensuring proper delivery; providing installation, maintenance, and service where appropriate; and other services designed to maintain close customer relationships throughout the value chain.

- *Legislative compliance reporting processes.* These relate to such private-sector activities as business development and performance management. They include managing change and innovation processes, adhering to reporting demands, and developing new and improved standards for routine processes.
- *Control and/or support processes.* These performance-measurement and reporting processes are designed to support all processes, monitor progress toward accomplishing mission objectives, and adjust process and services where required.

Box 8.1   How Change Was Botched at the GSA

An attempted merger of two General Services Administration (GSA) contracting divisions ran into a major roadblock that diverted the proposed merger to external mediation; the employee union and GSA administrators disagreed over many of the policies and processes that had to be merged into a single new agency.

The GSA Federal Supply Service (FSS) and the Federal Technology Service (FTS) were consolidated into the Federal Acquisition Service (FAS) in 2006. The FSS purchased office equipment and related materials for the federal government while the FTS provided government agencies with information technology products. The two GSA divisions had different polices and processes on pay, bonuses, telecommuting, and other personnel procedures. The National Federation of Federal Employees (NFFE) represented more than 2,000 of the combined agency's workers.

The president of the NFFE national council was quoted as attributing much of the blame for the difficulties with the GSA's decision to employ an outside contractor to be in charge of the negotiations, adding that employees of the private-sector contractor did not understand the culture of the agency and lacked concern for the welfare of the employees affected by the merger.

Source: B. R. Ballenstedt (2007)

The Difficulty of Changing a Functioning System

One of the greatest difficulties in changing a system that has been functioning for any time in a government organization is that the work processes employed within that system were established or evolved so that agency activities could be produced and delivered to constituents in an equitable way, time after time. Because the systems were designed to retain organizational stability under all conditions of risk and uncertainty, the existing systems and work processes they support have often proved to be a significant barrier to change. The example of the experience of the General Services Administration shown in Box 8.1 illustrates how such barriers to change can be enormously frustrating to public managers trying to implement major changes in their organizations.

To change work-process systems, agency administrators must first identify the elements that must exist in the process in order for the agency to succeed in its mission; these are the *critical success factors* that must frame the new strategy selection (Alter 1999). They are typically embedded in the operating environment of the agency and include such factors as complying with legislative mandates, meeting performance-measurement requirements, monitoring key client/customer satisfaction points, maintaining relationships with downstream agency partners, and ensuring that needed human-capital skills are available.

Process-Facilitating Systems

It is a truism that information and communications technology has transformed the way organizations function. A growing volume of technology-based systems now assist managers and administrators in nearly every activity of the organization, ranging from simple payroll processing systems to executive support systems that provide top-level administrators with the strategic information they need to develop strategic plans with time horizons of five or more years into the future. Governments and industries are rapidly integrating Internet capabilities into their service and product delivery process, supply-chain management, and other functional activities.

The IT systems employed in the public sector can be loosely grouped into four broad categories, each of which is designed to serve a different management level in the organization. These include executive support systems (ESS) for senior-level administrators, management information (MIS) and decision support (DSS) systems for mid-level managers, and transaction processing systems (TPS) that facilitate the day-to-day functions of the organization. Figure 8.1 includes brief definitions of the scope of each of these categories of ICT systems.

Changing Work with Integrative, Enterprisewide Systems

Enterprise management systems such as enterprise resource planning (ERP) systems have proved to be the most problematic of all systems-implementation strategies in government agencies. These systems have been developed to integrate *all* mission

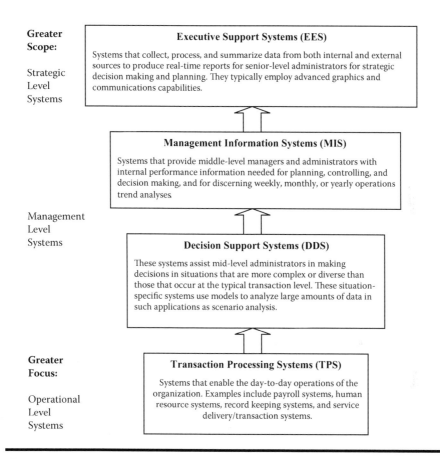

Greater Scope:

Strategic Level Systems

Executive Support Systems (EES)

Systems that collect, process, and summarize data from both internal and external sources to produce real-time reports for senior-level administrators for strategic decision making and planning. They typically employ advanced graphics and communications capabilities.

Management Information Systems (MIS)

Systems that provide middle-level managers and administrators with internal performance information needed for planning, controlling, and decision making, and for discerning weekly, monthly, or yearly operations trend analyses.

Management Level Systems

Decision Support Systems (DDS)

These systems assist mid-level administrators in making decisions in situations that are more complex or diverse than those that occur at the typical transaction level. These situation-specific systems use models to analyze large amounts of data in such applications as scenario analysis.

Greater Focus:

Operational Level Systems

Transaction Processing Systems (TPS)

Systems that enable the day-to-day operations of the organization. Examples include payroll systems, human resource systems, record keeping systems, and service delivery/transaction systems.

Figure 8.1 Major categories of ICT systems in agencies and organizations. (*Source:* Laudon and Laudon 2006.)

activities, processes, and procedures within an agency. They facilitate strategic planning, strategic management of human resources, and leadership development within the agency. Despite the many problems with early adoptions of the technology, however, they are slowly being adopted by government agencies for coordinative management. These are integrative software packages for the entire enterprise. They connect the processes of the organization across all functions. Figure 8.2 is a simplified information flow diagram in a typical public-sector ERP system.

The key feature of ERP systems is that they link all agency operations and processes through a common database. These systems have been defined by the Center for Digital Government (Ward 2006, 30) as

> business applications used by enterprises to manage and integrate best practice business, financial, administrative, and operational processes across multiple divisions and organizational boundaries. These

applications act as the backbone of the enterprise and are designed to
support and automate the processes of an organization.

Increased focus on more efficient and effective government, including better
managing of financial, technological, and human resources, is behind the use of
ERP in the public sector. However, governments in general lag behind the private
sector in implementing comprehensive ERP systems. Most agency administrators
are fully aware of the promised benefits from implementing an ERP system, but as
of 2006 few agencies had adopted complete ERP packages.

Complying with legislature-mandated performance measurements and
reporting processes is a big part of the factors supporting the adoption of

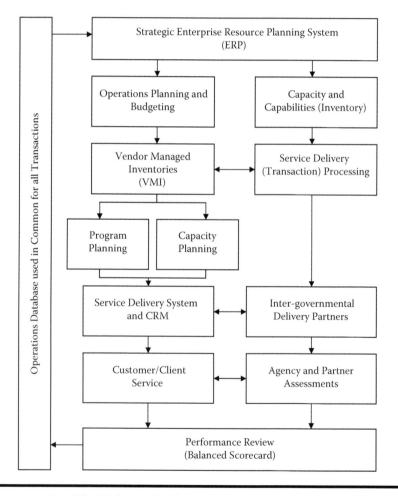

**Figure 8.2 Simplified information flows in a government ERP system. (*Source:*
Hamilton 2003.)**

operating systems that coordinate operations. Maintaining good relations with legislative bodies and regulators is important because of the impact those bodies can have on the ability of an agency to maintain long-term credibility and resource allocations.

One of the biggest gaps that must be filled before more government agencies fully adopt ERP solutions is the fact that their implementation goes beyond collaboration and coordination in technology and database consolidation. Such systems require a fundamental change in the operational culture of the organization. Acceptance of change at this level has not always been easy for government employees to accept. This is particularly so when the change agents involved promised to "improve productivity." In the past, this has been synonymous with reductions in staff. Naturally, government employees are not eager to give up their jobs so that the agency might become more productive. Federal employees in 2006 averaged more than 47 years of age; most have served more than 16 years. They are particularly sensitive to any change that threatens their livelihood (Ward 2006).

Changing Operating Systems: The Case of the DLA

The U.S. Department of Defense (DoD) is an example of a federal agency that has been implementing a comprehensive transformational change strategy affecting all of its units, programs, and operating systems. The Defense Logistics Agency (DLA) is one of the DoD units engaged in the overall transformation strategy. DLA provides one-source supply services of consumable items and technical and logistic support services to all branches of the U.S. military from its 26 separate distribution depots. The projected value of its 2005 sales and services was $31.3 billion. The agency fulfills more than 54,000 requisitions each day for items from a 5.2-million-item inventory.

The agency's transformation objective is to modernize its business model from the point where agency activities touch the defense department customer, all the way back through the supply chain to the smallest supplier (DLA 2005). This strategy may best be described as one of retooling rather than rebuilding (IBM 2004). By integrating its existing legacy systems with new applications rather than completely replacing the old, the agency is following a cost-effective transformation strategy.

An October 2005 report on DLA's contribution to the FY2005–2011 Department of Defense strategic plan described its progress on transformation efforts. That report included a transformation achievement timeline extending through 2010; the discussion in this section is taken from that document. The agency work plan targets 13 work elements as transformation initiatives. No single element will bring about transformation by itself, according to DLA director Vice Admiral Keith Lippert. Completion of all the initiatives is needed to achieve full transformation.

That DLA transformation strategy centers on a number of operating and service-delivery systems that are transforming the agency's relationships with its suppliers

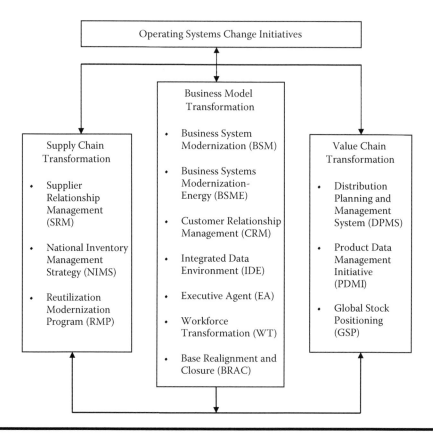

Figure 8.3 Strategic initiatives in the DLA transformation roadmap. (*Source:* DLA 2005.)

and customers as well as how and what work is carried out in the agency. The programs involved in the transformation initiatives are displayed in Figure 8.3.

The systems have been arranged according to whether their primary mission focus is backward in the supply chain, forward in the customer-value chain, or are more closely related to the business-process improvement taking place within the organization. The placement of these last elements is more or less arbitrary, as they are all interrelated, and many could be placed in any two or more of the categories, depending on the particular initiative aspect underway at the time or place of categorization.

Business Model Change Strategies

Transformation strategies are in place for six internal operations activities in the logistics agency's core business model: business systems and business systems-energy, customer relationship management, workforce transformation, integrated data management, and executive agent designation. These six strategic initiatives may be considered the core of the entire transformation strategy at the DLA. A seventh strategic activity—base relocation and closure (BRAC)—is included in the model but not discussed here.

The DSM strategy reaches into the very heart of the logistics agency, requiring a new organizational structure and the extensive retraining of agency workers to carry out new jobs that focus on relationships with suppliers or customers. Accordingly, a major change in the organizational culture is underway. This requires training of managers as well, for succeeding at a shift in organizational culture requires a strong change-management program in place. Readiness for change must be assessed, and employees must be prepared for their new roles in the changed agency.

Business System Modernization

The DLA considers business system modernization (BSM) to be the most significant information technology and business system transformation since the 1960s, when the agency's first computer-enabled management systems came on line. It is described (DLA 2005, 9) thus:

> This major re-engineering effort crosses all agency supply chains (e.g., subsistence, construction, medical, etc.) to provide greatly improved end-to-end material, financial and procurement management. BSM brings a commercially available business software solution that provides consistent and timely information for decision making and performance measurement; automates and integrates business processes; produces and accesses data in a near real time environment; and shares common data across the enterprise. BSM moves DLA from a manager of supplies to the much more effective manager of supply chains.

Business System Modernization-Energy

DLA's business systems modernization-energy (BSME) change strategy is closely related to the fundamental changes occurring in what work is done at the DLA. This information-management system uses commercial off-the-shelf software to plan, acquire, monitor the supply, and manage contracts and the global distribution network of DoD fuel supplies and related products.

The Customer Relationship Management System

The goal of the CRM strategy is to transform the logistics agency into a more customer-focused organization that is able to support its customers by providing more consistent delivery of value. This strategy is structured to accomplish four broad transformation objectives:

1. Changing from the traditional functional structure by transforming to a client-centric culture
2. Maintaining existing constituencies and, where appropriate, seek new constituencies through transforming from a "supply item" focus to a client-centered organization that values customer satisfaction, retention and, again where appropriate, client base expansion
3. Transforming from a generic "services warehousing" focus to an organization that builds "brand" loyalty by serving all constituents as honored and appreciated "customers"
4. Transforming from a take-it-or-leave-it philosophy to becoming the most effective supplier to delivery recipients by reducing the cost to serve

Integrated Data Environment Changes

The Integrated Data Environment (IDE) strategic initiative is the DLA's program for developing and managing its information technology architecture, using commercially available off-the-shelf technology. IDE units and systems provide DoD with centralized data sharing, reference, translation, business rule support, and master data access services that are vital to logistics transactions and knowledge management. The IDE transformation strategy focuses on reducing the number of system-to-system data interfaces and their associated costs, providing managed supply chain and centrally available metadata, as well as a centralized depository of DoD logistics business rules.

Executive Agent

As much a work-class transformation strategy as an organizational structure directive, the executive agent (EA) refers to the naming of the DLA as procurement point manager for a number of major DoD classes of supply items. The DoD defines EA status as the head of a department unit to whom the secretary of defense has assigned responsibilities, functions, and authority for the supply of items for two or more DoD units. Thus, as of August 2005, the DLA was integrating into its operations sole responsibility functions for subsistence products, clothing and textiles, bulk petroleum, construction and barrier materials, and medical materials. DLA's responsibilities include end-to-end supply-chain management, joint material management and requirements determination, increased standardization, and integration of commercial capabilities into military processes for these product classes.

Programs for Changing the Workforce

Another key change target is the transformation of the agency's workforce. This strategic initiative includes a set of long-term programs to deal with critical human resources issues, among which are such tactical activities as:

- *Enterprise Leader Development Program*: a training and development program to develop leadership skills in DLA employees and managers
- *Operating climate survey*: an assessment of employee morale and job satisfaction
- *Organizational culture survey:* identifies the desired culture, compares the DLA culture with the desired, and provides suggestions for improvements where appropriate
- *Multisource feedback*: provides a means for anonymous feedback to supervisors on their leadership behavior
- *New performance appraisals*: a revised system for measuring individual performance and linking performance with agency objectives

Supply-Chain Transformation

Supply-chain transformation initiatives include a supplier relationship management system (SRM), a national inventory management system (NIMS), and a reutilization and modernization program (RMP). These systems plus the overarching transformation strategy of business systems modernization (BSM) are designed to improve the five key functions of supply-chain management: planning for both the demand and supply side of the agency business, procurement, order fulfillment, financial management, and technical and quality management.

Strengthening Relationships with Suppliers

The SRM system involves synchronizing and modernizing supply chains to meet the mission support needs of the agency's "warfighting" customers efficiently and effectively. SRM is the DLA's strategy to strengthen relationships with key suppliers, thereby improving its ability to evaluate and manage supplier capabilities and jointly solve problems.

The SRM includes a number of different supplier management tools, among which are tailored vendor relationships (TVR) and supplier collaboration (SC) strategies. TVR is designed to standardize transactions for suppliers that have a direct connection with military customers. The TVR system makes it possible for orders to be transmitted over an electronic data interchange system. SC is a Web-based information technology system that facilitates and strengthens relationships between suppliers and the DLA. Suppliers and prospective vendors can review agency supply plans electronically.

Strategic Supplier Alliances

The agency has also formed strategic supplier alliances with more than two dozen important original equipment manufacturers (OEMs). These large firms typically require a high level of direct communication and day-to-day relationship management activities. These alliances are designed to improve communications between the agency and the OEMs. For smaller suppliers, the agency has implemented a *supply chain alliances* program that also promises to improve competitive bidding on supply items. To manage these and related supply-chain relationships with suppliers, DLA has developed a set of key performance indicators to be used to measure performance on a number of expected benefits, including:

- Reductions in delivery times
- Savings in inventory costs
- Lower total ownership costs (which include reliability, service, and replacement)
- Improvements in communications to and from suppliers
- Overall leveraged buying power across the DLA and the DoD

National Inventory Management Strategy

The National Inventory Management Strategy (NIMS) is the DLA's plan to extend its supply-chain responsibility for consumable items from the wholesale level to the point of consumption. The NIMS program is designed to enable the agency to accomplish a transformation of the type of work it performs by changing from a manager of supplies to a manager of supply chains. In this way, the DLA will now manage supply from the factory to the point where the warfighter customer takes possession. Some of the benefits expected from full implementation of this inventory management strategy include the following:

- Improved visibility and control of the complete supply chain
- Improved forecasting and reductions of overstocks and out-of-stocks
- Greater partnerships with customers, with improved customer support
- Greater partnerships with suppliers
- Lower overall inventory costs
- Elimination of redundant inventories
- Other related benefits

Reutilization and Modernization Program

The Reutilization and Modernization Program (RMP) is the DLA's program to integrate its Defense Reutilization and Marketing Service into its overall IT architecture and the DoD's supply-chain systems. Reutilization refers to the reuse and recycling of excess property and equipment. The goal is to provide greater visibility of its assets for potential users while also identifying and managing items that pose potential security risks. Another strategy involves collaborating with suppliers to gain early property information for disposal decisions while also ensuring the greatest possible use of reutilization of excess items in place of purchasing new inventory.

Customer Value-Chain Transformation Strategies

Transformations in the customer value chain include implementing a comprehensive distribution planning and management system (DPMS), a product data management initiative (PDMI), and a global stock-positioning system (GSP). The DLA's customers are the several branches of the military. In certain instances, the branches are able to seek other suppliers if the DLA cannot satisfy their requirements.

The Distribution Planning and Management System

The DPM system is a technology-based strategy for identifying, communicating, coordinating, and positioning inventory using commercially and government-available off-the-shelf software. A primary objective of this strategic transformation is to improve the flow of products and information from suppliers to the DLA and its customers. When fully implemented, the DPMS will enable continuous real-time information on the location, status, and movement of DLA-managed supplies and equipment through improved shipping, tracking, and traceability capabilities.

The Product Data Management Initiative

Product data management is the agency's strategy to transform technical and quality management processes by fully automating and reengineering knowledge management processes. The focus is to ensure the availability and delivery of the correct part for the customer's specific need quickly, reliably, and in a cost-effective manner. *Product data* refers to the technical specifications; description, operating, support, maintenance, and service information manuals; and product descriptions and engineering drawings needed for designing, purchasing, using, and servicing weapons systems and other supply items.

The Global Stock-Positioning System

The third strategic supply-chain management tool in development by the DLA is a global stock-positioning system. Given the global extension of U.S. military presence, the advance positioning of critical inventory is a particularly important strategy, and one that mirrors a revival of interest in the geographic component of strategy occurring in the private sector (Alcácer 2006).

This technology-enabled system incorporates a set of capabilities designed to guarantee that the right amount of inventory is at the right locations when needed and at the least cost. Managing inventory in this way is expected to significantly lower levels of inventory and maintenance while continuing to maintain the highest levels of warfighter readiness by balancing tradeoffs between responsiveness to customers, inventory levels, and distribution and transportation costs.

Changes to the DLA's Governance and Structure

The changes underway at the DLA are closely aligned with the agency's strategic management system and its strategic plan. Figure 8.4 displays the two primary thrusts of the agency's transformation initiative and the four goals of its strategic management and planning system. The ultimate strategic objective of the entire transformation process is the development of an integrated enterprise that

1. Delivers high-value customer-driven logistics
2. Manages a fully integrated supply chain for maximum added value
3. Is a best-practices exemplar in the procurement, supply, and delivery of supplies and services

In addition to the 13 strategic initiatives included in its overall transformation strategy, DLA is also transforming its governance structure to better accomplish agencywide and DoD strategic goals and objectives. This involves process reengineering, replacing old technology with commercial off-the-shelf applications that run on a single platform, and realigning DLA organizations, functions, and personnel.

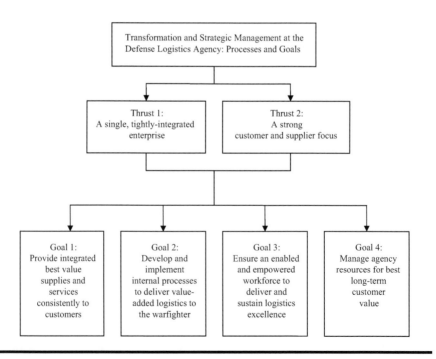

Figure 8.4   Major thrusts and goals of the DLA strategic transformation process. (*Source:* **DLA 2005.**)

Planning for ICT Systems at the Municipal Level

Planning for and implementing a new information systems strategy can be just as problematic at the municipal level as it is at the federal level (Smith et al. 2000). From 1995 to 2000, the city of St. Louis was engaged in a planning effort as part of a needed upgrading of its ICT systems.

The existing information systems of St. Louis at the time of the study provided services to more than 150 city departments or subunits. The legacy systems in place at the time were the cause of many organizational problems, including that of deciding how and when to upgrade the old systems. Faced with needs that could not be met with the existing system, individual organizations were developing their own client–server systems, geographic information systems (GIS), and local area network solutions—without a citywide strategy. Central MIS services were managed in the city comptroller's office, but with different groups having administrative control over applications support and developing and maintaining network applications. The strategic-planning consulting advice supplied by the research team addressed issues in these areas:

- Existing organization of MIS services
- Maintenance and sharing of data
- Design of a computing infrastructure
- Land records and GPS systems
- Information technology and service standards
- Staff development and training
- Planning and budgeting for MIS services, computing technology, and implementation scheduling

Five years after completion of the city's strategic plan, many of the recommended programs and actions were still not fully implemented. One of the most critical of the conclusions drawn by the authors (Smith et al. 2000, 154) was the continuing tendency to prefer single-use systems:

> In our judgment, the city (like many other organizations in the public and private sectors) must concentrate on finding effective methods for spanning formal organizational boundaries and information mechanisms in its information systems. The best combination of formal and informal mechanisms to effect such change begs further study.

Summary

The work of government organizations is carried out through a number of related systems, among which are:

1. The management systems that control the enterprisewide processes to coordinate and monitor all major operations of the organization
2. The supply-chain processes, which are routine activities that enable procurement, specification development, receiving, storing, and distributing products within the organization and to its stakeholders
3. The service-delivery processes that identify need, specify quality requirements, maintain customer information, design and monitor program configuration, and help manage other related value-chain activities
4. Systems for managing customer/client service-delivery processes
5. Systems for legislative-compliance reporting processes, including business-development and performance-management processes as well as control and support processes

These systems and processes can be grouped into three broad classes according to their primary objectives:

1. Those that facilitate the business operations of the organization
2. Those that facilitate delivery of the agency's products or services through the value chain
3. Those that maintain, enhance, and facilitate the flow of goods and services through the agency's supply chain

The chapter concludes with a description of the processes and systems involved in the transformation of the Defense Logistics Agency and of the strategic planning and implementation of changes in a large municipal information system.

Chapter 9

People and the Changing Face of Government

The future is not given. Especially in this time of globalization and the network revolution, behavior at the individual level will be the key factor in shaping the evolution of the entire human species. Just as one particle can alter macroscopic organization in nature, so the role of individuals is more important than ever in society.

Ilya Prigogine (2000)

Watson and Carte (2000) point to three fundamental differences between work in government and work in the private sector: in human resources management, management decision making, and in the design and application of information systems. They based their conclusions on three characteristics:

1. Environmental factors
2. The ways in which sector organizations interact with their environments and with their stakeholders
3. Fundamental differences in organizational structures and processes

Also, because government organizations have less interaction with the market, they are not as influenced by rewards and punishments associated with market controls. Finally, Watson and Carte found that government organizations:

- Were more constrained in their choices of procedures
- Perform activities that are mandated by political forces

135

- Face more external formal controls and specifications on their actions
- Deal with greater external influence on what they do and how they do it
- Gain approval from a wide variety of stakeholders
- Have multiple, often contradictory, objectives
- Have less autonomy and control over decision making and human resources
- Are less able to devise incentives for staff performance
- Are often forced to have their failures—large and small—aired in the public press

Four major shifts in the way that government functions have emerged from the transformation process now underway. First is the adoption of the strategic approach to managing human resources—what the federal government now refers to as *human capital*. An example of this change can be seen in the broadly based overhauls of the federal and local government Civil Service systems, including the use of incentive or merit pay for superior performance.

Administrators no longer focus on the internal detail associated with maintenance management. The second of these strategic shifts has resulted in changes in the way managers work in many government agencies. They are spending more time planning future actions than simply reacting to legislative mandates, for example. Strategic management concepts have made it possible for administrators to design and implement proactive agency strategies to meet the challenges that emanate from long-term trends in the demographic, economic, and social environments.

A third shift is the adoption of information and communications technology (ICT) by governments for the delivery of government services. One of the most far-reaching developments to emerge from this trend has been the continuing operational transformations that rapid developments in technology have forced upon governments. A major impact on the financial, tangible, and intangible assets of organizations has been the introduction of technology enabled e-government.

A fourth shift is the way that agencies manage and value their human capital—people and their skills. Without human capital, of course, none of the services that governments are supposed to provide could be done. People are needed to do the planning, implementing, and directing of operational strategies and tactics, including the transformation of government operations. However, a severe brain drain, caused by the thousands of government workers soon eligible for retirement, now threatens all levels of government.

In 1999, a group of 25 leading government managers and academicians met to discuss the state of the federal merit system. Also on the agenda was a call to produce an outline of how government needs to respond to changes in the labor market and in the delivery of public services. The participants agreed on four major points, the first of which was that the human resources of government must be valued more highly, and that government's human resources must be nurtured more carefully than the existing practices allowed (Ingraham, Selden, and Moynihan 2000).

The body of public managers belonging to the baby boom generation is also going to have to restructure the workplace to attract and keep the new generations of government workers (Yang and Guy 2006). The workers now beginning to replace the large number of retiring workers have different value systems, backgrounds, preparation, and motivations. Generation X workers (those born in the 1960s and 1970s), particularly, are believed to seek more intrinsic rewards, to demand participation in decision planning, and are more likely to change jobs and careers. In 2006, this group made up 38 percent of the U.S. workforce. In many skilled occupations, government organizations have had to adopt new and creative means of recruiting replacement workers (McNabb, Gibson, and Finnie 2006).

To address the challenges brought on by these changes in the government workforce, administrators are implementing *strategic human-resource management* to ensure that vital human capital is available when needed and applied in the most efficient and effective means available. This chapter addresses some of these human-capital challenges and the processes and procedures governments are adopting to deal with those challenges.

Human Capital and Transformational Change

Throughout the first years of this new century, the way that government workers deliver public services has undergone a revolutionary transformation. Governments everywhere are struggling to cope with profound changes in the three key elements of public management: people, process, and technology.

Comptroller General of the United States David M. Walker drew attention to the problem during a presentation before the U.S. National Commission on the Public Service when he called for greater attention to be given to the strategic management of human capital (Walker 2002). Walker began by making the connection between the need for government transformation and the role of human capital. Moreover, he identified human capital as a key driver of transformational change in government

The early years of the twenty-first century have seen a number of profound challenges emerge in the way that human capital is managed in government. These changes were driven by several key trends: global interdependence; diverse security threats; rapidly evolving science and technology; dramatic shifts in the age and composition of the population; important quality-of-life issues; changes in the economy; and changes in government structures and concepts. In the eyes of the comptroller general, these trends, although potentially damaging, present a wide range of challenges to administrators, which will require a variety of new and different responses. Accordingly, Walker urged that:

> Given these trends and long-range fiscal challenges, the federal government needs to engage in a comprehensive review, reassessment, and

reprioritization of what the government does, how it does business, and who does the government's business. We must re-examine a range of government policies, programs, and operations. The status quo is simply unacceptable. The long-range numbers do not add up. We must re-examine the base, including our current human capital policies and practices.

In Walker's opinion, such a reexamination is forcing government agencies to change their cultures and their overall orientations to bring about the following transformations:

- A shift from the traditional focus on processes to results
- A shift from stovepipes (single uses) to matrixes (broad applicability)
- A change from hierarchical to flatter and more horizontal structures
- Movement away from an inward focus to an external focus, in which citizens, customers, and stakeholders are recognized as primary recipients of agency attention
- Replacing the management control approach to one of empowering employees
- A change from reactive to proactive management behavior
- Embracing and leveraging new technologies rather than avoiding them as before
- A sharing of institutional knowledge rather than hoarding knowledge
- Managing risk rather than avoiding risk
- Instead of protecting turf, the forming of partnerships and collaborations

To address these and other people- and skill-related challenges, a *strategic human-capital initiative* now leads the federal government's drive to bring about a comprehensive transformation of government. The strategic management of human capital was the first goal stated in the 2002 President's Management Agenda (PMA).

Human-Capital Management in Government

Personnel, staffing, human resources, workforce management, and human capital: each of these terms have been used at different times to refer to the tasks of managing the human side of an organization. They all refer in one way or another to the activities associated with ensuring that enough people with the right skills and motivation are available when and where needed so that an organization can carry out its mission efficiently and effectively.

In the U.S. federal government, the term *human capital* is currently used to describe the intangible assets that people provide. According to the U.S. General Accounting Office (GAO), human capital is used in place of personnel or human-resource management because it includes two key principles that other terms omit

(Walker 2002). First, human-capital management looks at the people in an agency as *assets*, the value of which can be enhanced by proper investment. When that value increases, the ability of the agency to perform its mission also increases. This, in turn, increases the value of the service to clients and other stakeholders. The fundamental goal of management in all organizations is, after all, to maximize value.

Second, the human capital of the organization must be managed *strategically*. This means that it is managed in such a way that it supports the principles contained in the agency's overall mission, future vision, core values, objectives, and strategies. These are the means by which administrators and managers define the existence and expectations of the agency and its people. With such a plan in hand, determining how well the human-capital policies and programs of an agency were designed and implemented can be evaluated by weighing how successful they were in contributing to achieving desired results.

Strategic human-capital management is the management process of investing in people to improve the performance of the organization in both the short and the long term. These investments include improving management and leadership skills, assessing and anticipating workforce requirements and individual capabilities, and creating better systems and tools for the use of people in the organization. It also involves committing the energy and focus toward continuous career development. The goal is for these investments to help an agency develop stronger bonds between employee actions and desires and the performance of the agency.

Strategic workforce planning is the process that managers follow in planning how they are going to find, employ, utilize, and retain the people needed to achieve the missions of their organizations. It is a systematic way of ensuring that the organization now has, and will have in the future, the "right *people* with the right *skills* in the right *job* at the right *time* performing at their assignments *efficiently* and *effectively*" (Cotton 2007; emphasis in the original). A more formal definition of the process has been provided by the International Public Management Association for Human Resources (IPMA-HR 2006):

> Workforce planning is the strategic alignment of an organization's human capital with its business direction. It is a methodological process of analyzing the current workforce, identifying future workforce needs, establishing the gap between the present and the future, and implementing solutions so the organization can accomplish its mission, goals, and objectives.

Challenges Facing Human Resources Managers

In 2005, during testimony before a U.S. Senate subcommittee, Comptroller General Walker reported considerable progress in strategic human-capital management by government agencies. This issue had led the list of transformation initiatives in the

2001 President's Management Agenda. However, he also stated that much work still needed to be done; many agencies still have far to go in improving their strategic human-capital management programs. The human-capital problems that government administrators still faced included these four key challenges:

- *Leadership*: Agencies need long-term leadership with attention focused on completing transformations that extend over a number of years and administrations.
- *Planning*: Agencies need strategic workforce plans that identify and focus investments in human capital to encounter the strategic issues that constrain or contribute to long-term results.
- *Staffing*: The successful acquisition, development, and retention of talented personnel requires implementation of effective, flexible hiring processes; also, administrators need appropriate incentives that enable the retention of critical staff and, at the same time, reshape their workforce for the challenges of the future.
- *Culture*: Agencies need to improve their performance-management systems so that pay and rewards are linked to agency performance and results.

Box 9.1 The Federal Executive Leadership Program

The U.S. federal government, through the Office of Personnel Management (OPM), with other federal agencies, has established enterprise training and executive development and leadership programs to comply with strategic human-capital mandates. The Department of Agriculture Graduate School, for example, runs an OPM-approved nine-month leadership training program open to participation by personnel from other agencies.

Designed for government employees at the GS-11 and GS-13 levels with little or no supervisory experience, the program is designed to help participants learn or enhance their leadership abilities. Focusing on activities established in OPM's Leadership Effective Framework (LEF), learning activities include: individual needs assessments, leadership development plans, leadership development team activities, developmental work and shadowing assignments, executive interviews, readings in the leadership literature, and four residential training sessions.

Source: **DOE (2007)**

Government agencies will need three fundamental capabilities to deal with these human-capital challenges. First, they must adopt a process for human-capital development that joins staffing policies, strategies, and programs with agency objectives, mission, and outcomes. Second, agency administrators must develop the capacity to effectively forge and implement new systems of human-capital management. Third, administrators must put into place an effective and credible system for managing individual performance—a system with safeguards in place to guarantee fair, effective, nondiscriminatory, and efficient implementation. The following subsections examine in closer detail the four human-capital challenges facing government managers.

Box 9.2   Leadership at the U.S. Copyright Office

The mission of the U.S. Copyright Office is to promote creativity among the citizens and public and private organizations of the country by administering and sustaining an effective national copyright system. The office had a staff of 523 in 2004, organized into three key occupational categories: administrative, copyright specialist, and legal. Of these, 12 percent were eligible for immediate retirement; another 41 percent were eligible for early retirement. Only 2.7 percent had been at the office for less than 5 years. A major unit of the Library of Congress, the Copyright Office relies upon the library for its human resources services, including the leadership development program.

A key objective of the leadership program is to expose participants to "cutting-edge technology" and information systems, and prepare them for the next generation of librarianship in an expanding electronic environment. The 12-month leadership program includes library orientations, practical work experience, professional mentoring, needs assessments, professional development plans, training sessions on issues of leadership, librarianship, technology, and group and individual projects.

Specific Copyright Office strategic human-capital objectives include:

- Defining competencies and knowledge required for senior management positions
- Ensuring agency-level development programs for succession planning
- Training managers in strategic planning
- Working with managers and supervisors to set performance measures and performance targets

- Training managers and supervisors on how to measure performance and results
- Providing career incentives that include advancement and leadership opportunities where possible

Source: **USCO (2004)**

Challenges in Sustained Leadership

Public organizations in the United States and abroad agree that *strategic human-capital management,* with its concomitant transformation of the culture of government agencies, is an essential ingredient in any change-management program. This transformation will not take place overnight, however. Rather, it will take years to accomplish—extending far beyond the time most political appointees remain in office (GAO 2002). As a result, dealing with the challenge of finding a way to manage the exercise of leadership in government agencies is a critical early step in the desired transformation. Box 9.1 describes a government training program designed to improve leadership abilities and skills among existing agency personnel.

A Human-Capital Leadership Challenge

There are two aspects or tasks that shape the leadership challenge facing governments. One is finding, encouraging, and supporting long-term leadership within an agency to ensure that the proposed transformations are properly implemented and carried through to fruition. This becomes particularly problematic when there is a dearth of senior level administrators within the agency—a state of affairs that now exists in nearly every federal agency. Agencies are taking a variety of steps to rectify the leadership problems. Typical of these steps is the strategic human-capital plan the Federal Copyright Office (USCO) has implemented to address its leadership challenges (Box 9.2).

The lack of experienced leaders to step up to fill the growing numbers of vacant positions can occur for many reasons; the more probable cause of today's problem is the large numbers of federal employees electing to retire from government service. However, a related cause can be traced to the extensive cuts forced upon government agencies during the period of severe downsizing that took place during the decade of the 1990s. Downsizing resulted in the departure of many of the mid-level administrators who might now have been ready to fill the leadership needs in agencies.

During the height of the downsizing and reinventing government movement of the 1990s, Mark H. Moore (1995, 211) warned that government managers must seek, find, and exploit opportunities to create public value. Their task is not to increase the size of their organizations, institutionalize current policies, insulate their organizations from the demands of politics, or perfect the administrative systems that guide their organizations. Their task is to make their organizations more valuable, in the short and long run.

Increasing the agency's continuing capacity to respond to client needs and to innovate is one of the few ways that greater value can be produced. Moore and others are convinced that increasing agencies' ability to respond can happen only through the efforts of a dedicated, motivated, and satisfied workforce.

Also related to the dearth in personnel with strong leadership skills are such phenomena as a decline in the number of young workers seeking a career in public service, steep budget cuts that eliminated many executive development programs in agencies, and the need to train existing personnel in mastery of the rapid advances in information and communications technology that have helped to thoroughly transform the way government must function in the future.

The second major aspect associated with the leadership challenge facing government is the difficulty of truly transformational leaders to rise above the traditional hierarchical organizational structures that still characterize many government agencies.

The role of transformational leadership in facilitating change has been recognized for more than 20 years (Piccolo and Colquitt 2006). A transformational leader is one with the ability to enlist fellow workers in a drive to evoke an organizational change. Such leaders are able to appeal to followers' ideals and values in order to gain their commitment to a new vision for the organization. They are also able to inspire followers to develop new and innovative ways of thinking about organizational problems. For transformation to succeed in government agencies, leaders with the ability to inspire fellow workers to new and different ways of conducting the work of government must be found, encouraged, and assisted through leadership training and development.

Shin and Zhou (2003) found that the creativity of a sample of Korean employees was positively related to inspirational characteristics of leaders in their organizations. Their research also found that some of the responsibility for employees' willingness to follow the influence of a leader rested upon the values of the workers themselves. Leadership theory suggests that a leader's influence varies for subordinates who differ on how they value the relationship between the leader and themselves. Thus, the need to bring in leaders from outside because of a lack of "home-grown" leaders caused by the 1990s downsizing of government agencies adds to the problems of implementing transformational change.

Strategic Human-Capital Planning

A model of the concepts involved in a three-stage process for developing a strategic human-capital plan for government organizations is shown in Figure 9.1. Example activities are identified for each of the three key planning levels: staffing needs, staffing plans, and human-capital asset allocation and implementation.

One way to understand the strategic human-capital planning process is to look at it as occurring on three different levels. The first is the setting of strategic objectives that are relevant for a particular agency at that time. The second is the set of steps that result in identifying and developing relevant strategies. The third is the

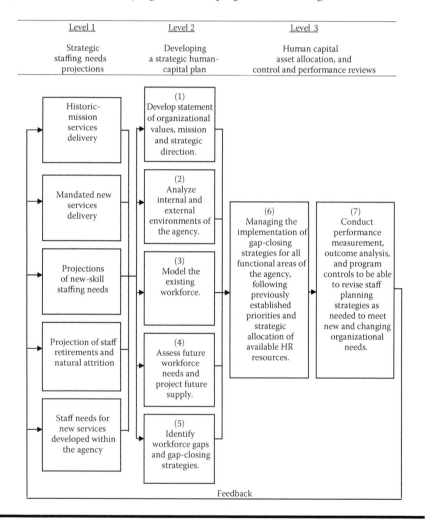

Figure 9.1 Components of a human-capital management planning process. (*Sources:* Berry 1994; Worrall, Collinge, and Bill 1998; Cotton 2007.)

level of implementing the strategy and monitoring progress, which includes establishing and applying controls and performance measurement processes.

The first level includes five categories of strategic processes (Berry 1994; Worrall, Collinge, and Bill 1998). The second level comprises the first five steps of the seven-step planning process suggested by Cotton (2007). Strategy implementation and performance evaluation and monitoring—the final two of Cotton's seven-step program—occur at the third level in the model. The following discussion of the seven steps occurring at the three levels is based largely upon Cotton's (2007) report.

Activities at the First, Preplanning Level

To ensure that staffing levels approach expected present and projected future needs, administrators are adopting a strategic management approach to managing human capital. This means looking at staffing in the light of how it contributes to the overall public value created by the agency. Administrators are making decisions in terms of what effects they will have on their agency's "bottom line" (Goldratt, Schragenheim, and Ptak 2000). This early research phase of the strategic human-capital planning process must relate agency human-capital policies and strategies, and tie in with the agency's mission goals and desired program outcomes.

- Evaluating the traditional services delivered by the agency or department and the historical rationale for its initial implementation
- Estimating staff needs for the new or significantly altered services or products provided by the agency, including services intended for a specific, short-term purpose that will not become an integral part of the agency's mission
- Forecasting human-capital needs for new or significantly altered services or products produced or provided by the agency that may reshape the fundamental mission of the agency (This step can even include dealing with recommendations for eventually discontinuing the agency itself.)
- Forecasting human-capital needs brought on by programs or services that may be added to or altered by client-generated requirements
- Forecasting human-capital needs for agency-developed actions introduced as a result of gaps identified by agency personnel

Planning Activities of Level Two

The first five steps of the seven-step strategic human-capital planning process occur during the second level, and these are:

1. Relating the human-capital function to the strategic direction of the agency
2. Evaluating the impact on staffing needs of events and trends in both internal and external environments

3. Modeling the existing workforce
4. Forecasting future workforce needs and workforce supply
5. Identifying and evaluating gaps between needs and supply and then developing strategies to close such gaps

Strategic Direction

Although some variant of strategic management and strategic planning exists in most larger public agencies today, aligning human resources to the strategic direction and the strategic plan is far less common (Cotton 2007). For this to be done, administrators must begin by reviewing the mission and performance requirements of the agency, while also specifying the human skills and competencies necessary for the accomplishment of the tasks and goals of the agency.

Environmental Analysis

Analysis of an agency's internal and external environment can identify potential constraints upon what an agency can do as well as producing new and improved methods and means of carrying out the tasks required by its mission. Cotton (2007) recommends reviewing the demographic, political, economic, and technological elements of the external environment for key issues and trends that may influence existing and future missions of the agency, the clients served, and other stakeholders. The internal analysis should focus on factors that affect the workforce, including workforce trends, HR transaction efficiencies, organizational structure and culture, operating climate, employee morale, and existing performance levels.

Model the Current Workforce

As with all planning activities, the process begins with a thorough understanding of things as they are now. This includes building a comprehensive picture of the characteristics, capabilities, skills, and knowledge distribution in the existing workforce, including permanent employees, supplemental direct-hire employees (i.e., employees not entitled to full benefits—workers hired on a temporary, seasonal, or on-call basis), and contract workers (such as workers employed by a staffing agency). This modeling enables the agency to construct a benchmark from which future workforce needs can be projected.

Assess Future Needs and Project Future Supply

Projecting workforce needs is founded upon the goals and objectives outlined in the agency's strategic plan. Future workforce demand is shaped by projected programmatic activities to meet the needs and characteristics of a forecast client base. The workforce-demand forecast is an estimate of the number of employees and types of skills expected to be needed in the future. Naturally, these forecasts are estimates, and should not be considered hard and fast. Workforce needs will vary as demand, environmental forces, and available assets vary. Therefore, staffing requirements will seldom exactly follow the plan.

Gap Analysis and Gap-Closing Strategies

Gap analysis is simply estimating the deficit or surplus between the expected supply of workers and the forecast workforce demand. This difference is the gap between what is needed and what is available. Gap analysis focuses on the particular skills, knowledge, and leadership abilities that are expected to be needed at some point in the future. This typically involves identifying critical professions for which a shortage is expected (such as scientists or engineers) and a projection of the new skills that will be needed but that are not now available in the agency or the local labor market. Gap-closing strategies are the activities that the agency plans to undertake to erase the gap. Gap-closing strategies can include programs to

- Retain good employees with needed skills
- Recruit good employees with needed skills
- Develop employees internally
- Collect and retain organizational knowledge
- Reduce overstaffing

Implementation Activities of Level Three

The final two closely related strategic workforce planning activities occur in level-three planning. These include first implementing the selected gap-closing strategies and, second, monitoring progress and measuring the effectiveness of the strategies, followed by any necessary revision of the strategy or strategies.

Implementing Gap-Closing Strategies

The best strategies in the world are of little value unless they are successfully implemented and judiciously supported through the full life of the initiative. Implementation is the task of the agency workforce, but workers must have the support and guidance of agency leadership and the resources needed to carry out those tasks.

Transformational strategies are particularly difficult to implement without widespread commitment of all stakeholders. Workers must be kept informed of the need for the change and the benefits that change is expected to achieve. This requires extensive communications both up and down the organizational hierarchy and across functions, groups, and teams.

State agencies that have been most successful at workforce planning have had good human-resources systems in place prior to planning and implementing a change. Managers and administrators have benefited from centralized support and guidance systems and workforce data.

Evaluating Effectiveness and Strategy Revision

The final step in the strategic workforce planning process described by Ann Cotton (2007) involves evaluating the success of the implemented gap-closing strategies—and the timely revision of those strategies if and when redirection is needed. Regular progress monitoring and performance measurements serve as an "early warning system" to administrators responsible for carrying out the planned strategies. Monitoring of both the plan implementation process and of the results of the implementation is necessary. Evaluation metrics include workforce characteristics, the distribution and availability of critical occupations and positions in the agency, present and projected gaps in the workforce, turnover rates, employee satisfaction, and organizational culture and climate.

Key Principles in Human-Capital Planning

Strategic workforce (or human capital) planning meets two important needs (GAO 2003b). First, the process makes it possible to align an agency's human-capital program with its existing and future mission and program goals. Second, the end product of the planning process results in long-term strategies for finding, developing, and retaining the workforce needed to conduct the business of the agency. Recognizing that not all agencies will develop their workforce plans in the same way, the GAO has recommended that all agencies address five key planning principles:

1. Top management, employees, and other stakeholders should be involved in developing, communicating, and implementing the strategic workforce plan.
2. The critical skills and competencies (capabilities) needed to achieve existing and future mission results should be determined.
3. Strategies should be developed that specifically address gaps in numbers, deployment, and approaches to workforce management so that the contribution of all critical skills and competencies is sustained.
4. Agencies should build the capacity to meet administrative, training, and development needs required to support workforce strategies.
5. Strategic workforce plans should include provision for monitoring and evaluating agency progress toward its human-capital goals and the contribution that human capital makes toward achieving program goals and objectives.

Box 9.3 Staff Shortfalls at the Nation's Forensic Laboratories

Forensic science is undergoing a technology-driven revolution, creating unprecedented opportunities to collect and examine criminal evidence. This has created backlogs in forensic laboratories, particularly in DNA analyses. The need for an adequate supply of trained forensic scientists to perform complex analyses is a significant challenge facing all law enforcement agencies. Staffing challenges in forensic laboratories exist nationwide. Staff turnover in Indiana laboratories, for example, created a one-year backlog despite a $1 million federal grant. Understaffing in the Massachusetts state laboratory system has been blamed for weakening its law enforcement capability. Similar stories can be found in other states.

Ralph Keaton, executive director of the American Society of Crime Laboratories, estimates that in 2001 there were about 10,000 forensic scientists is the United States. An additional 10,000 new forensic scientists are needed over the next decade to deal with the expanding case backlog. However, although job opportunities and funds for scientific research are increasing, the number of science degrees awarded continues to decline.

Forecasting staffing needs involves anticipating the workforce required to meet organizational objectives. Public agencies are usually poor planners, and laboratories are no exceptions. Forecasting staffing in public laboratories is problematic because estimating caseloads is difficult. Reliable and valid measures of productivity often do not exist, and there is a general lack of agreement on the definition of caseload, which can be configured as cases, items in a case, and other units of work. Variations from laboratory to laboratory in the use of batch processing and team analyses also make it difficult to accurately predict the personnel needed in scientific laboratories. Yet the importance of accurate and precise measurement is widely acknowledged in order to build effective human resource (human-capital management) systems.

Source: **Dale and Becker (2004)**

Challenges in Acquiring, Developing, and Retaining Talent

Many, if not most, government agencies in the developed world are experiencing declines in staff—whether mandated by budget cuts or legislative action, or through natural attrition due to retirements of workers among the baby boom generation. At the same time, a shortfall exists in the pool of possible replacement workers. As a result of these problems in the United States, a cornerstone of the enterprise-transformation initiative is the acquisition, development, and retention of talented replacement workers (Mihm 2007).

An example of how these problems affect government agencies is displayed in Box 9.3. The information was included in a report from a 2004 Federal Bureau of Investigation (FBI) publication describing the significant shortfall that exists in the number of scientists at the nation's forensic laboratories. At the federal level, existing bureaucratic rules and regulations have made addressing existing personnel shortages a difficult and time-consuming process. According to Mihm (2007), managing director of strategic issues at the GAO, these rules have put the federal government at a competitive disadvantage when recruiting workers, and particularly senior staff personnel.

The challenge of finding and hiring the thousands of talented men and women needed to fill the shoes of retiring government employees has many different facets. One of the main limiting aspects has been the traditional lengthy and complicated bureaucratic procedures through which prospective employees must pass.

The potential for breaking through this barrier exists, however. Congress, the Office of Personnel Management (OPM), and individual agencies have taken steps to significantly streamline the process. Referred to as *flexibilities*, agencies now have available exemptions from pay and classification restrictions. Moreover, OPM and government agencies are participating in job fairs, recruiting on college campuses, and using television commercials to attract prospective recruits. OPM has developed a hiring tool kit to help administrators through the hiring process. Not all agencies are taking advantage of the flexibilities, however, and corrections and adjustments are still needed (Mihm 2007).

Governments are also trying to attract more minority candidates to government careers by offering scholarships, grants, and training and mentoring programs. Agencies have also transformed the training and development process. One important change is the new focus on ensuring that training and development activities are targeted to meet the strategic needs of the organization. Training and development are recognized as playing a key role in enabling agencies to meet their transformation challenges.

Challenges in Reforming Organizational Cultures

Possibly the biggest barrier to successful transformation of an organization is the strong force within the organization that works to retain the status quo. That force is the *culture* of the organization (Box 9.4). Organizational culture has been defined in many ways, but all seem to closely follow Schein's (1990) shorthand description of culture as "the way we do things around here." Farmer's 1990 description was nearly identical: organizational culture is expressed as "what is done, how it is done, and who is doing it."

Most people are not inherently open to revolutionary change: in the way that they work; in the things that are done by their group; in the values of their workplace; or in the way they are treated, motivated, and rewarded by their organization. They must be shown or convinced that the proposed change is good for them and for the long-term health of their organization. Writing about organizational culture and transformational change in higher education, Keup et al. (2001) conceded that transformations in colleges and universities are based on the assumption that change can occur despite the emphasis on tradition and maintaining the existing collegial culture.

Box 9.4   Organizational Culture at the SSA and Transformation

The Social Security Administration (SSA)—a very large government agency with a long history of providing personal service to U.S. citizens—has built up a huge infrastructure since the 1930s to support its mission. In the process, it has adopted as its organizational structure the traditional hierarchical bureaucracy that large organizations since the Industrial Revolution have accepted as a model of efficiency. However, the changes and efficiencies promised by information and communications technologies were not considered when this model evolved. Many at the SSA believe that the traditional structure and culture of high personal service is threatened by proposed implementation of electronic delivery of services. A feeling held by many staff is that the potential benefits of electronic delivery are outweighed by a concern over the impact that such a change may have on SSA users and beneficiaries.

The SSA workforce takes great pride in fulfilling its mission. Moreover, it has a long tradition of providing personal service tailored to individual clients. It devotes substantial resources to its face-to-face and telephone services. Cultural values within the agency seem to link electronic or online services with impersonal service, rather than considering digital delivery as having potential for being more responsive in terms of cycle time, convenience, user satisfaction, load reduction, and accuracy.

The authors of the report noted that this concern with cultural and organizational challenges associated with innovative programs is not unique to the SSA. The concern is particularly pressing over the implementation of digital services delivery. A 2001 government study found that cultural issues are important factors in determining the success of an organization's ability to innovate. The SSA, like other agencies, is still a heavily "stove-piped" organization. This tends to make cross-program communications difficult and complicates the coordination needed for success in such interorganizational initiatives as the PMA and enterprise architecture, among others.

Source: **Osterweil, Millet, and Winston (2007)**

This assumption, of course, is seldom true. Culture can significantly limit change and transformation. Eckel, Hill, and Green (1998) pointed this out when they identified organizational culture as one of four fundamental characteristics of planned change in an organization. All organizational transformations affect the organization in these ways:

1. By altering underlying assumptions and organizational processes, behaviors, and products, transformation changes the culture of the organization.
2. Transformation change is deep and pervasive, affecting the entire organization and, therefore, should not be entered into lightly.
3. Transformational change is intentional, not casual or unplanned.
4. The transformation occurs over some period of time; it is seldom if ever immediate.

Special attention was given to cultural barriers in a report on the strategic assessment of the ability of the U.S. Social Security Administration (SSA) to implement a major transformation in the delivery of its services. The assessment warned that the existing organizational culture was severely limiting the ability of the agency to implement electronic delivery of services. The committee included the findings and recommendations displayed in Table 9.1.

The National Research Council's Committee on E-Government Strategy and Planning for the Future conducted a study to assess SSA's ability to expand the scale and scope of its electronic information and services. It determined that successful service-delivery strategies must be grounded in an understanding of the strengths and weaknesses of the organization, its operational constraints, and the nature of

Table 9.1   Findings and Recommendations for Digital Service Delivery at the SSA

Findings:	Recommendations:
SSA may be missing important opportunities to make sustained improvements in service delivery because of potential risks of modernizing its service delivery strategy and a lack of emphasis on the long-term risks of not revamping the strategy.	When evaluating new electronic service delivery initiatives, SSA should seek to balance risks and rewards by recognizing such benefits from automation as cost reduction, fraud prevention, and customer satisfaction.
The existing SSA organizational structure does not support a strategic focus in electronic services that is sufficiently high-level and broad-based. SSA can be more proactive in reassessing its customer-service value chain and, wherever appropriate, focusing on potential substitution of electronic services for other delivery systems (such as paper mail and in person in field offices)	SSA should make an unambiguous, strategic commitment to electronic services as part of its long-term service delivery strategy, focusing on electronic services that provide timely and up-to-date information for users, partners, and beneficiaries.
The establishment of appropriate metrics and measures to evaluate the effectiveness of various services and delivery channels is an important component of an effective service delivery plan.	SSA should define and use metrics and measures to assess and improve its service delivery across all channels, including electronic services.
There are opportunities for SSA to partner with other government agencies and nongovernment organizations in ways that could provide mutual benefit.	SSA should make an effort to understand the identities, needs, and attitudes of its user communities and then use that information to establish effective relationships and ongoing interactions with users, potential partners, and third parties. SSA should also explore partnering opportunities and identify changes and initiatives necessary for it to enable interaction and cross-functionality with strategic partners and support data exchange with other government agencies while ensuring that security and privacy measures are in place.

Table 9.1   Findings and Recommendations for Digital Service Delivery at the SSA (Continued)

Findings:	Recommendations:
SSA faces significant ongoing change in technology, demographics, and public expectations as it conducts its activities, services, and interactions with user communities.	SSA should embrace change. It should evaluate emerging trends in technology and business practices to improve efficiency and effectiveness. It should also regularly evaluate changing societal attitudes and expectations, and form strategies for addressing those trends.

Source: Osterweil, Millet, and Winston (2007).

the resistance or support of a changed vision of service delivery. The committee also concluded that an understanding of the culture of the organization and its approach to technology and its services are required if the proposed transformation to greater use of electronic delivery of agency services is to be successful.

Summary

This chapter has addressed concepts involved in developing and implementing strategic approaches to manage human capital and the process of transforming government agencies. The chapter also examined a model that illustrates the forces and antecedents that have shaped the development of strategic thinking in public organizations.

Strategic human capital is a critical challenge facing federal, state, and local governments. At the federal level, human capital has been identified as one of nearly two dozen areas of high risk. This occurred after it was determined that the lack of attention being given by agencies to strategic human capital was limiting the ability of the federal government to effectively perform its designated mission.

Four workforce challenges still continue to face agency administrators: finding, developing, and applying proper leadership; preparing comprehensive strategic human-capital plans; acquiring needed staff with the proper skills to meet the challenges of governing in the twenty-first century; and transforming organizational culture from hierarchical bureaucracies to learning organizations that embrace change.

All government strategic human-capital plans are encouraged to incorporate five key principles into their planning processes:

1. Involve top management and stakeholders in the planning process
2. Identify critical skills and competencies needed now and in the future

3. Develop strategies that enable meeting existing and future human-capital challenges
4. Provide training and development programs that help build competencies
5. Monitor and evaluate progress toward achieving agency and human-capital goals and objectives

Chapter 10

Changing Government Work Processes

> We ... suggest that the transformations currently occurring in the nature of work and organizing cannot be understood without considering both the technological changes and the institutional contexts that are reshaping economic and organizational theory.
>
> **Wanda J. Orlikowski and Stephen R. Barley (2001)**

A fundamental emphasis of enterprise transformation is radical change in the way that work is done in organizations. Work is accomplished through processes incorporated in simple and complex systems, such as program service delivery systems, finance and accounting systems, marketing and customer relationship systems, production and operations systems, and human resources systems. Organization managers and administrators plan and allocate information, human, financial, and physical resources to these systems in order to satisfy program missions and achieve goals and objectives.

The *systems concept* comes into play at two levels. First, organizations—public, private, nonprofit—can be considered as complex systems organized to accomplish some activity. Enterprises, however, are seldom viewed as complete systems by the people who reside in them. People tend to align themselves with smaller, more intimate groups, such as accounting, finance, marketing, operations, and the like. This tends to produce what is known as "stovepipe" thinking and stovepipe systems, where the management emphasis is on maximizing unit productivity and effectiveness—at the expense of units outside of the primary group. William Rouse (2006) described this thinking as, "One makes sure to get one thing 'right' but, in the process, ignores everything else." He added that technology has destroyed the viability of the stovepipe mentality approach to managing:

> However, computer and communications technologies are leading to everything becoming more integrated—everything connects to everything. We decrease our potential success when we try to design and manage functions within the enterprise independently of each other. The interactions are important, indeed essential to fully leveraging the enterprise's assets—human, information, financial, and physical—to the greatest benefit of all stakeholders. This requires that we look at the whole enterprise as a system, rather than as a collection of functions connected solely by information systems and shared parking lots.

Information technology has facilitated the growth of knowledge and competition—both of which derive somewhat from technology. This, in turn, has broken down barriers within and around work centers and created boundaryless or "virtual" organizations, which makes it possible to remove intermediaries, speed up transactions, and distribute power to organizations' stakeholders. When internal and external boundaries are removed, the result can be the creation of fundamental change in the context, scope, and very nature of work (Howard 1995).

Systems and Work Processes

At the second level, systems also refer to the various collections of processes by which the work of the organization gets accomplished. In this way, an organization can be considered a system of systems (Rouse 2006). Finance, management information, and accounting systems are examples of organized means of accomplishing certain tasks in organizations. Information systems have revolutionized the organization and performance of work in the private and public sectors (Davis 1995).

This chapter focuses on organizational and human adaptations taking place at this second level of systems; it examines several of the key transformations in work processes that are occurring within government organizations. Some of these work changes include such processes as shared services, service delivery privatization and collaboration, e-government, and knowledge-management systems. These and similar systems are the forces driving the transformation of government.

Value Deficiencies as Drivers of Transformation

Organizations engage in transformation initiatives because of discrepancies between the values of their primary stakeholders and what the organizations can provide. Rouse refers to these as "value deficiencies." When these value deficiencies occur in government organizations, a state of disequilibrium emerges in the agency's operating climate. Results can be employee dissatisfaction, high turnover, failure to achieve desired or projected program performance, and other organizational culture-related negative results. When this happens, senior administrators must develop strategies to change the business model and return the agency to the desired performance path.

One body of strategies focuses specifically on changes in work processes. Three approaches to work-process transformation are possible. One is to improve how work is performed in the organization. A second is to perform the same work differently. And a third is to perform different work altogether. Each of these approaches is discussed in greater detail in the following subsections.

Improving Current Work Processes

Because change in organizations focuses upon the what, how, and why work gets done, transformation demands change in work processes. A work process has been defined as a "repeated and repeatable set of activities that collectively create and deliver value" (Nadler, Shaw, and Walton 1995). Another way to describe the set of activities that make up a work process is to consider it a system. Clearly, work processes and systems are closely related.

Improving the way work is currently done in organizations is the goal of *business process improvement* (BPI). Although BPI may be less transformative than performing work differently or performing different work, it has been widely adopted by both private and public organizations as a way to get change started. Although it is more common today to refer to this process as BPI, it became a popular movement in the 1990s under the label of *business process reengineering* (BPR). BPI is also sometimes referred to as *business process redesign* (Rouse 2006; Hammer 1996).

Neither BPI nor BPR are really anything new; they both have their roots in the *work simplification* studies that Frank B. Gilbreth pioneered early in the last century (Graham 1999). Gilbreth considered work simplification to be nothing more than applying common sense to eliminate waste and find better and easier ways of doing work.

Business process reengineering was proposed as a way to bring about improvements in products and services, customer service quality, and operational efficiency to enhance organizational effectiveness. These processes require managers and administrators to look at all aspects of job design as they relate to the critical processes used to produce and deliver products and services. Managers and employees are involved in evaluating every element of the firm's operations in order to rebuild the enterprise system by improving efficiency, eliminating redundancies and non-value-adding activities, and eliminating all waste. The result is a significant impact on the way that jobs are designed (Lewis, Goodman, and Fandt 2001).

BPI in Government

The U.S. Army's Enterprise Solutions Competency Center defines business process improvement as a way of focusing change in a business process. These changes occur by analyzing the process as it is (AS-IS), and then using process models and other tools to develop a streamlined future (TO-BE) process. Since the late 1990s, the work process improvement more often than not includes addition of automation (technology) to produce better, faster, and cheaper processes. For the U.S. Army, BPI cost-reduction goals range from 10 to 40 percent (ESCC 2007).

Many government organizations in the United Kingdom have accepted BPI tools to implement improvements in the efficiency and effectiveness of the delivery of their services. Local governments particularly appear to believe that BPI can help them meet citizen expectations and achieve mandated efficiencies and service improvements, while also improving their management of tax revenues. For example, results of a 2006 survey of U.K. local governments revealed that nearly 80 percent of the respondents agreed that BPI is critical to the modernization of public services, and 90 percent said that they were going to do more BPI projects in the immediate future (RSeconsulting 2006).

Box 10.1 BPI Successes in U.K. Local Government

After reengineering work processes and using smarter scheduling, the Peterborough City Council was able to manage 20 percent more proprieties to higher standards with 50 fewer staff and annual cost savings of nearly £2 million. The council replaced an old paper-based system for dealing with repair and maintenance services with a mobile technology-enabled system. Time to complete nonurgent repairs dropped from an average of 20 days to 7.

Social-services delivery was the subject of the work-process transformation initiated by the Blackpool Council. The council's social-services information system was changed from an inaccessible and difficult-to-manage paper-based system that left citizens and staff frustrated and dissatisfied. Costs were high, and it seemed that employees were there to serve the organization rather than their clients. The old system was replaced with a CRM system providing electronic social-care records. The change is expected to greatly improve service while also saving the council more than £1 million annually. All social-care processes are now managed by the electronic care process, which interfaces with the council's core human resources and financial systems. The change is achieving the goal of alignment of people, information, process, technology, and organizational change.

The business-transformation team at the Sefton Metropolitan Borough Council has implemented a plan to improve the efficiency of its human-resources and payroll processes. A new payroll system added to improve efficiency required a staff increase to cope with disconnecting the old system from the new. Also, the council's complex remuneration structure caused heavy reliance on manual intervention.

New processes, management structures, and job definitions—with paperwork modification—were adopted. Enabling software made it possible to process payroll more efficiently and provided a management information system that resulted in greater visibility of how staff spent their time, which in turn made it possible to schedule staff time for greater productivity. The new enabling systems improved internal communication, resulting in positive changes in the way staff view their jobs, thereby improving morale and performance. Total savings of nearly £350,000 were expected.

Source: **U.K. Office of Government Commerce (OGC; 2007)**

The U.K. government is strongly pushing for business process improvement among local government bodies. A U.K. Office of Government Commerce (Office of the Treasury) report promoted ten success stories with BPI programs that ranged from how communities transformed work process in public housing, benefits, procurement, taxes, development, cleaning, change management, human resources, and information technology (OGC 2007). Several of those successes are presented in Box 10.1.

Box 10.2   Enabling Transformation with E-Government in New Zealand

The New Zealand government published its initial e-government and strategic vision for information and communications technology in 2000, adding an e-government strategy a year later. The latest installment in its progress reports, "Enabling Transformation," followed in November 2006. That report described actions for improving the convenience and responsiveness of government information and services. It also described how changes in technology—particularly the growth in social networking on the World Wide Web—have affected the e-government program.

Government agencies have increased their use of the Internet to increase the value that citizens derive from the government. The Internet has also become an important channel for publishing information and delivering interactive services.

New Zealand administrators believe that implementation of the e-government has succeeded in facilitating change in many, if not most, government agencies. Applying network technologies has become part of the day-to-day business of government in New Zealand.

Source: **NZSSC (2006)**

Changing How Work Gets Done

Change in the way work is done can more often result in a transformational change in agency operations than is likely to occur by simply changing work processes. *Transformed government* really means that an agency, department, or jurisdiction has either adopted a completely different way of working or has shifted its focus to another mission entirely. In the new way of working, for example, delivering services and communication through digital networks has replaced traditional face-to-face transactions as well as the old bureaucratic hierarchical structure of government (NZSSC 2006).

The key to implementing sustainable changes in an organization's work processes remains the successful introduction of information and communications technology (Carnoy and Castells 1997). Two key benefits of technology in work systems are *flexibility* and *networking*. Technology makes possible the flexibility that organizations need to respond to rapidly changing conditions in their internal and external environments; networking facilitates exchange of information and leverages productivity through collaboration and cooperation. The product of these two changes in work processes is the development of learning-centered organizations. These impact the transformation of work in the following ways (Carnoy and Castells 1997):

> Flexibility and networking are facilitated by information technologies and have become key elements of the transformation of work. Flexibility means constant adaptation to changing [services], processes, and [stakeholder values]; it requires higher skill levels as increased autonomy and responsibility are vested in the workforce. Networking, a form of organization well suited to fluid conditions, operates internally among levels and actors in firms and externally among firms.

Examples of transformational changes in the way work gets done in government include shared services, outsourcing, and privatization. The term *shared services* refers to the consolidation of such administrative services or functions as finance, information technology, human resources, and procurement from two or more agencies or departments into a single entity to serve all partners more efficiently and effectively while lowering the cost of delivering the service (TBS 2005).

Shared services are becoming increasingly popular among governments in the United States, the United Kingdom, Australia, and New Zealand, among others. The idea of shared services has a long history in the United States. The first large-scale shared-services organization was the General Services Administration (GSA), established by President Harry Truman on July 1, 1949, at the recommendation of the Hoover Commission. The commission recommended that several small agencies be merged into one in order to reduce duplication, cost, and confusion in handling supplies and providing space for government agencies.

GSA: A Shared Services Pioneer

The first mission of GSA was to dispose of war surplus materials, manage and store government records (transferred to the independent National Archives and Records Administration in 1985), handle emergency preparedness (transferred to FEMA in 1979), and stockpile strategic supplies (transferred to the Defense Department in 1988). The agency was also charged with regulating the sale of office supplies to federal agencies. In addition to its wide variety of products and services, the GSA is currently a competitive source for space, building services, vehicles, information and communications technology, and office supplies to federal agencies. It provides access to government information to citizens via the Internet, e-mail, telephone, fax, or print. The agency is also responsible for five presidential e-government initiatives—e-authentication, e-travel, federal asset sales, integrated acquisition, and USA Services—and manages the federal government's official Web portal, USA.gov (GSA 2007).

Outsourcing Government Services

Outsourcing, a common practice in large private-sector organizations, is slowly becoming accepted in government organizations as well. Contracting with faith-based organizations for the delivery of social services is an example of privatization of government activities (U.K. Cabinet Office 2005). In a report describing the U.K. government's strategy for implementing a shared-services policy, Prime Minister Tony Blair explained that the new approach was needed to gain efficiencies across the United Kingdom's e-government systems and to support delivery of services that were more focused on citizen needs. Public-service organizations were expected to benefit from shared services through reduced waste and improved

efficiency by reusing assets and sharing investments with others. The shared-services initiative focused on eight key areas:

1. Customer-service centers for customer contact or payment processes
2. Human resources, finance, and other corporate services
3. Common infrastructure, with off-the-shelf technology solutions and leveraged investments
4. Data sharing needed to transform services and reduce administrative burdens
   on citizens and businesses
5. Information management for more-collaborative actions across agencies and
   levels as well as common standards and practices
6. Information assurance (security), risk and enterprise architecture management, and a public–private partnership to promote Internet safety
7. Identity management, moving toward biometric identity cards and the
   national identity register
8. Technology standards and architecture to ensure that technology is most cost
   effective through a consistent approach to standards and architecture across
   all government organizations

Two years after issue of the report, the shared-services concept was slowly finding some acceptance among local government leaders in the United Kingdom. In
late May 2007, the Chief Information Officer Council (CIOC)—the body responsible for overseeing implementation of shared services across Great Britain—was
holding shared-services briefing sessions every six weeks to assist agencies in developing shared-services plans. The purpose of the sessions was to bring to light key
issues and problems, promote the sharing of experiences within various sectors,
and help eliminate real or perceived barriers to shared services (CIOC 2007). The
U.K. public sector has more than 1,300 separate organizations, employing a total
of more than 5 million workers. Most of the organizations are small, autonomous
agencies—increasing the difficulty of achieving hoped-for success in implementing
the programs.

The idea of shared services is catching on in the United States as well. The
National Business Center at the U.S. Department of the Interior is an example
(Box 10.3). At the end of 2005, for example, a number of jurisdictions, agencies,
or governments around the world were well on the way toward implementation of
shared-services programs.

Examples include several U.S. states (such as Illinois, New Jersey, and
Massachusetts, among others), Canadian provinces of Alberta and Ontario, the
state of Queensland in Australia, and the governments of New Zealand and Ireland,
all of which have implemented shared-services initiatives.

Box 10.3 Shared Services at the U.S. Department of the Interior

The National Business Center (NBC) is an example of a shared-services center at the federal government level. NBC functions like a private business, providing a broad range of services and support to other federal agencies. NBC is the systems manager and general-purpose computer host for departmentwide budgets, procurement and contracts, personnel management, finance and accounting, e-government, and other services and systems at the Department of the Interior (DOI). NBC also provides such services for its clients as systems analysis, functional design, software development or acquisition, system implementation, user training, operations support, and software maintenance for administrative services.

Half of NBC's work comes from DOI. Other customers include the Social Security Administration (SSA)—a 20-year customer for payroll services, the Department of Transportation (DOT), the Department of Defense (DoD), and NASA. NBC has provided business management systems and services for more than 30 years, and now serves more than 150 small and mid-sized agencies. NBC's eight lines of business are:

1. *Acquisition services/GovWorks*: Acquisition services, including contract support, charge card oversight, leasing services, and indirect rate negotiation
2. *Appraisal services*: General appraisal, appraisal reviews, appraisal consulting, and concession valuations services to DOI bureaus
3. *Aviation services*: Aviation safety and mishap prevention policy and oversight in support of aviation functions
4. *Financial and business management services*: Financial services and systems support; financial management systems support or accounting operations services
5. *Human-resource services*: Four key service offerings: core HR services, payroll, expanded services (operational servicing), and random drug and alcohol testing
6. *Information technology (IT) services*: IT infrastructure, integration, disaster recovery, Web development, and IT security
7. *Training services*: Training programs in leadership and performance, online learning systems, and cultural resources and events

8. *Other DOI support services*: A wide variety of services such as communications, employee services, facilities management, property and asset management, and IT support services

Source: **Defense Consulting & Outsourcing—online edition (2006)**

The Canadian federal government was in the early stages of the adoption process in 2005, planning to introduce shared-services operations in human resources, financial and material services, and information technology (TBS 2005).

Shared Services in State and Local Government

The successful completion of the first phase and kick-off of the second (design) phase of the Illinois Shared Services Program was announced in 2007. Its goal is to put new technologies and streamlined basic fiscal and human resources–related operations to work in the shared-services approach (State of Illinois 2007). Illinois had two shared-services centers (SSCs) operating at the end of the year, with plans to implement at least three additional centers in the near future. In service were the Public Safety SSC, serving the state's designated public safety agencies, and the Administrative and Regulatory SSC. Future SSCs include one to serve the state social services agencies, a healthcare agencies services center, and an SSC for environmental and economic development agencies.

Progress on implementation of shared services in local governments is exemplified by the experiences of the state of New Jersey. New Jersey is encouraging local and regional governments to adopt shared-services programs and then backing up their support with financial grants for feasibility studies, planning, and implementation of shared services in counties, municipalities, and special-purpose districts. Nonprofit organizations assisting in program planning and implementation are also eligible for the grants. A description of progress highlights as of February 2007 presented by the New Jersey Department of Community Affairs commissioner Susan Bass Levin is displayed in Box 10.4.

Box 10.4   Shared Services Inducements in New Jersey

The State of New Jersey formed a Joint Legislative Committee on Government Consolidation and Shared Services in July of

2007 to establish the state government's role in encouraging shared services at the local level.

The New Jersey Department of Community Affairs's Sharing Available Resources Efficiently (SHARE) program provides financial assistance to local governments—municipalities, counties, fire districts, school districts, and nonprofits acting as regional coordinators—for the study or implementation of shared and regional services between local entities. In its first two years, more than $4.2 million in 86 grants has been awarded for feasibility study and implementation grants.

New guidelines were announced in 2007: (1) the local match requirement for feasibility grants, formerly offered up to $20,000 provided the applicant matched 50 percent, has been reduced to 10 percent; (2) the maximum amount for implementation grants, formerly up to $100,000, has been raised to $200,000, with the local match requirement eliminated; (3) a new county program aimed at county governments encourages the use of counties to coordinate shared services arrangements by local government groups and organizations. The annual ceiling for county grants remains $100,000. However, they have been extended from one-year to three-year grants, so that the maximum an applicant can receive is $300,000, with no matching funds required. As of February 2007, six counties had received grants that underwrite their efforts to find and implement new shared-service opportunities.

Atlantic, Camden, Cape May, Monmouth, Somerset and Union counties each have a full-time Shared Service Coordinator's position. Besides working to expand the county's capabilities in shared services, the coordinators work with local and school officials to identify, develop and implement new shared services between local units. They also plan county-wide and regional meetings on shared-service topics.

Source: **Levin (2007)**

Information and communications technology in local governments is often one of the areas included in proposed shared-services programs. The National Association of State Chief Information Officers (NASCIO) published an issue brief in March 2006 in which they outlined differences between consolidated and shared-services IT delivery modes. The consolidated or centralized approach is sometimes adopted for cost-containment purposes without offering shared services. The services or applications in existing agencies are taken away and combined into a single, central operation. Consolidations are typically conducted as a result of executive mandates, as when a new executive office is voted into office.

Shared services do not necessarily result in large-scale consolidation. Rather, a shared service can be one that an agency is already providing another agency. Rather than developing the service internally, an agency buys the service from another agency. Shared services are a way to control costs while improving the quality of internal services; quality improvements are usually not a planned objective of consolidations. Participation in shared services is usually voluntary (NASCIO 2006c).

In May 2005, NASCIO published results of a nationwide survey of state past and future plans to implement consolidations and shared services of information technology operations. Thirty-four states plus the District of Columbia responded to the survey. Initiatives planned or underway are displayed in Table 10.1.

Communications services and telephony were the functions most often reported (91.4 percent) as a consolidation action; Geographic Information Service (GIS) was least likely (58.8 percent) to be included in a consolidation. Respondents were most likely to include agency portals as implemented or planned for shared services (93.1 percent), with e-mail services least likely to be included in a shared-services initiative.

Table 10.1   IT Consolidations and Shared Services Completed or in Progress

Initiative	Consolidation (percent)	Shared Services (percent)
Payment engine	71.4	78.6
Communications services/telephony	91.4	85.2
Data center	77.7	84.7
Disaster recovery	68.6	86.2
E-mail services	71.5	61.5
ERP/Financial/HR	73.5	71.5
GIS	58.8	79.3
Network	85.7	70.3
Portals	77.2	93.1
Procurement	80.0	82.1
Security services	65.7	79.3
Servers	65.7	77.8

Source: NASCIO (2006d).

Shared Government Services in Australia

Queensland, Australia, is in the process of implementing a shared-services approach to managing administrative processes designed to standardize service policies, practices, and systems (SSI 2007). All Queensland government departments are participating in the Shared Services Initiative (SSI). Each agency has been assigned one of five shared-services providers. Providers include:

1. The Shared Services Agency, which supplies corporate services to 30 departments and agencies
2. Corporate and Professional Services, operating as an independent business unit within the Department of Education, Training and Arts
3. The Queensland Health Shared Service Provider, supplying corporate services for the Queensland Health Department
4. The Corporate Administration Agency, providing corporate services for a small number of agencies
5. The Parliamentary Service provider

In addition, Queensland operates CorpTech, an all-government technology center serving applications and systems in support of the shared-services providers. Shared Services Solutions, a unit within CorpTech, manages the implementation of standard human resources, finance, and document and records solutions for the Queensland government.

Transformation by Performing Different Work

Performing different work is the most transformational strategy of the three work-process strategies. Transformation at this level results in changes in the purpose, goals, and objectives, as well as the work performed by people in the agency. Because the changes are so extensive and have such an impact on the culture of an organization, this type of transformation is often very difficult to achieve. Rouse (2006) pointed out that changing the purpose of an agency or department is likely to be exceptionally difficult, time consuming, and risky. The greater the change, the more problematic will be the change process.

Outsourcing, privatization, and public–private partnerships for the delivery of traditional government services are examples of the types of transformational actions that are changing the work done in government; all are part of the government's drive to use competitive sourcing to make government more market-based.

The terms *outsourcing* and *privatization* are often used interchangeably, although they differ in several points (Bandoh 2003). Outsourcing refers to government contracts with an outside supplier (a vendor) to perform specific services. Contracts are typically signed after competitive bidding, although in certain emergencies, short-term contracts may be let without this process. This occurred early in the Iraq invasion for support of U.S. troops and by FEMA for emergency housing and other services in New Orleans immediately after Hurricane Katrina.

The purpose of competitive sourcing is to expose the activities to competition with the private sector. Competing with private business is supposed to make government focus on continuous improvement for improved performance with greater efficiency. According to Angela Styles, administrator of federal procurement policy, the objective of competitive sourcing is to ensure the most effective and efficient means of accomplishing an agency's mission, regardless of whether it is done by public employees or private contractors (Styles 2003). Her testimony outlined revisions made to Circular A-76 as they relate to requirements of the Federal Activities Inventory Reform (FAIR) Act of 1998.

FAIR requires all federal agencies to prepare and submit to the Office of Management and Budget by June 30 of each year a report outlining any commercial activities performed by federal employees and a list of government activities deemed to be inherently a government activity. Inherently governmental activities are activities that are "so intimately related to the public interest as to require performance by federal government employees" (OMB 1998). Examples include activities involving the acquisition, use, or disposition of U.S. property.

Circular A-76 describes federal policy for competition of commercial activities and lists procedures for determining whether government activities should be performed under contract with commercial organizations or done in-house by government employees (OMB 2003). A-76, originally issued in 1966, was revised in 1967, 1979, 2000, and again in 2003.

Most outsourced activities involve transferring responsibility for the management, operation, and maintenance of some infrastructure (such as a prison or hospital) to a contracted organization, with the government agency continuing to exercise a key role in program oversight. Three types of contracts are used in outsourcing:

1. *Fixed-price contracts*: The amount a contractor will receive for performing the service is set in advance and cannot be changed unless the contract is amended.
2. *Cost-reimbursement contracts*: Formerly known as cost-plus contracts, this type of contract reimburses the contractor for all costs associated with performing the service (typically with a percentage added to the costs for profit).
3. *Performance-based contracts*: These contracts provide for payment to the contractor as certain preestablished results are met. Performance can also be defined as certain outcomes achieved by clients. In addition, bonus payments are sometimes paid when performance or results exceed minimally accepted levels.

Outsourcing of human services has become common at all levels of government.

As states and municipalities encounter budget crises and taxing limitations, they are finding that the new FAIR block grants go farther with delivery under outsourced contracts. Faith-based organizations (FBOs), charitable agencies, and private-sector companies are increasingly being used to provide human services under contract with some level of government. Engaging FBOs in the delivery of human services has been one of the major initiatives that make up the President's Management Agenda. Today, such large nonprofit organizations as Goodwill Industries, Catholic Charities, the YWCA, and Lutheran Social Services have joined such private businesses as Lockheed-Martin in moving from providing only some selected functions to controlling entire human services processes.

Outsourcing Internal Services

The outsourcing of internal function services is not progressing as rapidly in the public sector as anticipated. As of February 2007, fewer than 20 percent of public-sector organizations surveyed by the Public Management Association for Human Resources outsourced any significant portion of their human-resources function (McCrossan 2007). The sample consisted of 100 senior-level HR officials from federal, state, county, and local agencies. This is expected to turn around in the near future, as 53 percent of the respondents said they planned to outsource some HR functions in the near future. Some of the HR functions being outsourced include payroll processing, benefits administration, retirement plan management, and prospective employee recruiting and screening.

Privatization, Contracting Out, and Public–Private Partnerships

Privatization, contracting out, and public–private partnerships are processes that are changing the work done in government agencies. Privatization consists of transferring programs entirely from the public sector to a nongovernmental provider. The Government Accountability Office (GAO) defines privatization as "any process aimed at shifting functions and responsibilities, in whole or in part, from the government to the private sector." Contracting out is the hiring of a private-sector firm or nonprofit organization to provide goods or services for the government. The government controls financing the activity and has management and policy control over the type and quality of goods or services provided. Contractors not performing to expectations or contract requirements can be quickly replaced. Public–private partnerships were described by GAO in a special report on terms used in privatization activities and processes (Box 10.5):

Box 10.5   Federal Public–Private Partnerships

Under a public–private partnership, sometimes referred to as a joint venture, a contractual arrangement is formed between public- and private-sector partners that can include a variety of activities that involve the private sector in the development, financing, ownership, and operation of a public facility or service. It typically includes infrastructure projects or facilities. In such a partnership, public and private resources are pooled and responsibilities divided so that the partners' efforts complement one another.

Typically, each partner shares in income resulting from the partnership in direct proportion to the partner's investment. Such a venture, although being a contractual arrangement, differs from typical service contracting in that the private-sector partner usually makes a substantial-cost, at-risk equity investment in the project, and the public sector gains access to the new revenue or service-delivery capacity without having to pay the private-sector partner. Leasing arrangements can be used to facilitate public–private partnerships.

Source: GAO (1997, 4)

Public–private partnerships are often found in local governments, where construction and operation of important—and very expensive—infrastructure facilities might exceed or strain the jurisdiction's financial capacity to secure a bond. These infrastructure projects include electricity and gas public utility projects, water and wastewater treatment systems, toll roads and bridges, recreational facilities, and similar high-cost projects. The contracts typically include provisions for full ownership of the facility to revert to the public-sector agency at the end of some time period.

The nongovernment provider in any of these three approaches may be from either the private sector or the nonprofit sector, including faith-based organizations. The provider may also be a combination of private and nonprofit organizations working in collaborative ways to provide a service. A key characteristic of privatization is the provision of government services by nongovernment organizations. It can take several different forms:

1. Government can get out of the business entirely.
2. The service can be outsourced but still overseen by the government agency.
3. The service can take the form of a private–public partnership.

State governments are particularly engaged in contracting out the delivery of services (Choi et al. 2005). A study of more than 1,100 state agencies from all 50 states found that approximately 60 percent used contracts with other governments, 70 percent contracted with nonprofit organizations, and 80 percent contracted out with private firms. It is important to remember that the establishment of contracts between governments is not a new issue. State and local governments have wrestled with the problems of cooperative delivery of government services through contracts with other government units for at least 70 years, when the state of California found that the rapid growth it was experiencing demanded intergovernmental cooperation (Stewart and Ketcham 1941).

Becker and Patterson's analysis (2005) of the effect of financial returns, financial risks, and the roles of the various partners in a case study of conservancy management stressed the importance of the following two aspects of the partnership:

1. There should be a strong, positive association between risks and rewards for the private-sector partner; higher risk should be accompanied by the potential for higher rewards for the private partner (and the opposite).
2. A strong positive association must exist between risk and the level of involvement by the private partner in the development, operation, and ownership of the contracted program. A greater degree of involvement in managing the program may be warranted in exchange for assuming higher risk by the private partner (and vice versa).

Accordingly, the more that public–private agreements vary from these two factors, the more important it is for decision makers to show that the variance is justified by some overriding social purpose.

Public–private partnerships are increasingly popular outside of the United States, where they display the same mixed rate of performance success. Hodge and Greve's (2007) international review of partnerships found that, although some of the "glowing policy promises" that preceded their implementation have been achieved, other results suggest contradictory indications of their effectiveness. The authors concluded that greater performance monitoring by contracting agencies is warranted.

Summary

The transformation of work is made possible through strategies based on the integration of human resources and information and communications technology, working together in new and creative ways to improve the efficiency and effectiveness of organizations while also delivering higher value to the stakeholders of an organization (Robertson 1999). There are three primary ways in which the transformation of work and work systems occurs. One way is by improving how work is performed. This is the least likely to result in a major cultural shakeup and is, as a result, less likely to result in transformational change occurring in the organization. Business process improvement and reengineering are methods of implementing these changes.

A second way of changing work process is to perform the same work in a different way. Advances in information and communications technology are making this the intervention of choice in governments around the globe. Enterprise architecture initiatives, knowledge management, the Internet, and enterprise resource planning are some of the tools now being used to implement these changes. Requiring workers to learn to perform work in different ways has significant impact on the organization's work culture. It can, therefore, be highly problematic in implementation. When successful, it results in transformational change in an organization.

A third means of generating transformational change in organizations is to introduce revolutionary change in an organization by completely changing the work done by the workforce of a department, an agency, or a group. This type of change is often the most difficult to achieve; it is without doubt the most transformational. Examples of technology-enabled holistic change include turning over an agency's work to other public or private organizations. This can be done through privatization, outsourcing, or collaborative agreements.

Chapter 11

How Delivery Changes Are Reshaping Government

> E-government is about transforming the way government interacts with the governed. Critical to the success of e-government transformation is the understanding that e-government is not just about the automation of existing process and inefficiencies. Rather, it is about the creation of new processes and new relationships between the governed and governor.
>
> **Bruno Lanvin (2003)**

E-government and e-learning are two of the key strategic initiatives of the global movement to transform government. This phenomenon is revolutionizing the way that governments deliver services and collect revenues, although not to the degree that was predicted at the start of the twenty-first century (Coursey and Norris 2008). Some see this digital revolution as representing one of the most far-reaching delivery paradigm shifts ever to occur in the ways that governments function; it is making government accessible to everyone, at all times, and perhaps most importantly, accessible from whatever location is most convenient to citizens. Others are less sanguine, pointing to recent studies that found e-government—particularly at the local level—to be mainly transactional, with virtually none of the high-level functions upon which it was predicated.

Nevertheless, e-government has produced many benefits both for governments and citizens (Chen and Thurmaier 2008; Robbins, Simonsen, and Feldman 2008; Tolbert, Mossberger, and McNeal 2008). Government agencies are finding that, as more people become connected and more programs are brought online, they are able to do more even with declining resources. At the same time, businesses and other organizations are increasingly finding that e-government helps resolve many problems that once soured their relationships with the bureaucracy. In a nutshell, e-government is bringing about changes in ways never anticipated; it is helping government become more representative and responsive to the needs of the people and, in the process, it is also becoming more streamlined and resourceful.

What Is E-Government?

E-government has been defined as consisting of actions to produce and deliver government services to citizens, not in the traditional face-to-face manner, but instead through the use of communications technology. A more inclusive definition would include the application of any information or communications technology used to "simplify and improve transactions between governments and other actors, such as constituents, businesses, and other governmental agencies" (Moon 2000). Thus, e-government involves the use of information and communications technologies (ICT) to ensure that citizens and businesses receive better-quality services, mainly through such electronic delivery channels as the Internet, digital TV, mobile phones, and related technology.

The term *e-government* thus covers a variety of government programs associated with the application of technology and information to accomplish the greatest possible gains in productivity, service, and results. Overall, the underlying objectives of e-government are to achieve greater operational savings, produce better program results, and enable better delivery of services. The federal government (GAO 2003a, 1) officially describes this digital strategy as:

> The term *electronic government* (or e-government) refers to the use of information technology (IT), particularly Web-based Internet applications, to enhance the access to and delivery of government information and service to citizens, to business partners, to employers, and among agencies at all levels of government.

Government Accountability Office (GAO) program examiners believe that the current e-government program, which did not take off in earnest until passage of the E-Gov Act of 2002, is off to a good start. By 2006, improvements in the delivery of government services facilitated by the act were being experienced by citizens and throughout the government. In the tax-filing season, for example, 5.1 million citizens filed tax returns online using the no-cost IRS Free File. This and other customer-service reforms that have occurred at the Internal Revenue Service (IRS) under the leadership of Charles Rossotti, who headed the agency from 1997 to 2002, helped the IRS achieve customer-service ratings higher than those earned by McDonald's restaurants (Rainey and Thompson 2006).

In other government programs, more than 17,000 grants applications were received electronically; disaster management interoperability services were accessed electronically in 111 disasters and 624 training exercises; and federal job seekers had filed more than 1,900,000 resumés online. Annual reports of federal department, agencies, and bureaus for FY 2006 can be accessed through the URLs in Appendix B.

Developing a coordinated federal, state, and local policy on the use of e-government and information and communications technology was a key strategy of the George W. Bush administration. Working with state, local, and tribal governments, the general public, and the private and nonprofit sectors, the federal e-government office was charged with finding innovative ways to

1. Improve the performance of governments in collaborating on the use of information technology to improve the delivery of government information and services
2. Set standards for federal agency Web sites
3. Create a public directory of government Web sites

It is important to remember that e-government is not simply a technology-driven change in government. Temple University professors Blackstone, Bognanno, and Hakim (2006b, 5) make this point emphatically in the introduction to their book of essays on e-government by city and state government officials:

> E-government is a move from an inefficient and mainly unaccountable bureaucracy to a new entrepreneurial and accountable culture. It enables workers at lower levels of the hierarchy to take part in and be accountable for decision-making. E-government is being used to improve the management of cities and the more efficient use of resources. In the long run, opportunities exist for e-government to bring about a reorganization [i.e., a transformation] of government, one that would reduce excessively bureaucratic processes and organizational structures. It is these changes that may ultimately bring the biggest cost savings to taxpayers.

Evolution of E-Government

Talk of implementing e-government strategies in the United States began in earnest during the last years of the Clinton administration. In a 1999 report, the President's Information Technology Advisor Committee addressed the issue of how greater application of ICT could make significant improvements in the way the federal government functioned. One of the key sections in that report highlighted strengthening relationships between government and businesses. Although the study focused

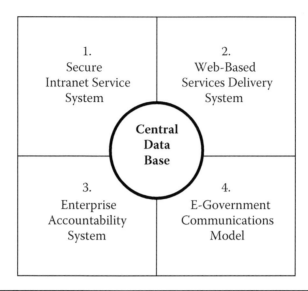

Figure 11.1   Key components of early e-government systems.

on the value of e-government for business, the report also mentioned in passing that e-government could improve relationships with private citizens as well. Originally, e-government included just four fundamental components. Figure 11.1 illustrates how these four components of e-government systems interact with a planned central database (Moon 2002):

1. A secure government intranet and central database was established to enhance communication and collaboration between agencies.
2. A system for the Web-based delivery of government services was developed.
3. Taking a page from the private sector, an e-commerce model customized to fit governments' needs was developed to provide greater efficiency in transactions such as government contracts and procurement.
4. Provisions for gaining greater and more open accountability were included. These components were supported by such technologies as electronic data interchange, electronic filing systems, interactive voice response, voice mail, e-mail, Web service delivery, virtual reality, and many others.

The adoption of e-government at the federal level became more of a reality in February of 2002, when President George W. Bush included a President's Management Agenda (PMA) in his annual budget submission to Congress. PMA was offered as a way of getting government to be more focused on citizens and results. Two key components of the PMA (OMB 2005a) were

1. A focus on Internet-based technology in an effort to make it easier for citizens and businesses to interact with government agencies and departments
2. A Federal Enterprise Architecture initiative that aimed to transform government to be more like business

The E-Government Act of 2002 established the Office of E-Government and authorized appointment of an e-administrator within the Office of Management and Budget (OMB). A key goal of the program was to develop a coordinated federal, state, and local policy on the use of information technology. Working with state, local, and tribal governments, the general public, and the private and nonprofit sectors, the Office of E-Government is charged with finding innovative ways to

1. Improve the performance of governments in collaborating on the use of information technology to improve the delivery of government information and services
2. Set standards for federal agency Web sites
3. Create a public directory of government Web sites

E-government consists of actions to produce and deliver government services to citizens, not in the traditional face-to-face manner, but instead through the use of communications technology. A more inclusive definition would include the application of any information and communications technology (ICT) used to "simplify and improve transactions between governments and other actors, such as constituents, businesses, and other governmental agencies" (Moon 2002). Thus, e-government involves the use of ICT to ensure that citizens and businesses receive better quality services, mainly through such electronic delivery channels as the Internet, digital TV, mobile phones, and related technology.

In the form established in the PMA, the 2002 e-government initiative was designed to improve the management and performance of the federal government by focusing on operational areas where deficiencies are most apparent and where the government could begin to deliver concrete, measurable results. The PMA included the five federal governmentwide initiatives and ten program-specific initiatives that apply to a subset of federal agencies. For each initiative, the PMA established clear, governmentwide goals (termed *standards for success*) and developed action plans to achieve the goals. The standards in place for the federal government are just as relevant for state and local governments. The five governmentwide standards for success for e-government are:

■ *Budget and Performance Integration* (BPI): BPI includes efforts to ensure that agency and/or program performance is routinely considered in funding and management decisions, and that the programs are monitored to make sure they achieve expected results and work toward continual improvement.

- *Competitive Sourcing* (CS)*:* This initiative calls for agencies to regularly examine activities performed by the government to determine whether it is more efficient to obtain such services from federal employees or from the private sector (often referred to as *outsourcing*).
- *Improved Financial Performance* (IFP): IFP is concerned with accurately accounting for the taxpayers' money and giving managers timely and accurate program cost information to improve management decisions and control costs.
- *Strategic Management of Human Capital* (SMHC): SMHC consists of processes to ensure that the right person is in the right job, at the right time, and is not only performing, but performing well. It is closely associated with Human Resources Planning (HRP).
- *Expanded Electronic Government* (EEG): This refers to actions designed to ensure that the federal government's $65 billion annual investment in information technology (IT) significantly improves the government's ability to serve citizens, and that IT systems are secure, delivered on time, and on budget.

Monitoring E-Government Progress

To monitor and maintain agency progress, OMB publishes a governmentwide quarterly scorecard, in which it reports individual department and agency progress on the five initiatives. An example of how the scorecard is used to push for compliance with the five-point agenda is a published e-mail warning from OMB that the scorecard of the U.S. Agriculture Department (USAD) would be downgraded from a yellow to a red—the lowest rating—on the competitive-sourcing section of the quarterly management scorecard unless the U.S. Forest Service, a USAD agency, allowed outside suppliers to bid on at least 100 information and communications technology jobs by the end of the 2005 fiscal year.

To improve the development and use of common technology solutions for e-government and other programs across the federal government, the OMB has developed e-government implementation plans with each agency to promote and monitor their adoption and utilization of governmentwide solutions in order to avoid unnecessary redundant systems.

A Single-Entry Point for E-Government

One of the most visible accomplishments for the benefit of the public was the development of a single-site entry point for accessing federal agencies; this is the PMA's firstgov.gov Web site (now named www.usa.gov). This Web site has made it possible for citizens to change their addresses, file taxes online, and access information from nearly all agency branches of the federal government. The Web site received more than 6 million visitors per month in 2006. A typical example of the benefit of e-government was the author's filing for and receiving Fulbright Senior Specialist status in 2006, all from his office computer.

OMB has been pushing for a number of years for one federal enterprise architecture framework for use by all agencies. The problem, however, has been that different agencies have used at least four major frameworks as they bring their technology architectures to maturity. Although the actual differences between those frameworks are not great, digital translators will be necessary to harmonize terminology for the different frameworks, thus defeating one of the chief purposes of the exercise. Because of this glitch, not all agencies will be able to achieve the e-government goals originally conceptualized by the strategy.

Unlike their counterparts in business and industry, federal, state, and local government agencies have been required by laws and organizational (often presidential) initiatives into absorbing electronic information and communication systems into every possible aspect of their operations as a way of becoming more efficient and effective. Interestingly, this mandate to improve the way government operates is a global pattern, not exclusively a North American phenomenon.

Even while governments are being told to become more efficient and technologically savvy, there is also a global movement underway to shrink government, to make it more responsive to citizens' needs, and to improve its accountability. In brief, the mandate is to reform government along the lines of business. This reform includes the privatization of programs and activities wherever possible. Globally, these initiatives are collectively referred to as *electronic government*, or simply *e-government*.

E-Government at the State and Local Levels

Implementation of e-government strategies has expanded across all levels of government since the early, tentative steps in the late-1990s to transform government through the application of information and communications technologies. Typical of the progress achieved by the states is that of the state of Washington, one of the early leaders in the digital strategy process. Washington was awarded the Sustained Leadership Award for its e-government progress by the Center for Digital Government and the Progress & Freedom Foundation in 2003 (Dinin 2003). Washington was selected for the award after a five-year study of the progress made by the states toward implementation of e-government. That study reached the following conclusions:

- All 50 states had implemented e-government to some extent.
- States with the largest populations were behind the medium/small states in their progress, particularly in the level of digital services provided to aid businesses.
- Three-fourths of the states had fully implemented digital archiving, with the remaining 25 percent using digital archiving to some degree.

■ Almost all states used online storage for tax records, with only four states still using paper-based storage.

Adoption of e-government by governments below the national level has moved at a rapid pace since 2003, when the federal government permitted all state and local governments and Native American Indian Tribes to use the dot-gov domain in their Internet addresses. Prior to April 2002, the dot-gov domain was reserved for the federal government. However, that year the General Services Administration extended the use of this naming convention to Native American tribes.

A year later, the right was extended to all state and local governments in the United States. Today, most U.S. territories, states, and the more than 3,000 counties and 19,000 municipal governments that have active Web sites up and running use the dot-gov domain. As of 2007, only Minnesota, Pennsylvania, and South Dakota continued to use the dot-us domain in their portal URLs.

All of the states have gone beyond their initial Web site development and now have established more elaborate Web portals. Web portals bring together both information and processes across government agencies and branches. Two examples of state government-to-business portals are displayed in Box 11.1.

Box 11.1   Winning State Government-to-Business (G2B) Portals

In 2006, NASCIO awarded its outstanding achievement award to the state of Michigan for its business-services portal; in the same year, the state of South Carolina received an honorable mention award for its business–one-stop portal.

Michigan
The designers of the Michigan portal had two objectives in mind when developing their portal:

1. Significantly reduce the time needed to begin operating a new business in the state
2. Simplify subsequent transactions with state government

The system has reduced the time it takes to begin operating a business by as much as six to ten weeks and now processes quarterly and annual state business and unemployment taxes online. At 2006 usage rates, the state estimated it saved 11,520 staff hours in processing business registrations. To increase usage of the online filing system, the state initiated a marketing campaign that included Web-site links with a number of private and public Web sites, press releases with user testimonials, and outreach activities. Michigan developed its system internally, using open systems and technology.

South Carolina

South Carolina introduced its Business One-Stop portal in 2005 as the first step in its strategy to improve the business-registering and electronic-filings processes. The mission statement established for the portal is "to develop a gateway for business and professional registration incorporating services offered by state and local governments within South Carolina."

Four objectives were established for the strategy:

1. Present a unified electronic interface
2. Shorten the time and reduce the cost for obtaining business licenses, permits, and registrations
3. Answer inquiries more quickly with fewer resources
4. Process licenses, permits, and registrations faster and with fewer resources

The South Carolina system originally involved the collaboration of seven state agencies, the Municipal Association of South Carolina, and the Association of South Carolina Counties. A variety of other public and private agencies and organizations later joined in the development of the portal. These included chambers of commerce, small business development centers, and several additional state agencies.

Source: **NASCIO (2006b)**

According to NASCIO (2007a), the states have made significant progress since 2000 in organizing the portals along paths that are considered to be "intuitive to users." Their expanded digital portals typically include some or all of the following features:

- "Utility" applications, such as employee and department directories
- Content and document management, including archiving
- Search-engine and navigation functions or site users
- Personalization options
- Collaboration tools

Box 11.2   Cleveland Named to Digital Government-to-Communities List

In August 2005, a dozen or more international technology companies joined with the Intel Corporation to assist communities in installing wireless infrastructures to improve delivery of basic services. Called the Digital Communities Initiative, the program identified 13 cities around the globe for pilot installations. The first four cities included were Corpus Christi, Texas; Cleveland, Ohio; Philadelphia, Pennsylvania; and Taipei, Taiwan. Follow-on cities included Portland, Oregon; Mangaratiba and Rio de Janeiro, Brazil; Düsseldorf, Germany; Gyor, Hungary; Jerusalem, Israel; Seoul, South Korea; Osaka, Japan; Westminster, London; and the principality of Monaco (Wilson 2005).

Like many communities around the globe, Cleveland was ill-equipped to implement the needed transformation in systems, procedures, and technology that was necessary for successful implementation of e-government programs. Cleveland mayor Jane Campbell was quoted in the industry journal, *Telephony Online,* as saying, "Before, days and weeks would pass before the information was fed into the ... system. We have had a rough economic time, so we had to make do with 700 fewer employees. We had to be more efficient."

Prior to implementing the change, the city used more than 15 different systems and manual processes to oversee such activities as issuing permits, renewing licenses, managing inspections, and reviewing development plans; more than 135,000 permits were issued by the city each year, but none of the departments doing the issuing could interact with one another (Accela 2006). The city implemented an application, computing, and networking system to remedy its stovepiped system

Sources: Intel (2005), Wilson (2005), Accela (2006)

In addition to these digital strategy features, many of the states have made significant progress in making their Web portals easier to use (Box 11.2). Most states now include a link to online services on their portal home page, in which they list the online services available to citizen and business users. This makes it easy for users to find a service even if they are unaware of the government agency providing the service. Other states have added language-translation services for high-demand services. In addition, some states also include multiple access points, including toll-free numbers, e-mail assistance, online voting instructions, traffic and weather alerts, and even online chat functions (NASCIO 2007b).

The Global E-Government Movement

Many governments worldwide are developing and implementing e-government strategies and programs (Borras 2003). International examples of e-government reforms include such programs as Public Service 2002 in Canada, Next Steps as well as Modernizing Government in the United Kingdom, Renewal of Public Service in France, Financial Improvement Program in Australia, Administrative Management Project in Austria, Modernization Program for the Public Sector in Denmark, and the Major Options Plan in Portugal (Haque 2001). The European Union is providing encouragement and incentives for such programs to all EU member states through its eEurope initiative (Aichholzer 2003).

An interesting multidimensional model of citizen participation in the New Public Management environment was proposed by Vigoda and Golembiewski (2001), in which they identified four types of citizen behavior: micro-citizenship, midi-citizenship, macro-citizenship, and meta-citizenship. They concluded that the idea of citizenship is a missing component of the New Public Management paradigm, and offered their model as a way of planning and implementing programs for improving citizen participation.

The results of an international study of e-government jointly sponsored by the United Nations and the American Society for Public Administration contained the following description (Moon 2000, 425) of e-government:

> E-government includes the use of all information and communication technologies, from fax machines to wireless palm pilots, to facilitate the daily administration of government ... [and] improves citizen access to government information, services and expertise to ensure citizen participation in, and satisfaction with the government process.... It is a permanent commitment [by] government to improving the relationship between the private citizen and the public sector through enhanced, cost-effective and efficient delivery of services, information and knowledge. It is the practical realization of the best that government has to offer.

The drive to implement e-government has clearly become a global phenomenon. However, not all attempts to bring the public to taking advantage of the many opportunities e-government affords them have been as successful as desired. The United Kingdom, for example, has been having "surprising difficulties" in getting the public to use the e-government Web sites established for citizen transactions. Nearly all of the 400 local governments in the U.K. had established e-government services by the end of 2005. However, a "digital divide" still exists between the U.K. citizens who have access to computers and those who do not.

The U.K. government reports that e-government use is low even among those who do have access. One of the mistakes contributing to this low usage rate is the failure of the U.K. e-government designers to take full advantage of the potential in their first contact Web site, Directgov; this site was the U.K. equivalent of the U.S. first access site, firstgov.gov. Rather than containing links to local government Web sites, the content of Directgov was mainly limited to policy statements.

Although there are differences among strategies adopted by different governments, Bresciani, Donzelli, and Forte (2003) have identified a "common roadmap" that government agencies are following on their path toward e-government implementation. Four common checkpoints on that roadmap include: (1) establishment of a governmentwide communications infrastructure to enable cooperation among the different public-sector components, both at the central and local levels; (2) creation of the appropriate ICT infrastructure; (3) establishment of relevant channels for service delivery. Fundamental for the first three steps and recognized as the key for efficiently managing e-government evolution is (4) transformation of the public agency into a learning organization, in which high knowledge sharing, information reuse, and strategic application of the acquired knowledge and lessons learned regularly occur.

The e-government movement in the United States can be seen as a logical extension of the reinventing government movement that began in the late 1980s, and which achieved widespread distribution with the publishing in 1992 of David Osborne and Ted Gaebler's *Reinventing Government*. E-government moved from concept to reality during the administration of President Bill Clinton, who professed the belief that e-government offered a means of overcoming the time and space barriers that in the past had limited delivery of government services. The very nature of the public sector has resulted in mixed signals regarding the benefits of knowledge management, as one study (Bresciani et al. 2003, 51) has indicated:

> Public [sector organizations] … are characterized by the presence of very diverse kinds of actors (e.g., citizens and businesses, employees and administrators, politicians and decision-makers—both at the central and local level), each of them with its own objectives and goals. Thus, in general, eGovernment applications have to operate in a social environment characterized by a rich tissue of actors with strong interdependent intents. Due to this complex network of interrelated objectives, synergies and conflicts may be present.

Government E-Learning Strategies

Closely related to the federal e-government mandate is the federal government's e-learning initiative. E-learning may be defined from both an educational and a technological point of view. From the instructional view, e-learning is seen as the use of print or electronic media to deliver instructional content when learners and teachers are separated in time or place. From the point of view of technology, e-learning has been defined as the means of getting people together (including through video conferencing) in the same electronic space, thereby facilitating mutual learning (Kerka 1997).

Under its original title of GoLearn.gov, this program was instituted under the original Office of Personnel Management's e-Training Initiative, which was one of the first 24 e-government initiatives included in the PMA. The GoLearn.gov site was launched in July 2002 to make available a wide variety of free, high-interest, and agency-mandated courses. By the end of FY 2004, the site had recorded 314,952 completed courses out of the 441,537 registrations since its beginning (OMB 2005b). The GoLearn.gov site was renamed as USALearning.gov to become "the official learning and development site for the U.S. federal government" (USALearning 2005). USALearning has become the portal for access to all federal government e-training and e-learning products and services.

E-learning has a role to play in many of the PMA-influenced initiatives, including strategic personnel management, knowledge management, information architecture, and e-government. It is also coming to be seen as an important tool for implementing and maintaining the momentum of government transformation.

According to Al Corbet, a U.S. Department of Energy spokesman, the original goals for the e-learning initiative were (Corbet 2002):

- To support and move forward the PMA by unifying and simplifying e-training programs across all government agencies
- To improve the efficiency and effectiveness of government operations by providing training as and where it is needed
- To support federal agency human-capital initiatives by leveraging existing e-training resources
- To serve as a focal point for e-training access across agencies
- To aid in the transformation of government by providing learning opportunities to all employees
- To push lifelong learning as a strategic goal, improving agencies' ability to react to changes and challenges and to become more cost effective in the performance of their services

By 2006, these goals had been amended to go beyond just offering e-training courses, as seen in the following OPM (2006, 2) statement on e-training:

> The goals of the e-training initiative extend far beyond offering e-training courses. The Gov Online Learning Center is evolving into an online learning center of excellence focused on easily accessible, high quality

learning and performance support. In addition to the myriad e-training course and e-mentoring offered through GoLearn [now USALearning], employees can obtain targeted learning objects on demand and make use of performance support tools for research and career management; supervisors and managers can use performance support tools to provide skill gap analysis and integrate into plans for the strategic development of human capital.

Expanded Access to Information

Developments in the capacity, functionality, and declining cost of information and communications technology (ICT) have greatly increased access to and the availability of information for everyone (Dirr 1999). Moreover, ICT has shown itself to be an effective medium for delivering instructional content. ICT and the Internet have resulted in e-learning that is "constructivist, interactive, collaborative, learner centered, and just in time" (Wonacott 2002).

Both the rate and extent of change occurring in the economic, social, and technological foundations of higher-education delivery systems are increasing dramatically. In addition, the knowledge base in many disciplines is expanding so rapidly that it is almost impossible for most people to stay current in a field. At the same time, existing knowledge becomes obsolete often before it can be fully absorbed. Imparting information and sharing knowledge among government workers at all levels involves imparting practical experience with current e-government applications, including the ability to diagnose, prescribe, and monitor the design and application of solutions to management problems. The E-Training Initiative was included in the 2002 President's Management Agenda to meet these challenges; it is one of five e-government initiatives managed by the Office of Personnel Management.

E-learning is often considered to be synonymous with distance learning (or distance education), with the terms used interchangeably. However, this is not entirely correct. Distance education does not necessarily involve computers, the Internet, or any electronic media at all; e-learning, on the other hand, does involve computers. E-learning has been defined as a "process of delivering instructional material to remote sites via the Internet, intranet/extranet, audio, video, satellite broadcast, interactive TV, and CD-ROM" (Holsapple and Lee-Post 2006). For most of its history, distance education meant correspondence courses, with student–teacher interaction taking place via the mails.

The Internet in E-Learning Strategies

The Internet has brought about significant changes in the way business, government, and education transfer knowledge. Today, government organizations increasingly use such strategies as e-procurement, e-government, and e-learning to deliver content to their respective constituencies. Personal computers, the

Internet, the World Wide Web, and other technologies have entirely reshaped the way that products and services are developed, produced, and delivered (Sternstein 2006). The Internet is also the chief component in many e-learning systems, resulting in what is often referred to as Internet-based, Internet-enhanced, or Internet-enabled learning. Internet-based instruction can take many forms.

Instructional delivery systems range across a continuum, with traditional classroom-based systems at one pole and completely external delivery systems at the other. The exclusively distance-learning model is positioned at the opposite pole of the content-delivery continuum. The combined models are sometimes collectively referred to simply as *e-learning*. They have been defined as "education created and delivered by using technologies related to [the] computer, the Internet and telephony, in combination or in isolation" (Chadha and Kumail 2002). Clearly, if judiciously applied, distance or online learning is not a substitute for the classroom, but an extension of the classroom.

The central positions on the continuum employ many of the best components and pedagogies of both of the two opposite approaches. The use of the World Wide Web and the Internet is a cornerstone of these combined approaches. These combinations benefit from the chief strength of the Internet by overcoming the barriers of time and space in teaching and learning. Moreover, they also maintain the important benefits that accrue from on-site learning by enabling face-to-face student–teacher interaction.

Whether it occurs in the classroom or at a distance, Internet-based learning typically takes one or more of the following forms (Kerka 1997):

1. Electronic mail, including delivery of course materials, assignments, giving and receiving feedback, participation in discussion groups, and other interactive activities
2. Electronic bulletin boards serving newsgroups and special-topic discussions
3. Student accessing and downloading of course materials, handouts, or tutorials
4. Interactive tutorials on the Web
5. Real-time, one-on-one or group interactive conferencing
6. Intranet Web sites with limited access
7. Sharing of online databases, catalogs, and other library information
8. Sharing or contributing to research related to specific study issues or questions

Summary

E-government and e-learning strategies together contribute a large proportion of the federal government's drive to transform the way government works, the way it communicates with the electorate, and the way it delivers services of all types to the public and other stakeholders. E-government constitutes a complete revolution in the way government agencies interact with the public and their other constituencies. Governments have had to implement major changes in the dynamics of their organizational culture: They have had to become customer oriented.

In part as a response to the President's Management Initiative calling for strategic management of human resources, government agencies have adopted many of the latest training and development processes collectively referred to as *e-learning*. The Internet and other technological advances have thoroughly transformed traditional distance education to make it available to present and prospective government workers where they want to receive it, at the time of their choosing, and with the most current content possible. E-learning has helped to solve one of government's biggest worries in the early years of the new century: how to capture, retain, and share knowledge that will be lost with the high numbers of retirements expected during the next ten or so years.

Chapter 12

Expanding the Delivery Structure of Government

> The traditional model of government agencies administering hundreds of programs by themselves is giving way to one-stop services and cross-agency results. This transition implies collaboration—within agencies; between agencies; between levels of government; and between the public, private and nonprofit sectors.
>
> **John M. Kamensky, Thomas J. Burlin, and**
> **Mark A. Abramson (2004)**

Identifying and implementing a variety of governance strategies to cope with changes in their operating environment has once again become an issue for public managers (Goodsell 2006). Restructuring, unbundling, deregulation, privatization, wholesale and retail competition, and outsourcing are all having an impact on the already complex governance system. What is emerging is a hybrid system of governance that incorporates the best of administration and management practices from both the public and private sectors. This chapter reviews events that are shaping the trend toward collaboration among various jurisdictions in the development of infrastructure and the delivery of public services. It examines four different manifestations of the collaboration trend and presents two case examples.

Changes in Public Responsibilities

A series of revolutionary changes in the governance environment has resulted in a number of dramatic changes in the regulatory responsibilities of public administration. The deregulation of once-highly regulated industries that began in earnest in the 1970s has brought revolutionary changes to aviation, trucking, communications, energy production and distribution, public utilities, and other public and quasi-public enterprises. In addition, a wave of executive malfeasance (Weisberg 1996), criminal behavior by managers and administrators, and the costly failures of such organizations as Enron and WorldCom, to name just two, have brought about a crisis in the public's trust in such institutions as government, industry, voluntary organizations, and organized religion.

A wide variety of scandals have swept across corporate America since the late 1990s, including improprieties in accounting, market manipulation, misappropriation of shareholder funds, outright theft, and executive corruption (Genieser 2004). Together with the as-yet unmet promised benefits of deregulation, these excesses and breakdowns in morality among leaders and managers, particularly in the energy and telecommunications industries, have had a deleterious effect upon citizens' confidence in government and quasi-governmental organizations. In many cases, this has limited government's ability to meet its public-service obligations. Public managers and administrators have been forced to adopt a new approach and develop new and different strategies. One of these new strategies entails replacing bureaucratic dictatorial mandates with strategic management and collaborative problem solving.

New Governance Strategies

Governance is not, and never has been, a static principle. Demands for change and for greater or less control over public utility governance, for example, have been aired over three major waves of activism. These demands first appeared during the Progressive Era and reached their peak during the early 1900s with the trust-busting activity of President Teddy Roosevelt's administration. At that time, the issue was at the top of proposed reforms of the American economic system. The drive for better governance saw passage in 1887 of the act that established the Interstate Commerce Commission and, subsequently, the near-unanimous passage of the Sherman Antitrust Act of 1890 (Bruchey 1990).

The second wave coincided with the Great Depression of the 1930s. Demands for better governance resulted in passage of the Securities Exchange Act in 1934 and the Public Utilities Holding Company Act in 1935.

The third wave in governance reform began during the 1980s with restructuring of the utilities industry. It reached its apex with the California deregulation failures in 2000 and 2001 and the collapse of Enron, once the largest energy trading company in the world.

Until the first few years of the twentieth century, the trend in governance was leading away from government ownership and control toward deregulation and privatization of government-owned enterprises. Since then, plans for further restructuring—and its controversial offspring, deregulation—have been put on hold, where they may remain for the foreseeable future. The credit crisis that emerged in 2008 resulted in a renewed drive for greater regulation of the financial industry.

Governance Strategy Defined

Keohane and Nye (2002) define governance as "the processes and institutions, both formal and informal, that guide and restrain the collective activities of a group." That definition is used here to refer to the internal and external exercise of direction, control, management, and policy shaping of public agencies. Governance is also the term used to define the process of controlling the operations of organizations and their relationships with their internal and external stakeholders.

In most organizations, strategy is decided by directors and senior officers, while the responsibility for carrying out operations is delegated to managers and supervisors. These operators are generally free to run the organization without fear of excessive external interference from government.

Variations in Governance Strategy

Johnston Birchall (2002) has identified six separate governance strategies prevalent today, four of which lie between what he termed "the extremes" of private ownership on the one hand and public ownership on the other. Between these poles are four ownership variations:

1. A nonprofit trust or company
2. A public interest company
3. A consumer mutual society
4. A public authority (such as the New York Water Authority)

Nonprofit firms function in the same manner as for-profit organizations, with the same ability to turn to the bond market to raise long-term capital and to borrow from banks for short-term funding. Prices charged by nonprofits may be the same or less than or greater than organizations who seek and distribute profits to investors.

In a nonprofit organization, some surpluses are retained for future expenses, but most nonprofits try to avoid earning greater than minimally needed profits in order to keep prices low and retain their federally granted nonprofit status. Most nongovernment organizations (NGOs) are nonprofits. Because the nonprofit company can issue membership shares, its governance can become widely community based. As more shares are issued in the community, the more this model comes to resemble a mutual society.

Public-interest companies are designed to reap the social benefits of public service with the economic benefits of entrepreneurship. Like a nonprofit, the public-interest company has public-benefit goals permanently etched into this charter. However, this type of organization is also able to distribute surplus earnings to investors or entrepreneurs. The public-interest company is a model that is sometimes used to govern water and wastewater utilities.

The mutual-society form of utility governance is a form of the basic consumer cooperative (co-op). The co-op model has its roots in associations of farmers and ranchers in the western United States for building irrigation projects. Many farm cooperatives still provide an important function in the supply and distribution of agricultural products and for the marketing of farm products.

Mutual societies are similar to consumer cooperatives. Mutual societies are registered as businesses, but only for specific purposes, and they are owned by their customers. Each customer has an equal voting right, thus making it difficult for any single individual or group to gain control of the operation. Directors are elected by the membership. Earnings surpluses are distributed to members as annual dividends or percentage discounts on future purchases. Dividend amounts received by utility customers are based upon the amount of business done with the society, not on ownership. This governance model is very popular in the United States, where there are nearly 1,000 electricity co-ops and more than 700 telecommunications co-ops, the majority of which operate in rural areas.

Public-authority agencies are quasi-governmental institutions established to provide one or more public services to customers within a specific—often a regional—taxing area. Such authorities have the same power to tax property in their service areas as do other levels of government. However, they function independently of all other government jurisdictions in their service area. Public authorities also have the power to issue government bonds and to borrow on the value of the property in their service area.

Moving toward Greater Cooperation

Seldom can any government organization function without interacting with and gaining the cooperation of other organizations. In the past, this interaction was sometimes coercive—compliance was dictated by law or by the power of the purse. In the long run, however, this governance model has been shown to be less effective than a collaborative approach.

Organizational cooperation can be established through several different means, including collusion, overlapping fields of operations, and dependence on the expertise available only in other organizations' specialization (Bozeman and Straussman 1991). In the field of public service, collusion is not often found. Rather, the cooperative interdependence model is most common.

The evolution in the way that various levels of government are approaching their operational and regulatory activities suggests that a major governance paradigm shift is underway in all levels of government (Agranoff and McGuire 2001). Government managers are finding new ways to deliver services through what is becoming a new public-service environment: outsourcing traditional activities to private-sector contractors, such as seen in many infrastructure construction projects and such services as medical, corrections, and public-safety activities.

Top-Down Governance Strategies

Traditionally, the management of public service has operated under a top-down or donor-recipient governance strategy. These strategies emphasize higher-level control over subordinates' actions and emphasize the enforcement of laws, regulations, standards, and guidelines. An example of a top-down strategy is national governance in which the federal government manages its policies and programs through implementation by state and local governments. Federal laws such as the Public Utility Holding Company Act of 1935 ensured that utility operations at the customer-delivery interface would forever be controlled by elected or appointed state public utility commissioners. Equally, local administrators are responsible to ensure that rules, regulations, and standards are followed. Federal laws established policy; agencies such as the FERC (Federal Energy Regulatory Commission), EPA (Environmental Protection Agency), and SEC (Securities and Exchange Commission) interpreted the policy and set operating policies; state legislators developed specific rules from those standards; and local utility commissions approved industry-suggested ways of implementing the rules.

Donor-Recipient Strategies

The donor-recipient management strategy addressed some of the pitfalls inherent in an authoritative top-down management approach. This strategy presupposes the existence of a mutually dependent relationship among the various intergovernmental and private enterprise actors functioning cooperatively, but still working toward accomplishing the objectives of the superior (typically federal) organization. This model is exemplified in the way lower-level agencies have organized their activities to comply with standards established by grant-disseminating higher-level agencies. It is an implied "do it our way or no way" model.

Two New Governance Models

Today, two new collaborative governance models seem to be replacing the traditional strategic approaches: a network- and a jurisdiction-based model. Both are more collaborative than are the top-down or donor-recipient models. Multiple independent government and nongovernment organizations pursuing similar goals characterize network strategies. This strategic approach is found in situations where a group of different participants, none of whom has the power to shape the strategies of others in the group, form a loose network to accomplish some specific goal. Under this scenario, the boundaries between public and private operations are often blurred.

An example of a network strategy is that of the EPA and local water utilities. All participants share a common goal of providing only clean, safe drinking water to the public. To ensure the safety of the water supply, the EPA has issued a large number of standards and regulations that require utilities to test for and remove toxic chemicals and other pollutants. A growing number of cities are negotiating directly with EPA to modify the workload and cost burden placed upon them by federal water-quality rules. EPA requires even very small water utilities to regularly test for and remove a long list of toxic chemicals, minerals, and other pollutants from their drinking water. In some locations, however, it is highly unlikely that certain pollutants on the list will appear in the local water supply. A number of the community organizations have proposed to the EPA that they be permitted to develop their own water-quality standards, with their own priorities for removal of toxic substances. EPA has approved the proposals.

This network of municipal utilities and the EPA has resulted in a collaborative strategy that is based on the assumption that "not everybody will comply and not everybody will defy" (Agranoff and McGuire 2001). Under such parameters, it is far more efficient for EPA to focus its corrective efforts on the few who do not comply, simply receiving periodic reports from others in the network.

Clearly, this governance strategy allows far greater flexibility than the top-down and donor-recipient models. The network model is based on the interdependencies of the participating organizations, agencies, or individuals. Interdependence means that all participants will benefit in some way because of their mutual interest in some program or activity. It also implies that a problem cannot be solved unless all participants freely collaborate.

The jurisdiction-based governance strategy model is found most often in highly complex situations where significant intergovernmental and interorganizational cooperation is required. This model is seen in situations where one government jurisdiction requests and incorporates contributions of other public and private participant organizations. The plan developed by the initial jurisdiction includes the contributions and adjustments proposed by other jurisdictions.

Collaborative Governance Models

Four blended versions of these governance models dominate government efforts at sharing power and responsibility today (Figure 12.1):

1. Partnering
2. Collaboration between government agencies and one or more private organizations

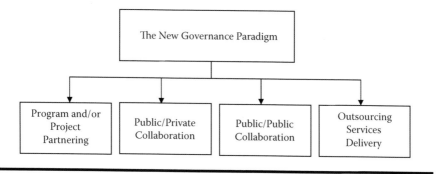

Figure 12.1 Extension of government reach into new action approaches.

3. Collaboration between government agencies at different levels (federal-state, state-local, etc.)
4. Total outsourcing of delivery of government services to private firms

Working with others to deliver government services is referred to as *third party government* (Berry and Brower 2005).

Program/Project Partnering

Partnering refers to a type of agreement between contractual parties to share management. The agreement typically includes several key clauses (Seddon 1999):

1. Mutual objectives are formally identified in the agreement.
2. Methods for resolving problems that arise during the length of the project or program are agreed to in advance.
3. All parties agree to actively search for and implement measurable improvements in the project or program.
4. Many partnerships stipulate that all parties share the risks, such as in cost overruns, and the potential rewards of bringing a project in under budget.

Two types of partnering agreements exist: longer-term (lasting as long as ten years or longer) strategic partnering, similar to joint ventures in the private sector, and shorter-term project partnering. Examples include partnerships formed by the U.S. Corps of Engineers on some public-works projects and partnerships between the U.K. government and the North Sea oil and gas industry for lowering costs because of a drop in oil prices.

Box 12.1   A State Collaboration Strategy to Save the Children

In 2000, the California Department of Health Services (CDHS) kicked off a program to replace its 20-year-old legacy system for prenatal and newborn screening. The existing system screened for 39 genetic diseases, but could not be expanded to take advantage of new developments in technology. The upgrade strategy was designed to accomplish two objectives: (a) to enhance the existing system and (b) to expand the number of rare genetic diseases screened for by the system.

California launched its new Screening Information System (SIS) in 2005. The new system screens for 75 inherited and congenital disorders instead of the earlier 39. If detected quickly, these diseases are often treatable; changes as simple as altering the diet of an infant can mean the difference between living a normal life instead of mental retardation or even early death. Without the upgraded system, CDHS estimates that annually 20 newborns would suffer severe mental retardation, 20 would suffer mild to moderate retardation, and 20 would die. SIS improves collaboration among testing laboratories, case coordinators, health counselors, doctors and staff, and follow-on specialists.

The SIS was developed to transform the way screening was conducted as well as how information was distributed to all relevant stakeholders. SIS provides solutions to problems that the legacy system was incapable of resolving. The new system is Internet based, allowing for easy access and expansion to new types of testing and new disorders as well as addressing many patient privacy and information reporting requirements. In addition to providing direct online access for medical users, the system also improves security and private protection.

In 2006, the National Association of State Chief Information Officers (NASCIO) gave the program its Cross-Boundary Collaboration and Partnerships Award for Outstanding Achievement in Information Technology.

Source: **NASCIO (2006b)**

Private/Public Collaboration Strategies

Private/public collaborations have become an increasingly common governance model (Agranoff and McGuire 2005). This approach to problem solving and service delivery often emerges after some national or regional emergency, such as terrorist attacks, natural disasters, threats of a pandemic, or crises in national programs such as defense, health, and education (NASCIO 2006a). Responding to the crisis brings participants from both sectors together to solve a problem. These arrangements can be informal collaborations or formal cooperative arrangements (see Box 12.1).

Two definitions have been offered for collaborative arrangements. The Canadian Council for Public-Private Partnerships, for example, defines them as "a cooperative venture between the public and private sectors, built on the expertise of each partner, that best meets clearly defined public needs through the appropriate allocation of resources, risks and rewards" (CCPPP 2007). The National Association of State Chief Information Officers (NASCIO 2006a, 2) has adopted a definition suggested by W. C. Lawther (2002), in which these partnerships are defined as:

> relationships among government agencies and private or nonprofit contractors that should be formed when dealing with services or products of highest complexity. In comparison to traditional contractor-customer relationships, they require radical changes in the roles played by all partners.

According to NASCIO, collaborative partnerships are extralegal working relationships that bring members of both the public and private sectors together to achieve a common purpose or solve a common problem. Often, the glue holding the partnership is enlightened self-interest mixed with goodwill, commitment to meeting a public need, and a desire to collectively leverage resources for a common purpose. Examples of such arrangements abounded during the response to the devastation resulting from Hurricane Katrina and Hurricane Rita.

Cooperatives, on the other hand, are usually more-or-less formal systems held together by contractual agreement. They are a form of collaboration that can be either public/public or public/private. Most co-operatives are small, local organizations owned by their customers/clients, with all decisions made by locally elected board members (Burr 2004). This local control is seen by some as one of the strengths of the cooperative system. However, local control often limits a co-op's ability to achieve its primary mission—that of providing its customers reliable service at the lowest possible price.

Some critics have argued that co-ops waste their customer-owners' money by not consolidating and economizing administrative costs. Those critics are calling for a new collaborative approach, one that includes elements from both the private and the public sectors. Basin Electric Power Cooperative (BEPC) in Bismarck, North

Dakota, is an example of the new public/private collaborative model emerging in the co-op governance picture (McNabb 2005).

BEPC is a cooperative of cooperatives. The co-op operates coal-fired electricity-generating plants with a total capacity of 3,373 megawatts, providing power to 124 rural local government electric cooperatives, which in turn serve 1.8 million consumers in nine states from North Dakota to New Mexico. Much like an investor-owned holding company, BEPC controls five subsidiaries: Dakota Gasification Co., which produces natural gas by a coal-gasification process to produce chemicals and fertilizers; Dakota Coal Co., which purchases coal for its power plants and owns a lime-processing plant; Basin Telecommunications, Inc., which provides customized Internet service through BTInet; Basic Cooperative Services, which owns and manages properties in North Dakota and Wyoming; and Granite Peak Energy, Inc., a for-profit subsidiary for marketing electricity in Montana under that state's 1997 customer-choice program.

Consolidation and collaboration in this way is apparently the wave of the future. BEPC is involved in two examples of changes underway in this sector: It has joined with three other utilities—two municipals and one investor-owned—to conduct a transmission study to help establish the best location for a new 600-megawatt coal-fired power plant and a 100-megawatt wind farm. BEPC has also joined a group of about 550 U.S. cooperatives in 1998 to form a nationwide alliance, Touchstone Energy, to provide retail-marketing resources for co-ops expecting to face retail competition (Burr 2004; BasinElectric.com. 2004).

Local Area Public/Public Collaboration

An example of a governance model based on different levels can be seen in the utility extension plan of a small, rural community in a western state. The utility department is the lead agency in a multijurisdictional plan to extend water and sewer service to other jurisdictions outside of the city boundaries. The city earlier entered into an interim intergovernmental agreement in partnership with the local port, the state department of corrections and its nearby correction center, the state patrol's training academy, the county, and a local power cooperative that provides power to the area to be served. Other organizations such as local Native American tribes, the EPA, and state and federal fish and wildlife agencies are also tangentially involved in the outcome of the project. The agreement covers extension of city sewer and water lines, expansion of the city's sewage treatment plant, sinking new wells, and installing new water-treatment facilities.

As lead agency in the more than $42-million proposal, the municipality is responsible for record keeping and recording. It has set up two special business funds to account for the project, with each fund having four "customers": the city, the port, the state patrol training academy, and the corrections center. The project is financed through a mix of grants and loans. Each of the four chief partners is to pay a proportionate share of the construction costs and normal usage rates. This example of a jurisdiction-based activity follows the governance model described by Agranoff and McGuire (2001, 675), who describe jurisdiction-based management as providing significant benefits for all project participants:

> Jurisdiction-based activity emphasizes local managers taking strategic action with multiple actors and agencies from various governments and sectors.... Bargaining and negotiations are important instruments of jurisdiction-based management. Bargaining by local managers within programs of vertical (state or federal government) or horizontal (metropolitan, regional, or intersectional) origin provide alternatives to unilateral concession, resulting in a "mutually beneficial solution."

Although in a classic multiorganizational agreement no one unit is deemed to be superior or subordinate to others and no central participant provides guidance or control, in the interorganizational agreement, the city has assumed the role of lead agency. Whether this was by default or by plan, the delays and cost escalation experienced clearly show the need for someone to be in charge. The agreement may thus be said to incorporate parts of both the network and jurisdictional governance models. This may be a portent of the nature of other such cooperative and collaborative utility ventures, regardless of the formal ownership or governance model of any or all of the participants.

Federal/Local Public/Public Collaboration

Collaborations between government agencies at different levels (interagency collaborations) suffer from many of the accountability problems that plague other types of collaborative agreements (Page 2004). Accountability problems tend to fall into four major administrative areas: legal, administrative (hierarchical), political, and professional. The Department of Homeland Security, along with its state and local partners, has had to work its way through many of these accountability and other related issues since its formation after September 11, 2001 (Donley and Pollard 2002; Wise and Nader 2002).

The Department of Homeland Security (DHS), formed in response to the terrorist attacks of September 11, 2001, resulted in the merger of a variety of security-related federal agencies. One of the primary reasons for the merger was to improve information sharing to avoid similar disasters. However, more than five years after 9/11, DHS had not completely implemented congressionally mandated policies and processes for sharing terrorism information. However, it had come up with a strategy for putting in place the overall framework, policies, and architecture for sharing that information with its critical partners. This incomplete action has resulted in DHS being named to the GAO (2007a) list of high-risk federal agencies.

The Intelligence Reform and Terrorist Prevention Act of 2004 required that action be taken to facilitate the sharing of terrorist information by the establishment of an information-sharing environment (ISE); as of 2007, the ISE was still in the planning stage. Completing the information-sharing plan is described as a complex task that will take many years under long-term administration and congressional support and oversight. Moreover, successful implementation will only occur with major transformations in the cultures of the various organizations. Overcoming the operational and technical challenges facing the DHS will require a collaborative effort between agencies at the federal, state, and local levels.

Outsourcing Delivery of Services

Outsourcing refers to the practices of contracting with private-sector providers to supply one or more services either to an agency or government unit, or for delivery of services to a citizen clientele. An example of a large outsourcing contract occurred in 2000 with what was then the "richest IT outsourcing deal ever signed by a state government" (Madden 2000). The state of Connecticut signed a seven-year, $1-billion contract with Electronic Data Systems (EDS) of Plano, Texas, for developing, installing, and operating computer systems and networks for all of the state's departments. At the time, San Diego County, California, was planning to issue a request for bids on a ten-year, $1-billion outsourced contract for similar IT services.

The Connecticut contract included developing 150,000 square feet of office space in Hartford for the state's IT operations; establishing three computer training centers for state employees; and guaranteeing jobs for two years for state IT workers, with similar or better salaries and benefits.

What may be the most controversial manifestation of government outsourcing its services is the contracting with private companies to provide combat services (Brayton 2002; Quirk 2004). Contracts for such items as logistics supply and personal services such as housing and feeding military forces have been around for decades. However, contracting for private corporate soldiers is a relatively new phenomenon—and it is increasingly becoming a global event. Examples include:

- A five-year contract for $831 million for the Vinnell Corp. to train and supply the Saudi Arabian National Guard (The Vinnell Corp. also received a contract for $48 million in 2003 to train nine battalions of a new Iraqi army.)
- A $293-million three-year contract with Aegis Defense Services in 2004 to provide security for the office monitoring reconstruction in Iraq

- A \$52-million contract with DynCorp for security for Afghan President Hamid Karzai; a one-year contract for DynCorp for \$50 million for creating a new Iraqi police force

Brayton (2002) critiqued contract operations in Sierra Leone, Angola, and Bosnia-Herzegovina. He suggested that the growing use of private contractors in national security has created a "clientele politics" in which civic and political loyalty has been passed to nongovernment military contractors with their own motives. This shift of power to private, nonstate military interests is seen most often in so-called failing states, where local authorities cannot, or will not, protect citizens. A good example of this phenomenon is the use of private security contractors in Iraq.

The Downside of Government Outsourcing

There are certainly downsides to cross-sector and cross-level cooperative approaches such as outsourcing (Bryson, Crosby, and Stone 2006). One is the fact that managing these many different models of collaborative government requires a skill set that differs from those skills customarily employed by public managers. The required skills include negotiation, contract writing and management, monitoring and enforcing external partners' performance, knowledge of information and communications technologies such as enterprise resource planning systems, and others (Kettl 2006).

Australian attorney Bernard Collaery (1999) discussed some possible downside results of outsourcing some tasks that had previously been performed by public workers. His chief example was the March 1998 near disaster at the Dounreay Nuclear Plant in Scotland. After the incident, a team of investigators reported that the near-complete failure of electrical equipment at the plant occurred because outsourcing of some key tasks had weakened the management and technical skill base at the plant, resulting in a loss of special skills once held by specialists at the plant. Moreover, the existing rule-based organizational culture also contributed to the failure.

The government agency responsible for plant oversight felt that it was forced to accept the lowest bids for contracts, despite some questions regarding reliability. That mindset was traced to the operating agency's overwhelming concern with cost control; government fines levied for occupational health and safety issues were lower than civil damages awarded for not complying with government-competitive bidding rules.

In this instance, outsourcing led to accepting the lowest bid instead of the optimal bid, resulting in a loss of critical and hard-won operational knowledge about reliability testing, and nearly causing a major accident at a nuclear plant. Collaery (1999, 99) identified the following additional set of problematic outcomes associated with outsourcing:

- Because governments are able to use executive power to issue contracts for services, contracts thus become a form of *de facto* legislation, bypassing the process of checks and balances that apply to laws enacted by Congress.
- Contracts commit future governments as well as the current one to a policy.
- Contracts provide less flexibility than government-provided services; to redress failures to perform under contract often requires extensive and costly contract negotiations.
- Contracts can increase the risk of litigation.
- Contracts can increase the risk of loss of control over public expenditures.
- Public managers may become contract administrators, without training in the necessary skills.

Summary

Six governance strategies were discussed in this chapter, together with four models of collaborative or partnering strategies. Two of the strategies fall at the extremes of private ownership and public ownership. Between these poles are four strategy variations:

1. Nonprofit trusts or companies
2. Public-interest companies
3. Consumer mutual societies
4. Public regulatory authorities

Two new governance strategies appear to be replacing the traditional top-down or donor-recipient management approaches. These are a network model and a jurisdiction-based model. Both are more collaborative than are the top-down or donor-recipient models. Multiple independent governments and nongovernment organizations pursuing similar goals characterize the network model; it is applicable in situations where a group of different participants, none of whom has the power to shape the strategies of others in the group, form a loose network to accomplish some specific goal.

The jurisdiction-based governance model is found most often in highly complex contexts, such as those situations where significant intergovernmental and interorganizational cooperation is required. This strategic approach is often seen in situations where one government jurisdiction requests and incorporates contributions of other public and private participant organizations. The chapter concluded with examples of a large, multistate traditional collaborative operation and a local, network-based collaborative energy delivery operation.

A new paradigm of governance has emerged in government. This new concept is replacing the traditional top-down bureaucratic model of governance, promoted by Max Weber, with a variety of strategies that are characterized by shared responsibility, risk, and services delivery. The four most commonly seen shared strategies include contractual partnering, collaboration between government agencies and one or more private or public organizations, collaboration between government agencies at different levels (federal-state, state-local, etc.), and outsourcing of delivery of services to government and the delivery of government services to private citizens and firms.

Chapter 13

How Knowledge Facilitates Change in Government

The management information system revolution has provided us with technology that allows the design of information practices to support individual and organizational learning. With the ready availability of computerized information programs and interactive telecommunications, tasks involved in organizational learning—monitoring individual and organizational performance, storing information in easily accessible forms, retrieving relevant information, and measuring actual performance over time—are accomplished with relative ease and in a timely manner.

Chris Argyris (1999)

This chapter is about how government organizations identify and implement knowledge management (KM) strategies to (a) facilitate organizational change, (b) improve the ways government agencies operate, and (c) enhance how they deliver public services to citizens. Knowledge is important for each of these purposes for two primary reasons. First, the processes of KM involve collecting the information needed to assess the necessity for a change and to provide the data needed to design and implement a change initiative. Second, knowledge management ensures that complete news of innovations and changes planned or taking place in government are disseminated throughout the organization. For this reason, this chapter includes a brief discussion of the role of knowledge management and the processes by which this element of strategic management is implemented.

The goal of improving organizational performance is to make it possible for agencies to become more innovative in how they carry out their missions and, at the same time, become more accountable to the publics they serve. Information about past and present best practices in government agencies is needed to achieve this and similar goals. Knowledge-management processes abet the organizational drive to harness the existing knowledge held by the people in government agencies, thereby fostering creative problem solving by government workers at all levels. Knowledge management is thus a key component in this new way that governments function.

What KM Can and Cannot Do

KM is one of the latest components in the government's 50-plus-year effort to integrate information and communications technology (ICT) into operations. The goal of that integration has been to improve performance and make government more accountable. This has become a global movement to transform the services they provide and the way governments serve their citizens. One important global strategy is the drive to implement e-government. One leading enterprise software and knowledge-systems industry spokesperson (McKinnon 2005) described the foundation for this movement in these terms:

> Governmental organizations worldwide are facing several challenges as administrative, executive and judicial bodies continue to evolve into an electronic work environment. Pushed by paperwork-reduction mandates, requirements to handle increased workloads with fewer personnel and the rapid adoption of electronic communication channels by taxpayers and citizens, governments are often on the forefront of adopting new approaches to electronic information management.

The KM Process

KM refers to the process of gaining maximum benefit from the knowledge in an organization. It involves applying the knowledge that exists in an organization to find and apply innovative answers to old and new questions. The KM process is built on three fundamental building blocks. One is information and communications technology. Another is the people who use knowledge. And the third is the processes that have been developed to enable and enhance knowledge capture, sharing, and archiving.

Technology has made it possible for KM to evolve into a key management tool necessary for agencies and institutions to function and flourish in today's knowledge economy. Peter Drucker (1994) explained that the world has entered a postindustrial economy characterized by globalization, increasingly sophisticated information and communications technology, and a knowledge society. Nonaka (1991) added that, in this new economy, the only certainty is that knowledge is the only sustainable source of competitive advantage.

The Evolution of KM and KM Systems

When examined objectively, KM and knowledge-management systems (KMS) may be considered the latest manifestation in a long progression of governments' concerns with data, information, and knowledge.

The federal government's concern with improving the performance of government agencies through better management of information can be traced as far back as 1943, when the first call for local governments to collect data by measuring their performance offered guidelines for the government to follow. However, government reformers had to wait until July 1993 for the federal government to act on that recommendation with passage by Congress of the Government Performance and Results Act (GPRA) (Aristigueta 2002).

The first wave in the transformation of how the government collects and uses information began in the late 1950s and 1960s with installation of mainframe computers to process large amounts of data. Among the heaviest users of computers for this purpose were the Census Bureau, the Department of Commerce, and the Department of Defense. During the decade of the 1970s, as computer hardware and software gained more power and new applications were developed, more agencies looked to the new promise of computers to store, process, codify, process, and synthesize the reams of data governments must collect and retain. A key development at this time was the appearance of a variety of vertical management information systems.

Early Problems

A problem with the early systems was that they tended to be largely agency or application specific and, therefore, unable to communicate with other government systems. Those overly customized systems are unable to meet today's performance requirements; access to the information they contain remains restricted to members of the unit. It is impossible for others to share others' information and, more importantly, learn from earlier mistakes.

A solution for some of these difficulties was the internal development in the late 1970s of a few broadly based executive information systems (EIS) in the private sector. It was not until the mid-1980s that these commercial executive information systems became available to government agencies (Watson and Carte 2000). Although the early EISs were developed for only a few of the highest-level executives, they quickly evolved to be able to support all members of top management and, in some large firms, were able to serve hundreds or more users. The importance of those executive systems to the development of comprehensive knowledge-management systems in the late 1990s cannot be overemphasized.

The Drive for Control

By the 1990s, it was clear that some higher-level coordination and control was needed over the acquisitions and applications of information technology (IT) systems by agencies. A single organization was needed to oversee IT resources (Lee and Perry 2002). The federal government's answer was to place information resources management (IRM) under the auspices of the Office of Management and Budget (OMB). Tasks and responsibilities included oversight of planning and budgeting for all federal agency activities associated with acquiring, storing, processing, and distributing data and information.

Although OMB began its coordination and control over IT in federal agencies, others in government were envisioning an even greater role for IT in all levels of government. They dreamed of putting the lessons learned in the private sector's use of IT to introduce the same private-sector productivity gains in government. Government was to be more businesslike if it could use the same systems used in business and industry. This would bring higher performance standards, stronger performance measurement, and stricter accountability for results. Their vision became codified in the Reinventing Government initiatives issued from the Clinton White House. President Clinton included a number of e-government initiatives in his June 2000 Webcast address. A key proposal revealed in the address was a plan to put all online resources offered by the federal government on a single Web site, www.Firstgov.gov. Not long afterward, many state and local governments expanded their adoption of IT for similar purposes.

The National Performance Review (NPR) Act, which gave life to the Reinventing Government movement, may have been the most important reform of the twentieth century. It came at a time when there was higher than ever demand for changing the way governments function (Qiao and Thai 2002).

How KM Helps Reshape Government

Knowledge management has been defined in a number of different ways—a fact that many authors point to as being one of the reasons why KM has not achieved greater acceptance among organizational managements. One of the more commonly seen definitions is that provided by Nonaka and Takenchi (1995), who defined KM as the substantiated understandings and beliefs in an organization about the organization and its environment.

They also differentiated between two types of knowledge: explicit and tacit. Explicit knowledge is codified facts and information that are easily translated and shared; it exists in reports and other documents. Tacit knowledge is personal knowledge that is hard to confirm and share with others; it is the private understanding and *knowing* that people have about issues, problems, services, and products. A major task of KM is to turn tacit knowledge into explicit knowledge.

Tiwana (2002) defined knowledge management as a changing mix of workers' experience, values, expert insight, and intuition that provides an environmental framework for evaluating and incorporating new experiences and information. It resides in the minds of workers, but is often expressed in the culture of the organization, including its routines, processes, systems, and norms. (This definition is similar to many of the definitions for human capital.)

It is important to remember that KM has both a social and a technological side, and that it is a management discipline that is still evolving. Thus, the arguments of both its critics and its champions are worthy of consideration. To the many government managers now involved with KM programs and processes, it is far from the "just another management fad" described by some authors and public managers (Fuller 2002; Wilson 2002). However, because knowledge-management practices focus on the human side of *using* information, KM was soon considered a critical tool in the management of information and communications technology. For these administrators, KM represents a major paradigm shift in management thinking from the role of caretaker to that of innovator. The knowledge held by its human capital is now an organization's most important resource. Its loss represents the waste of billions of dollars in creative investments; therefore, it must be collected, retained, managed, and utilized wisely.

The Two Worlds of KM

Traditionally, the practice of knowledge management has united the orbits of two worlds: the world of information and communications technology, and the world of people at work. This second aspect is often referred to as the "people side" or "soft side" of the knowledge-management discipline. It is the least understood and most problematic, but it is also now considered the most important side of KM. The ability of an organization to grow its knowledge base depends upon the extent to which members exchange and combine existing information, knowledge, and ideas (Smith, Collins, and Clark 2005).

The technology side of KM has long been where the money is, however. As a result, suppliers (or *vendors*, in government parlance) of computer hardware and software dominated the literature, conferences, and spending on KM for the first decade of its development. Beginning in the first years of the new century, however, this trend began a shift to a greater emphasis on applications. This has meant that applications integrators and KM systems consultants, including a growing number of academics, are contributing significantly to the growth of the human side of the KM discipline.

Conventional wisdom suggests a caveat for anyone hoping to pin reductions in spending and improvements in government performance and accountability to any rationality imposed on the government's purchase and use of technology. This was pointed out in *Public Administration Quarterly* in 2002 (Nicolay 2002, 65):

> Two issues are clear: there exists no theoretical underpinning for the use of information technologies as an agent of change in the public service and, two, at the federal level, technology itself is regarded as a positive investment while human capital is not.

Developing KM Strategies

Five fundamental processes that are central to the process of formulating and implementing a knowledge-management strategy are depicted in Figure 13.1. These are

1. Knowledge mapping within the organization
2. Capturing both tacit and explicit knowledge
3. Transferring or sharing for maximum returns

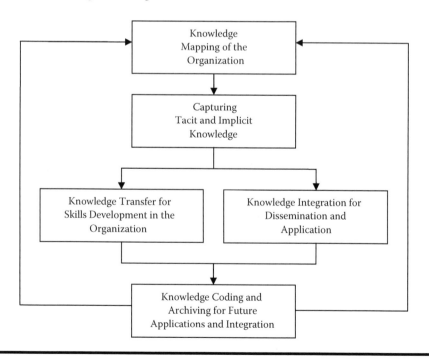

Figure 13.1   Fundamental processes in KM strategy. (From concepts in Tiwana 2002.)

4. Integrating knowledge-management processes and procedures into the culture of the organization
5. Classifying and storing or archiving the knowledge for future access and application

Knowledge Mapping

Knowledge mapping is the first step in the process. Knowledge mapping is a way of identifying the sources of knowledge and fixing the location of key holders of knowledge within an organization. Such knowledge is often held in the memories of a few long-time employees who have developed their knowledge and skills over long periods of trial and error on the job. This tacit knowledge can rarely be described in words, but instead must be shared through application or integration into a work process. Many organizations are now using videotaped stories to collect this tacit information before it is lost to the organization for good.

Public managers are increasingly turning to social network analysis (SNA) to locate holders of tacit knowledge within their agencies (Provan et al. 2005). SNA is a tool for establishing relationships between individuals in an organization or group. An example of a social network analysis is establishing how often or when individuals turn to one or more other workers for answers to work-related questions. A number of easy-to-use software programs are available to produce the network plots that illustrate the relationships. These network maps use what are known as *nodes* and *ties*. Figure 13.2 is an example of a hypothetical SNA diagram. Nodes represent people; ties illustrate the connections between nodes. Many different types of relationships can be identified and illustrated in this way.

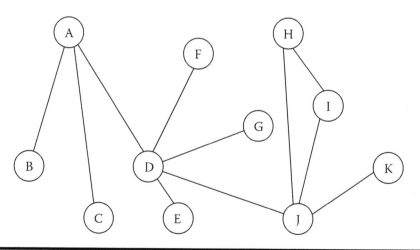

Figure 13.2   Illustration of a simple SNA diagram.

Knowledge Capture

Capturing tacit and explicit knowledge typically occurs during application of a knowledge audit. The knowledge audit performs a series of important tasks: It tells managers what knowledge they need to complete a task or carry out a mission. At the same time, it tells managers what portion of that information they have and do not have. Once you know what you know and, more importantly, what you do not know, you must then determine the best way to go about collecting the information that fills the knowledge gap.

During this search stage of the knowledge audit, the audit team will also be able to record the organization's knowledge assets—the combination of people, data, and technology that exists within the organization and which are necessary to carry out the agency's mission. The people side may be the most important element in this portion of the audit because it is easy to lose an asset when an employee leaves or retires.

Transferring and Integrating Knowledge

Knowledge transfer and knowledge integration are the applied elements in this process. Although closely related, they perform different functions. Knowledge transfer occurs as learning, as when a senior administrator helps a new employee understand how to work around a misleading written procedure in order to carry out a task. The new employee is receiving new knowledge for a specific application. Knowledge transfer, on the other hand, is a more passive way of capturing and sharing knowledge. It occurs when individuals are encouraged to record their experiences for a collected synthesis of information or experiences. Thus, knowledge integration is a strategy that promotes synthesis of the knowledge held by individuals at a project or task level while keeping cross-member learning down to a minimum; it stresses existing but disconnected knowledge.

Knowledge sharing is another way of describing knowledge transfer and integration. Many governments now recognize the importance of free and effective sharing of knowledge in the success of their organizations (Kim and Lee 2006; McNabb 2007). In 2000, for example, the government of South Korea formed a special committee to develop knowledge-management systems in the public sector and to implement knowledge-management strategies. Australia, New Zealand, and the United Kingdom have long employed knowledge-management programs and systems.

Coding and Storing Knowledge

The final element in this abbreviated knowledge-management process is coding (categorizing), recording, and archiving the knowledge so that future administrators do not have to repeat earlier failures or "reinvent the wheel" when developing solutions for problems that have been successfully dealt with in the past. This is the most information-technology-dependent aspect of the knowledge-management system.

KM in Local Government

A cultural and economic environment that is permanently shaped by global access to information is increasingly influencing today's world. More and more, this means access to information via the Internet. Over the last decade and a half, the economies of many industrialized nations underwent a wave of technological change that has significantly reshaped nearly every aspect of both the private and public sectors. Information-age technologies are changing people's values and the nation's interests (Acs 2002; Fast 2002; Ho 2003). Access to information—and to the knowledge that results from the application of information and communications technology to problem solving and decision making—has influenced the way that businesses operate, how consumers purchase good and services, and the ways that government at all levels provides public services.

Before the growth of the Internet, the federal government was already applying information and communications technology to improve operating efficiency, but primarily for internal communications and managerial purposes. The growth in Internet usage and e-commerce that occurred during the 1990s in the private sector soon pressured the public sector to serve citizens electronically in what is recognized globally as the e-government initiative (Ho 2002).

Use of Web Sites by Local Governments

An international survey on the extent of e-government at the local level was sent to nearly 3,000 local governments with populations greater than 10,000; only a little more than half (51 percent) responded. The results showed that 85.3 percent of the municipalities responding had a Web site and 57.4 percent had an intranet. Only 46 cities reported having had a Web site longer than five years. Despite these encouraging results, the survey was less sanguine about local governments moving farther toward adoption of full e-government programs; only 114 cities (8.2 percent of respondents) reported having a comprehensive e-government strategy or master plan to guide their future e-government initiatives (Moon 2000).

The slow growth of knowledge management among local governments has been echoed by a number of studies that report a local perception that investments in the technology do not result in commensurate positive gains in productivity and performance. Lee and Perry (2002), however, found this conclusion to be erroneous. They blamed that misconception on several genuine factors, among which are redistribution of benefits within the organization, poor measurement tools and processes, time lags in benefits, and mismanagement.

The redistribution argument states that IT may not improve the productivity of the entire public sector; rather, it only redistributes benefits within government, such as giving one organization a competitive advantage. Poor measurement, the most commonly reported reason, refers to the use of labor productivity measures that track only the number of outputs, not their quality. The lag in time required for an organization to receive full benefit from its investments in IT might be because such investments often require extensive restructuring of workflow and infrastructure before full benefits are seen. Additionally, not all workers may participate in the use of the IT at the same time; some administrators and workers will remain emphatically computer illiterate.

This leads to the last argument: investing in IT will not by itself support organizational change nor will it improve productivity. Training and a cultural change are often needed. Moreover, the investment may be larger than actually needed, thus contributing to poor results.

After studying data from all 50 states, Lee and Perry (2002) concluded that, although IT does have a positive impact on economic performance (as measured by gross state product) alone, it was not found to significantly increase agency productivity. Far greater economic benefits appear to accrue to those organizations that marry information and communications technology with knowledge-management theory to build knowledge-management systems that synergistically magnify the benefits of each item alone (Butler et al. 2003).

The President's Management Agenda (PMA) reference models discussed in Chapter 7 incorporate a number of different domains, or business activities, under its umbrella. Each domain frames a distinct set of capabilities or tasks that contribute to achieving the mission of that domain. For example, four capabilities are included in the Digital Asset Services Domain: content management, document management, knowledge management, and records management. The eight primary functions or responsibilities that fall under the knowledge-management set of capabilities and their definitions are displayed in Table 13.1.

Summary

KM is a set of processes, practices, and management philosophies that exist to collect, process, store, and make available the organizational knowledge that enables government agencies to be more proficient and competitive in the delivery of public services. Key uses of KM by government agencies include a means of collecting, processing, and disseminating the information needed to facilitate a change, to ensure the availability of data needed to improve agency operations, and to enhance the delivery of government services to citizens.

Three converging trends are driving public-sector organizations to gain better control of their information infrastructure and management of the tacit and explicit knowledge held by their personnel. The first is the expected high turnover

Table 13.1 Changing Information into Knowledge

Service Component	Defines the Set of Capabilities That
Information retrieval	Allows access to data and information for use by an organization and its stakeholders
Information mapping/ taxonomy	Supports the creation and maintenance of relationships between data entities, naming standards, and categorization
Information sharing	Supports the use of documents and data in a multiuser environment for use by an organization and its stakeholders
Categorization	Allows classification of data and information into specific layers or types to support an organization
Knowledge engineering	Supports the translation of knowledge from an expert into the knowledge base of an expert system
Knowledge capture	Facilitates the collection of data and information
Knowledge distribution and delivery	Supports the transfer of knowledge to the end user
Smart documents	Supports the interaction of information and process (business logic) rules between users of the document, i.e., the logic and use of the document is embedded within the document itself and is managed within the document parameters

in knowledge workers as large numbers of the baby boom generation retire; a number of studies have cited the coming loss of senior project and technical managers as the greatest risk facing government agencies.

The second is a global push to implement e-government; agencies at all levels of government have been increasing the amount and variety of online services available to citizens. Many government agencies are also providing a mobile communications capability for their knowledge workers. Electronic tools such as personal handheld devices, smart phones, tablets, and laptop computers provided to field workers have freed knowledge workers from the tyranny of being chained to a desk.

The third is continued emphasis on enterprise architecture initiatives (i.e., shared services) to achieve greater operational efficiencies and implement Web-based service delivery. Agencies must comply with enterprise architecture analysis mandates before moving to acquire new or replacement IT. Agencies had to establish common network platforms, operating and e-mail systems, and knowledge-management systems.

KM and knowledge-management systems (KMS) may be considered to be the latest manifestation in a logical progression of governments' concerns with data, information, and knowledge. By the late 1980s, the push to reinvent government allowed government leaders to take advantage of the widely available computer capabilities in government agencies to introduce private-sector management practices into government, including total quality management, performance appraisals, and cost controls. This information transformation is still underway.

Chapter 14

Preparing for Change: Trouble at the Sheriff's Office

No organization in the emerging world of 2015 can survive without, at the very least, an acceptance of change and, at best, an enthusiasm for it. Where it is hardest to build this is where there are generational differences, such as where workers have grown up in a generation used to a fixed way of operating, combined with government policy that endeavors to protect workers' security.

Paul Taffinder (1998)

Administrators and managers at all levels of government face the same needs to revitalize their organizations as their counterparts in the private sector. This drive for change took on a heightened urgency over a decade ago with the move to "reinvent government." It quickly became apparent that successful transformations are difficult to achieve. McNabb and Sepic (1995) reported on a series of public- and private-organization transformation diagnoses conducted during the last half of the 1990s and into the first years of the new century.

This transformation assessment instrument included in Appendix A was developed to provide a benchmark assessment of the culture and climate in public- and private-sector organizations. The culture/climate diagnosis instrument was first used in assessing organizational climate in a five-unit regional office of the General Services Administration (GSA). The instrument was later adjusted to meet the special needs of a regional law enforcement agency, and once again for a regional office of a federal fisheries and wildlife agency. It has also been used by other researchers in numerous private- and public-sector organizations in the United States, Europe, and Asia. The assessment instrument has most recently been translated into Norwegian for assessing organizational culture dynamics in a regional arm of an international environmental services organization.

This chapter describes results of the assessment of a countywide law enforcement agency. The agency serves several communities with contract public safety services across a county of 1.5 million citizens and manages a regional corrections facility. The need for a transformation process emerged after an acrimonious internal debate over management philosophy resulted in the departure of the chief executive officer.

A review of 13 different approaches to culture and climate assessment resulted in an instrument that grouped items into nine organizational culture dimensions (McNabb et al. 1997; Sepic et al. 1998). These dimensions included Structure, Responsibility, Risk, Rewards, Warmth and Support, Conflict, Organizational Identity, Approved Practices, and Ethics and Values.

Development of an Assessment Instrument

The 65-item core Organizational Culture Assessment Survey (OCAS) instrument developed for assessing organizational culture evolved over nearly a decade of trial and revisions. Developed originally for an analysis of a branch office of the GSA, the instrument contained 99 items. Items with low reliability scores after several applications were deleted or integrated into other items.

A review of more than a dozen different approaches to culture assessment resulted in a grouping of items into nine separate culture-dimension scales (McNabb et al. 1997): Structure, Responsibility, Risk, Rewards, Warmth and Support, Conflict, Organizational Identity, Approved Practices, and Ethics and Values. Definitions for each dimension follow.

- *Structure:* The feelings that employees have about structural constraints in the organization. It includes such aspects as how many rules, regulations, and procedures there are; whether "red tape" hinders the functioning of the organization; and whether the organization (a) requires employees to go through channels for decisions or (b) is characterized by a free-flowing informality.
- *Responsibility:* The feeling of being "your own boss," i.e., of not being forced to double-check all decisions with higher authority. The feeling that one gets when, given a job to do, you know that it is your job; you are not told how to do it.
- *Risk:* The sense of risks and challenge encountered in the organization. Is there an emphasis on taking calculated risks, or is "playing it safe" the best way to operate?

- *Rewards*: The feeling that you are being rewarded for a job well done; emphasis on positive rewards for personnel, rather than punishments; the perceived fairness of pay and promotion policies.
- *Warmth and Support*: The feeling of good fellowship that prevails in the workgroup atmosphere; emphasis on being well-liked; prevalence of friendly and informal social groups; perceived helpfulness of managers and other group employees; emphasis on mutual support from above and below.
- *Conflict*: The belief that managers and other workers welcome opinions that are different from their own; emphasis on getting problems out in the open, rather than smoothing them over or ignoring them.
- *Organizational Identity*: The extent to which members of the group identify with the organization, their fellow workers, and with the underlying mission and philosophy of the individual work groups, larger units within the organization, and the organization as a whole.
- *Approved Practices*: The perceived importance of implicit and explicit goals and performance standards; emphasis on doing a good job; the challenge represented in personal and group goals.
- *Values*: The extent to which members of the organization believe that (a) ethical principles are important to them personally and (b) the organization's core values and codes of conduct can and should be upheld in all circumstances; endorsement of ethical courses of action.

An experimental scale for measuring readiness for change has been added to the sample instrument in Appendix A.

Instrument Factors and Survey Administration

The survey instrument assessed dimensions on the above nine factors. Responses to all items were made on a seven-point scale. Responses to negatively worded items were reverse-scored so that a *low* score consistently indicated a more favorable culture. Several demographic questions were also included to make comparisons between subgroups. Responses to all questions were self-recorded on machine-readable forms.

A total of 650 survey instruments were distributed, accompanied by a letter signed by agents of the department's unions and by the newly appointed interim chief officer. Respondents were asked to mail completed surveys in postage-paid envelopes so that no responses could be seen by anyone in the department, thereby maintaining confidentiality and anonymity. After a follow-up letter, a total of 257 responses were received, for a response rate of 40 percent. Demographic characteristics of the sample are displayed in Table 14.1.

A series of one-way analyses of variance compared subsample group scores (i.e., respondents at different hierarchical levels, male compared to female respondents, corrections compared to law enforcement respondents). These analyses allow

Table 14.1 Demographic Characteristics of Assessment Study Sample

Respondent	Characteristic	N	Percent
Gender	Female	52	20.9
	Male	197	79.1
Level	Nonsupervisory	190	75.7
	First-line supervisor	43	17.1
	Middle management	11	4.4
	Upper management	7	2.8
Assignment	Law enforcement	138	55.0
	Corrections	92	36.7
	Service bureau	10	4.0
	Administration	11	4.4
Length of service	1–5 years	82	32.7
	6–10 years	77	30.7
	11–15 years	46	18.3
	16–20 years	30	12.0
	More than 20 years	16	6.4
Education	High school grad	12	4.7
	Some college	83	32.8
	College grad 2-year	61	24.1
	College grad 4-year	72	28.5
	Graduate work/degree	25	9.9

Note: Total sample size of 257 is reduced in some categories by missing data. Percents are based on full sample valid data for each characteristic.

comparison of mean scores on items and indexes, computation of F statistics, and *a posteriori* comparisons to identify statistically significant differences between specific subsample groups when more than two groups exist.

Dimension summary scores for all 257 of the study's respondents are compared in Table 14.2, listed in ascending order by mean score (most-favorable index scores are listed first). Six of the nine index scores fall within one half

Table 14.2   Dimension Index Score Means and Standard Deviations

Dimension	Mean	Standard Deviation
Approved Practices	3.50	0.94
Values	3.54	0.68
Responsibility	3.70	1.17
Organizational Identity	4.13	1.33
Warmth and Support	4.15	1.23
Structure	4.41	1.09
Risk	4.57	0.99
Conflict	4.64	0.98
Rewards	5.36	1.25

Note: A low mean score (1.0) indicates a favorable climate, a high mean score
  (7.0) an unfavorable climate (midpoint = 4.0).

point of the midpoint of 4.0 on the seven-point scales used for responses.
Three—Approved Practices, Values, and Responsibility—represent a moder-
ately favorable climate.

Three others—Organizational Identity, Warmth and Support, and Structure—
represent a slightly unfavorable climate. The remaining three dimension scores represent a less favorable picture. With respect to the Risk and Conflict indexes, the
climate is somewhat unfavorable. On the Rewards index, a mean score of 5.36
indicates a distinctly unfavorable climate. Respondents' most negative perceptions
of the climate of the department relate to the reward system.

Differences in the Department's Hierarchy

A number of significant differences were found on items within each dimension
between nonsupervisory respondents, first-line supervisors, and middle and upper
management (combined into one group because of subsample size). Significantly
different mean scores were found on four of the climate dimensions. Differences in
dimension scores are discussed below.

  Structure: First-line supervisors were most likely to disagree that opportuni-
    ties exist to participate in setting goals and objectives. However, the other
    two groups also disagreed that this opportunity exists. Similarly, differences
    between groups on the prevalence of red tape are overshadowed by the fact

that all three groups characterized the department as having excessive rules, administrative details, and red tape.

Rewards: Respondents below middle and upper management expressed considerable concern about several aspects of the reward system: that the best people do not rise to the top, that trying something new is not encouraged, and that the work climate does not encourage people to do their best. All three of these perceptions are serious impediments to individuals' commitment to excellence and quality customer service.

Conflict: Three issues are of concern particularly to nonsupervisors, who are more likely to perceive that conflict between competing units is not healthy, that disagreeing with supervisors is discouraged, and that open arguments and disagreements are avoided if one wants to make a good impression. This finding raises the question of whether these norms of behavior, which have become accepted in this bureaucratic system, are those that are most desirable for the department.

Values: Ethical concerns are at the core of the value system in the department. For two of the questions on this dimension, judgments made by middle and upper managers and those below them were in disagreement: Middle and upper managers disagreed more strongly about the need for stretching the law a little at times and about whether rules should always guide right behavior. For the first question, the difference was a matter of degree—all parties disagreed that the law could be stretched a little. For the second, nonsupervisory personnel and first-line supervisors tended to agree that sometimes it is best to do what you know is right, although middle and upper managers disagreed. The reasons for so large a difference in perception are worth exploring.

Approved Practices: Middle and upper managers were less likely to believe that making risky decisions when they prove to be wrong, and questioning why things are done, are disapproved of. That those below them believe these practices are highly disapproved of may diminish their willingness to exert themselves in the performance of their jobs. To the extent that these attitudes truly are debilitating to good performance, the norms of conduct in the department regarding these behaviors merit careful examination.

Administrative-Level Summaries

In most organizations, perceptions about various aspects of organizational climate differ according to hierarchical level. This department was no exception. Respondents at lower levels hold more negative views concerning the organization's climate. It is most critical to address differences that represent obstacles to good performance. Several themes in particular warrant scrutiny and action:

1. The message that red tape and bureaucratic rules impede getting things done
2. The need to engage in bureaucratic gamesmanship (not rocking the boat by asking questions or expressing opinions, not expressing one's genuine concerns for fear of creating personal difficulties)
3. Beliefs that good performance does not pay off in terms of promotions or other rewards

Gender Differences

Significant differences were also found for several dimensions for male and female respondents. Male and female respondents differed significantly on items within five of the climate dimensions. As above, specific comments about observed differences follow the results presented in Table 14.2, as do conclusions about gender differences. Differences included:

- Female officers were more likely to indicate that they had unclear job definitions, that policies and procedures were poorly communicated, and that they were unclear about to whom they should report. These differences raise the question of whether women were treated differently than men in regard to very basic organizational practices.
- Female officers were more likely to feel that they must get approval from their bosses before they take action—unlike men, who move ahead even without management approval when they think they have the right answer for a situation.
- Female officers were less likely than men to feel that people in the organization are friendly, that the organization is relaxed and easygoing, that the human factor is stressed in their departments, and that people encourage one another's best efforts. This may reflect a pattern within the department in which feelings are not emphasized and little concern is shown for the way female officers feel.
- Female officers were more likely to feel that they are not encouraged to disagree with their supervisors. This finding supports an interpretation that women feel they are being held back or not given the opportunity to participate in decision-making situations that could show their skills and abilities.
- On just one question within this dimension, female officers display a propensity to be more ethical than men; women were significantly less inclined than men to stretch the law.

Comparisons of responses by gender subgroups revealed statistically significant differences in perceptions of organizational climate. Women held more negative perceptions than did men concerning the way work is structured, how supportive managers and colleagues are, and how easy it is to express their own ideas and make their own decisions.

Organizational Climate and Readiness to Accept Change

The key to successful transformation initiatives lies in preparing the organizational culture and climate to accept change. As many administrators and managers will attest, this has never been a simple process. Typical of the reaction many managers have of the difficulty in implementing a change is this remark by a European manager: "It's my personal conviction that it's only possible to get change done and achieve a culture of change with new people" (Taffinder 1998).

The government workforce, as structured until big changes began to take place during the 1980s and 1990s, had more than a century of experience in building networks with legislators and their staffs. Fortunately (or perhaps unfortunately) for agency personnel, appointed legislative and senior-level agency heads tend not to change as often as elected officials. Organizations such as the Government Accountability Office (GAO) and the Office of Management and Budget (OMB) tend to remain committed to identifying waste and poor management practices—and rectifying poor governance practices regardless of who holds office. They monitor and report on all agencies' performance and progress toward transformation to the new government paradigm.

Government at all levels must deal with a number of rapidly changing and increasingly complex economic, demographic, social, technological, and security issues if the United States is to remain strong, competitive, and innovative. This chapter presented a proposed list of steps to take when planning or implementing a transformational change.

Survey responses to three of the dimensions—Rewards, Conflict, and Risk—represented the climate in the organization as somewhat unfavorable. Responses to questions regarding three other climate dimensions—Structure, Warmth and Support, and Organizational Identity—were also on average unfavorable, but slightly less so. The climate was characterized as somewhat favorable for the remaining three dimensions: Approved Practices, Values, and Responsibility.

Respondents below the rank of supervisor likewise saw a number of issues related to Structure, Rewards, Conflict, Values, and Approved Practices in somewhat more negative terms than did middle and upper management.

Specific strategies that might be considered to transform this public agency include training and organizational development activities; changes in communication, decision-making, and goal-setting practices; and providing a more structured opportunity for members of the department in all units and at all levels to have their concerns heard by their supervisors and by upper management.

To measure the behavior dimension of the organization's climate, further investigation was needed to identify idiosyncratic problems as well as those issues that should be addressed on an organizationwide basis. The presence of differences as distinct as those found during the assessment is likely to pose significant challenges to the success of change efforts aimed at making this a revitalized, higher performing, and more responsive organization.

The process of climate assessment itself can provide a foundation for building increased levels of commitment to the organization as well as to particular change interventions. The assessment process will signal to employees that the organization is willing to examine how it functions and that their inputs are desired and respected. Periodic repetition of the climate/commitment assessment process reinforces employees' perceptions that the organization continues to value their collaboration in pursuit of organizational improvement.

Summary

This was an abbreviated overview of the results of an organizational culture and climate assessment conducted to asses a large public safety organization's organizational culture and operating climate in order to identify sources of perceived disequilibrium in the organization. The assessment was conducted using a survey instrument developed and tested in public and private organizations. The assessment instrument measures organizational climate on nine dimensions. The instrument is attached in Appendix A.

References

Abramson, M. A. 1996. Transforming public service. *Government Executive Online* (May 1). Retrieved October 10, 2008 from www.govexec.com/archdoc/0596/0596book.htm

Abramson, M. A., J. D. Breul, and J. M. Kamensky. 2003. *Four trends transforming government*. Washington, DC: IBM Center for the Business of Government.

Abramson, M. A., J. D. Breul, and J. M. Kamensky. 2006. *Six trends transforming government*. Washington, DC: IBM Center for the Business of Government.

Accela. 2006. Cleveland, Ohio transforms its community with enterprise land management solution. Dublin, CA: Accela, Inc. Retrieved March 25, 2007 from www.accela.com/products/includes/assets/casestudy.cleveland.pdf

Ackerman, F., N. R. Goodwin, L. Dougherty, and K. Gallagher, eds. 1998. *The changing nature of work*. Washington, DC: Island Press.

Adams, G. B. 2000. Uncovering the political philosophy of the new public management. *Administrative Theory & Praxis*. 22 (3): 498–499.

Agranoff, R. 2007. Enhancing performance through public sector networks. *Public Productivity and Management Review,* 31(3): 320–340.

Agranoff, R. and M. McGuire. 1998. Multinetwork management: collaboration and the hollow state in local economic policy. *Journal of Public Administration Research and Theory.* 8 (1): 667–91.

Agranoff, R. and M. McGuire 1999. Managing in a network setting. *Policy Studies Review.* 16 (1): 18–41.

Agranoff, R. and M. McGuire 2001. American federalism and the search for models of management. *Public Administration Review.* 61 (6): 671–681.

Agranoff, R. and M. McGuire 2003. *Collaborative public management: new strategies for local governments*. Washington, DC: Georgetown University Press.

Agranoff, R. and M. McGuire 2005. Managing collaborative performance. *Public Productivity and Management Review,* 29(1): 18–45.

Aichholzer, G. 2003, *BISER-Workpackage 1: e-Europe Regions Development Model*. Information Society Technology Programme. Retrieved December 17, 2008 from www.biser-eu.com/resultsdoc%20-%Biser%20D1-3.pdf

Alcácer, J. 2006. Location choices across the value chain: how activity and capability influence collocation. *Management Science,* 52 (10): 1457–1471.

Alford, S. 2002. Transforming public administration: realizing the benefits of technology for government. Paper presented at the 36th annual ICA Conference, Singapore. Retrieved October 10, 2008 from http://unpan1.un.org/intradoc/groups/public/documents/APCITY/UNPAN011279.pdf

229

Alter, S. 1999. *Information systems: a management perspective,* 3rd ed. Reading, MA: Addison-Wesley.

Altshuler, A. A. and R. D. Behn. 1997, The dilemmas of innovation in American government. In A. A. Altshuler and R. D. Behn, eds. *Innovation in the Public Sector.* Washington, DC: Brookings Institution: 3–37.

Amirkhanyan, A. 2008. Privatizing public nursing homes: examining the effects on quality and Access. *Public Administration Review,* 68(4): 665–680.

Andrews, R., G. A. Boyne, and R. M. Walker. 2006. Strategy content and organizational performance: an empirical analysis. *Public Administration Review,* 66(1): 52–63.

Applebaum, E. and R. Batt. 1994. *The new American workplace: transforming work systems in the United States.* Ithaca, NY: ILR Press.

Argyris, C. 1999. Initiating change that perseveres. In R. C. Kearney and E. M. Berman, eds, *Public Sector Performance.* Boulder, CO: Westview Press: 57–64.

Aristigueta, M. P. 2002. Reinventing government: managing for results. *Public Administration Quarterly,* 26(2): 147–173.

Ashkanasy, N. M., P. M. Widerom, and M. F. Peterson, eds. 2000. *Handbook of organization culture and climate.* Thousand Oaks, CA: Sage

Backoff, R., B. Wechsler, and R. E. Crew, Jr. 1993. The challenge of strategic management in local government. *Public Administration Quarterly,* 17 (2): 127–144.

Balfour, D. L. 1996. Organizational commitment. *Public Productivity and Management Review,* 19 (3): 256–277.

Balfour, D. L. and J. W. Grubbs. 2000. Character, corrosion and the civil servant: the human consequences of globalization and the new public management. *Administrative Theory & Praxis.* 22 (3): 570–584.

Balfour, D. L. and B. Wechsler, 1990. Organizational commitment: a reconceptualization and empirical test of public-private differences. *Review of Public Personnel Administration,* 10 (3): 23–40.

Ballenstedt, B. R. 2007. Union, GSA at odds over personnel policies after merger. *Govexec. com* Daily Briefing (May 15, 2007). Retrieved March 20, 2007 from http://www.gov-exec.com/story_page.cfm?articleid=36379

Bandoh, E. 2003. Outsourcing the delivery of human services. *Economic Success Clearinghouse* (formerly the Welfare Information Network). 7 (12). Retrieved December 3, 2007 from www.financeproject.org/Publications/outsourcinghumanservicsIM.htm

Barras, J. 2003. E-government challenges and perspectives—the UK perspective. London: Office of the e-Envoy. Retrieved December 17, 2008 from john.borras@e-envoy.gsi. gov.uk

Barzelay, M. 2001. *The new public management.* Berkeley: University of California Press.

Basinelectric.com. 2004. Basin Electric Power Cooperative. Retrieved December 17, 2008 from www.basinelectric.com

Batley, R. and G. Larbi. 2004. *The changing role of government: the reform of public services in developing countries.* Houndmills, UK: Palgrave Macmillan.

Becker, F. and V. Patterson. 2005. Public-private partnerships: balancing financial returns, risks, and roles of the partners. *Public Performance and management Review,* 29(2): 125–144.

Beckett, J. 2000. The 'Government should be run like a business' mantra. *American Review of Public Administration,* 30(2): 185–204.

Beckhard, R., and R. Harris, 1987. *Organizational transitions,* 2nd ed. Boston: Addison-Wesley.

Beer, M., R. A. Eisenstat, and B. Spector. 1990. Why change programs don't produce change. *Harvard Business Review*, 68 (6): 158–166.

Belbin, R. M. 1996. *The coming shape of the organization.* Oxford: Butterworth-Heinemann.

Berg, A. M. 2006. Transforming public services—transforming the public servant? *International Journal of Public Sector Management*, 19 (6): 556–568.

Bergson, H. 1946. *The creative mind.* New York: Carol Publishing.

Berman, E. M. 1997. Dealing with cynical citizens. *Public Administration Review*, 57(2): 104–123.

Berman, E. M. and J.P. West. 1998. Productivity enhancement efforts in public and non-profit organizations. *Public Productivity and Management Review*, 22(2): 2076–219.

Berry, F. S. 1994. Innovation in public management: the adoption of strategic planning. *Public Administration Review*, 54 (4): 322–330.

Berry, F. S. and R. S. Brower. 2005. Intergovernmental and intersectoral management. *Public Productivity and Management Review*, 29(1): 7–17.

Berry, J. M. 2005. Nonprofits and civic engagement. *Public Administration Review*, 65 (5): 568–578.

Bingham, L. B., T. Nabatchi, and R. O'Leary. 2005. The new governance: practices and processes for stakeholder and citizen participation in the work of government. *Public Administration Review*, 65 (5): 547–558.

Birchall, J. 2002. Mutual, non-profit or public interest company? An evaluation of options for the ownership and control of water utilities. *Annals of Public and Cooperative Economics.* 72 (2): 181–213.

Blackstone, E., M. Bognano, and S. Hakim. 2006a. *E-Government at the state and local level.* Retrieved March 24, 2007 from http://sbm.temple.edu/ccg/documents/e-governmentBookIntroduction.swf

Blackstone, E., M. Bognano, and S. Hakim, eds. 2006b. *Innovation in e-government: governors and mayors speak-out.* Lanham, MD: Rowman & Littlefield.

Bowler, S. and T. Donovan 2004. Evolution in state governance structures: Unintended consequences of state tax and expenditure limitations. *Political Research Quarterly,* 59(2): 189–196.

Boyne, G. and J. S. Gould-Williams. 2003. Planning and performance in public organizations. *Public Management Review*, 5 (1): 115–132.

Bozeman, B. and J. D. Straussman. 1991. *Public management strategies.* San Francisco: Jossey-Bass.

Brayton, S. 2002. Outsourcing war: mercenaries and the privatization of peacekeeping. *Journal of International Affairs*, 55 (2): 303–329.

Brazil, J. J. 2007. Mission: impossible? *Fast Company*, 144 (April): 92–109.

Bresciani, P., P. Donzelli, and A. Forte. 2003. Requirements engineering for knowledge management in e-government. *Proceedings of the 4th Working Conference on Knowledge Management in electronic government.* Rhodes, Greece.

Broadbent, B. 2002. *ABCs of e-learning.* San Francisco: Jossey-Bass/Pfeiffer.

Brown, M. E. 1969. Identification and some conditions of organizational involvement. *Administrative Science Quarterly,*14 (3): 346–355.

Bruce, H. W. 1998. User satisfaction with information seeking on the Internet. *Journal of the American Society for Information Science*, 47 (2): 541–556.

Bruchey, S. 1990. *Enterprise: the dynamic economy of a free people.* Cambridge, MA: Harvard University Press.

Bruel, J. B. 2007a. Three Bush administration management reform initiatives: The President's management agenda, freedom to manage legislative proposals, and the program assessment rating tool. *Public Administration Review,* 67(1): 21–26.

Bruel, J. B. 2006b. What is transformation? In M.A. Abrahamson, J C. Breul and J M. Kamensky, *Six trends transforming government.* Washington, DC: IBM Center for the Business of Government.

Bruel, J. B. 2006. GPRA—A foundation for performance budgeting. *Public Productivity and Management Review,* 30(3): 312–331.

Bruhn, J. G., Zajac, G., and Al-Kasemi, A. A. 2001. Ethical perspectives on employee participation in planned organizational change: a survey of two state public welfare agencies. *Public Performance and Management Review,* 25 (2): 208–228.

Bryson, J. M. 2004. *Strategic planning for public and nonprofit organizations,* 3rd ed. San Francisco: John Wiley & Sons.

Bryson, J. M., F. Ackerman, and C. Eden. 2007. Putting the resource-based view of strategy and distinctive competence to work in public organizations. *Public Administration Review,* 67(4): 702–717.

Bryson, J. M., B. C. Crosby, and M. M. Stone. 2006. The design and implementation of cross-sector collaborations: propositions from the literature. *Public Administration Review,* 66(December Supplement): 44–55.

Bunning, C. R. 1992. Effective strategic planning in the public sector: some learnings (sic). *International Journal of Public Sector Management,* 5 (4): 54–59.

Burr, M. T. 2004. Consolidating co-ops. *Public Utilities Fortnightly.* 142 (June): 71–76.

Butler, T., J. Feller, A. Pope, P. Barry, and C. Murphy. Promoting Knowledge Sharing in Government and Non-Government Organizations Using Open Source Software: The pKADS Story, *Electronic Journal of E-Government*(2:2). 2004.

Callahan, R. 2007. Governance: the collision of politics and cooperation. *Public Administration Review,* 6(2): 290–301.

Cammarano, B. 2004. Facing the challenges of enterprise transformation. Retrieved March 10, 2007 from www-126.ibm.com/developerworks/rational/library/4346. html

Cappelli, P., L. Bassi, H. Katz, D. Knoke, P. Osterman, and M. Useem, 1997. *Change at work.* New York: Oxford University Press.

Carnall, C. A. 1995. *Managing change in organizations.* London: Prentice Hall.

Carnall, C. A. 1982. *The evaluation of organizational change.* King's Lynn, UK: Gower.

Carnoy, M. and M. Castells. 1997. Sustainable flexibility: a prospective study on work, family, and society in the information age. Abridged segments of *OECD Working Papers,* 5 (29) reprinted in F. Ackerman, N. R. Goodwin, L. Dougherty and K. Gallagher, eds. *The changing nature of work* (1998). Washington, DC: Island Press: 208–213.

Carr-Chellman, A. A., ed. 2005. *Global perspectives on e-learning: rhetoric and reality.* Thousand Oaks, CA: Sage.

Catherall, P. 2005. *Delivering e-learning for information services in Higher Education.* Oxford: Chandros.

CCPPP. 2007. About PPP: Definitions: Canadian Council for public-private partnerships. Retrieved March 31, 2007 from www.pppcouncil.ca/aboutppp.definition.asp

CEDEFOP. 2003. *E-learning and training in Europe.* Thessalonica, GR: The European Centre for the Development of Vocational Training.

Chadha, G. 2002. *E-learning: an expression of the knowledge economy.* New Delhi: Tata McGraw-Hill.

Champy, J. 1995. *Reengineering management.* New York: HarperCollins.

Chen, Y. C. and K. Thurmaier. 2008. Advancing e-government: financing challenges and opportunities. *Public Administration Review*, 68(3): 537–548.

Childress, A. and P. Owen. 2000. Strategic management for mine action operations: a case for government-industry partnering. *Journal of Mine Action*, 4 (1): np. Retrieved December 9, 2006 from http://maic.jmu/Journal/4.1/feature_childress.htm

Choi, Y. S., C. L. Cho, D. S. Wright, and J. L. Brudney. 2005. Dimensions of contracting for service delivery by American state administrative agencies. *Public Productivity and Management Review*, 29(1): 46–66.

Choi, S. O. and B. T. Kim. 2007. Power and cognitive accuracy in local emergency management networks. *Public Administration Review*, 67(December Supplement): 198–209.

Christensen, C. M. and M. Overdorf. 2000. Meeting the challenge of disruptive change. *Harvard Business Review*, 78 (2): 66–76.

Christensen, T. and P. Lægreid. 2002. *New public management: the transformation of ideas and practice.* Aldershot, UK: Ashgate.

Christensen, T. and P. Lægreid. 2007. The whole-of-government approach to public sector reform. *Public Administration Review*, 67 (6): 1059–1066.

Cigler, B. A. 2007. The 'big questions' of Katrina and the 2005 great flood of New Orleans. *Public Administration Review*, 67(December Supplement): 64–76.

City of Buffalo. 2007. Mayor Brown's citizens participation academy graduates second class. City of Buffalo: Office of Citizen participation and Information. Retrieved June 23, 2008 from www.ci.buffalo.ny.us/Home/Mayor/Archive_Press_releases/Leadership/2007

City of Phoenix. 2007, How do citizens participate in city government? City of Phoenix. Retrieved June 23, 2008 from http://phoenix.gov/EDUCATN/citizen.html

Clerkin, R. M. And K. A. Grønbjerg. 2007. The capacities and challenges of faith-based human service organizations. *Public Administration Review*, 67(1): 115–126.

Cohen, A. 1996. A crisis of trust. *Enlightenment Magazine*, 9 (Spring/Summer). Retrieved January 9, 2007 from www.wie.org/jp/andrew_crisis.asp?pf=1

Cohen, S. 2001. A strategic framework for devolving responsibility and functions from government to the private sector. *Public Administration Review*, 61 (4): 432–440.

COIC. 2007. Shared services in government. London: Chief Information Officer (Cabinet Office). Retrieved November 30, 2007 from http://www.cio.gov.uk/shared_services/ss_in_govt.asp

Col, J. M. 2007. Managing disasters: the role of local government. *Public Administration Review*, 67(December Supplement): 114–124.

Collaery, B. 1999. The future direction of specialist advice in the public sector. *Journal of Contingencies and Crisis Management*, 7 (2): 98–101.

Comfort, L. K. 2007. Crisis management in hindsight: cognition, communications, coordination, and control. *Public Administration Review*, 67(December Supplement): 189–197.

Conaway, R. N., S. S. Easton, and W. V. Schmidt. 2005. Strategies for enhancing student interaction and immediacy in online courses. *Business Communication Quarterly*, 68 (1): 23–35.

Corbet, A. 2002. *The president's management agenda: e-learning Initiative.* PowerPoint presentation, Department of Energy Office of Training and Human Resource Development. Retrieved May 21, 2006 from www.doeal.gov/gtd/internet/trn-conf/tc-presentations/The%20Presidents%20Management%20Agenda.ppt

Cotton, A. 2007. *Seven steps of effective workforce planning.* Washington, DC: IBM Center for the Business of Government.

Coursey, D. and D. F. Norris. 2008. Models of e-government: are they correct? An empirical assessment. *Public Administration Review*, 68(3): 523–536.

Cox, R. W. III, S. J. Buck, and B. N. Morgan. 1994. *Public administration in theory and practice.* Englewood Cliffs, NJ: Prentice Hall.

Daft, R. L. 2004. *Organization theory and design,* 8th ed. Cincinnati, OH: Thomson South-Western.

Dale, W. M. and W. S. Becker. 2004. A case study of forensic scientist turnover. *Forensic Science Communications* 6(3). Np. Retrieved November 18, 2007 at www.fbi.gov/hq/lab/fsc/backissu/july2004/research/2004_03_research04.htm

Davis, D B. 1995. Form, function, and strategy in boundaryless organizations. In A. Howard, ed. *The changing nature of work.* 112–138. San Francisco: Jossey-Bass.

Defense Consulting & Outsourcing. 2006. Interior agency provides acquisition, financial management and human resources support to its federal customers. September 18. Retrieved December 3, 2007 from www.defense-consulting-outsourcing.com/print_article.cfm?DocID=1661

DELG. 2006. *DELG mission statement and vision.* Retrieved December 29, 2006 from http://michigan.gov.cis/0,1607,7-154-10573-42377-,00.html

DeLone, W. H. and E. R. McLean. 2003. The DeLone and Mclean model of information systems success: a ten year update. *Journal of Management Information Systems,* 19 (4): 9–30.

DeLone, W. H. and E. R. McLean. 1992. Information system success: the quest for the depended variable. *Information Systems Research,* 31 (1): 60–86.

Deming, W. E. 1986. *Out of the crisis.* Cambridge, MA: MIT Press.

Dept. of Finance Canada. 2005. *Strengthening and modernizing public sector management.* Ottawa, Ontario: Department of Finance Canada. Retrieved October 10, 2008 from www.fin.gc.ca/budget05/pdf/bkmgte.pdf

Derthick, M. 2007. Where federalism didn't fail. *Public Administration Review,* 67(December Supplement): 36–47.

Dinin, M. 2003. Washington State wins leadership award. Center for Digital Government. Retrieved December 17, 2008 from www.centerdigitalgov.survey

Dirr, P. J. 1999. Distance and virtual learning in the United States. In G. M. Farrell, ed., *The development of virtual education: a global perspective.* Vancouver, BC: Commonwealth of Learning: 23–48.

DHS. 2007. *Report of the homeland security culture task force.* Washington, DC: Department of Homeland Security. Retrieved February 22, 2007 from www.dhs.gov/xlibrary/assets/hsac_ctfreport_200701.pdf

DIS. 2000. *Washington state digital government plan.* Olympia, WA: Washington State Dept. of Information Services. Retrieved May 20, 2006 from http://www.public.iastate.edu/~ycchen/eGovernment/IT_Plan/Washington_State_DGPlan_0200.pdf

DIS. 2005. *Washington state enterprise architecture program, Version 1.0.* Olympia, WA: Washington State Dept. of Information Services. Retrieved May 20, 2006 from www.dsis.wa.gov/enterprise/enterprisesearch/releaseplanjune2006.doc

DIS. 2006. *Enterprise architecture update.* Olympia, WA: Washington State Dept. of Information Services. Retrieved May 20, 2006 from www.dis.gov/technews/2006_01/20060111.aspx

DLA. 2005. *Transformation roadmap.* Washington, DC: The Defense Logistics Agency. Retrieved January 17, 2007 from www.dla.mil/library/DLATransRoadmap.pdf

DLA. 2006. Transformation roadmap: Transformation in support of the future force. Washington, DC: Defense Logistics Agency. Retrieved January 17, 2007 from www.dla.min/library/DLATransRoadmap.pdf

DOE. 2007. *Executive leadership program.* Washington, DC: U.S. Department of Energy Office of Human Capital management, Office of Innovations and Solutions, Enterprise Training Services. Retried November 18 from http://humancapital.doe.gov/Training/docments/Ececutive_Leadership_Program.pdf

DOL. 2006. *Veterans' employment & training service (VETS).* Retrieved December 29, 2006 from http://www.dol.gov/vets

Donley, M. B. and N. A. Pollard. 2002. Homeland security: the difference between a vision and a wish. *Public Administration Review, 62*(Special Issue): 138–144.

Donohue, A. K. and S. O'Keefe. 2007. Universal lessons from unique events: perspectives from *Columbia* and Katrina. *Public Administration Review, 67*(December Supplement): 77–81.

DOS. 2005. *FY 2005 performance and accountability report.* Washington: U.S. Department of State. Retrieved January 5, 2006 from www.state.gov/s/d/rm/rls/perfrtp/2005/html/56267.htm

Driscoll, M. and S.Carliner. 2005. *Advanced web-based training strategies: unlocking instructionally sound online learning.* San Francisco: Pfeiffer.

Drucker, P. F. 1993. *The post capitalistic society.* New York: HarperCollins.

Duck, Jeanie D. 2001. *The Change Monster.* New York: Crown Business.

Durst, S. L., and Newell, C. 1999. Better, faster, stronger: government reinvention in the 1990s. *American Review of Public Administration, 29* (1): 61–76.

Dysard, J. A., II. 2001. How competition is changing the face of the public water resources industry—trends in privatization, management competition, and other alternative delivery systems. In W.C. Lauer, ed., *Excellence in action: water utility management in the 21st Century.* Washington, DC: American Water Works Association. 85–90.

ECEL. 2002. The European conference on e-learning. Proceedings of the First International e-Learning Conference. November 4–5, 2002. Uxbridge: UK: Brunel University: np.

Eckel, P., B. Hill and M. Green. 1998. *En route to transformation. On change: an occasional paper series of the ACE project on leadership and institutional transformation.* Washington, DC: American Council on Education.

EDS. 2006. *Government transformation.* Electronic Data Systems Corp. online Government Journal, 1(1). Retrieved December 8, 2007 from www.eds.com/services/whitepapers/downloads/govt_journal_v1-1.pdf

Eikenberry, A. M., V. Arroyave, and T. Cooper. 2007. Administrative failure and the international NGO response to Hurricane Katrina. *Public Administration Review, 67*(December Supplement): 160–170.

EOB. 2002. *The president's management agenda.* Washington, DC: Executive Office of the President. Office of Management and Budget.

ESCC. 2007. *President's management agenda.* U. S. Army Enterprise Solutions Competency Center. Retrieved January 5, 2007 from www.army.mil.ESCC/cm/hcm1.htm

Farazmand, A. 2007. Learning from the Katrina crisis: a global and international perspective with implications for future crisis management. *Public Administration Review, 67*(December Supplement): 149–159.

Farmer, D. W. 1990. Strategies for change. In D. W. Steeples, ed. *Managing change in higher education.* San Francisco: Jossey-Bass: 7–18.

Farris, M. T. and R. J. Sampson. 1973. *Public utilities: regulation, management, and ownership.* Boston: Houghton Mifflin.

Feiock, R. C., M. J. Moon, and H. J. Park. 2008. Is the world 'flat' or 'spiky'? Rethinking the governance implications of globalization for economic development. *Public Administration Review*, 68(1): 24–35.

Felts, A. A. and P. H. Jos. 2000. Time and space: the origins and implications of the new public management. *Administrative Theory & Praxis*. 22 (3): 519–533.

Ferlie, E. 2002. Quasi strategy: strategic management in the contemporary public sector. In O. Pettigrew, H. Thomas, and R. Whittington, eds., *Handbook of Strategy and Management*. London: Sage Publications: 279–298.

Ferlie, E., L. Ashburrner, L. Fitzgerald, and A. Pettigrew.1996. *The new public management in action*. Oxford: Oxford University Press.

Fernandez, S. and H. G. Rainey. 2006. Managing successful organizational change in the public sector. *Public Administration Review,* 66 (2): 168–176.

Finnie, B. W., L. K. Gibson and D. E. McNabb, 2007. Reform of the general mining law of 1872: a case study in charting public policy. Unpublished case study. Tacoma, WA: Pacific Lutheran University.

Flemming, S. 2007. Progress and challenges in planning and implementing the transformation of the national airspace system. Testimony before the U.S. Senate Subcommittee on Aviation Operations, Safety and Security (March 22). GAO Report No. 07-649T. Washington, DC: US Government Accountability Office.

Flett, P., A. Curry, and A. Peat. 2007. Reengineering systems in general practice—a case study review. *International Journal of Information Management,* 28 (2008): 83–53.

Fox-Penner, P. and G. Basheda. 2001. A short honeymoon for utility deregulation. *Issues in Science and Technology,* 17 (Spring): 51–57.

Freiock, R. C. 2004. Introduction: regionalism and institutional collective action. In R. C. Freiock, ed. *Metropolitan governance: conflict, competition, and cooperation*. Washington, DC: Georgetown University Press. 3–17.

Friedman, T. L. 2006. *The world is flat: a brief history of the twenty-first century,* 2nd ed. New York: Farrar, Strauss, and Giroux.

Frühling, S. 2006. Uncertainty, forecasting and the difficulty of strategy. *Comparative Strategy,* 25 (1): 19–31.

Fuller, S. 2002. *Knowledge Management Foundations*. Burlington, VT: Butterworth-Heinemann.

GAO. 1997. *Terms related to privatization activities and processes*. Washington, DC: Government Accountability Office. Report No. GAO/GGD-97-121, July.

GAO. 2000. *Determining performance and accountability challenges and high risks*. Washington, DC: U.S. Government Accountability Office, Report No. GAO-159SP (November).

GAO. 2002. *Charitable choice: overview of research findings on implementation*. Washington, DC: U.S. Government Accountability Office, Report GAO-02-337 (January).

GAO. 2003a. *Electronic government: potential exists for enhancing collaboration on four initiatives*. Washington, DC: U.S. Government Accountability Office, Report GAO-04-6 (October).

GAO. 2003b. *Key principles for effective strategic workforce planning*. Washington, DC: U.S. Government Accountability Office, Report GAO-03-39 (December).

GAO. 2005a. *21st century challenges: reexamining the base of the federal government*. Washington, DC: U.S. Government Accountability Office, Report GAO-05-229T (February).

GAO. 2005b. *21st century challenges: transforming government to meet current and emerging challenges*. Washington, DC: U.S. Government Accountability Office, Report GAO-05-229T (July 13).

GAO. 2006. *Defense business transformations: a comprehensive plan, integrated efforts, and sustained leadership are needed to assure success.* Washington, DC: U.S. Government Accountability Office, Report GAO-05-325SP (November).

GAO. 2007a. *High risk series: an update.* Washington, DC: U.S. Government Accountability Office, Report GAO-07-310 (January).

GAO. 2007b. *First responders: much work remains to improve communications interoperability.* Washington, DC: U.S. Government Accountability Office, Report GAO-07-301 (April).

GAO. 2007c. *Forces that will shape America's future: themes from GAO's strategic plan.* Washington, DC: U.S. Government Accountability Office, Report GAO-07-467SP.

GAO. 2007d. *President's management agenda: review of OMB's improved financial performance scorecard process.* Washington, DC: U.S. Government Accountability Office, Report GAO-07-95.

GAO. 2007e. *State and local government: Persistent fiscal challenges will likely emerge within the next decade.* U.S. Government Accountability Office, Report GAO-07-1080SP.

Garnett, J. L. and A. Kouzmin. 2007. Communicating throughout Katrina: competing and complementary conceptual lenses on crisis communication. *Public Administration Review,* 67(December Supplement): 171–188.

Garrison, D. R. and T. Anderson. 2003. *E-learning in the 21st century: a framework for research and practice.* London: RoutledgeFalmer.

Gazley, B. 2008. Beyond the contract: the scope and nature of informal government-non-profit relationships. *Public Administration Review,* 68(1): 141–154.

Genieser, K. 2004. Boardroom evolution. *Public Utilities Fortnightly.* 142 (June): 67–70

Golat, M. 2004. Personal interview with the author. Shelton, WA: Office of the Director of Public Works.

Goldberg, B. 2005. Retirement woes. *The century foundation* (March 15). Retrieved February 23, 2007 from www.tch.org/print.asp?tyle=NC&pubid=933

Goldratt, E. M., E. Schragenheim, and C. A. Ptak. 2000. *Necessary but not sufficient.* Great Barrington, MA: The North River Press.

Goldsmith, S. 1997. Can business really do business with government? *Harvard Business Review,* 75 (3): 110–121.

Goodsell, C. T. A new vision for public administration. *Public Administration Review,* 66(4): 623–635.

Gouldner, H. P. 1960. Dimensions of organizational commitment. *Administrative Science Quarterly,* 4 (4): 468–490.

GPO. 2004. *A strategic vision for the 21st century.* Washington, DC: U.S. Government Printing Office.

Graham, B. 1999. *Business process improvement methodology.* Tipp City, OH: Ben Graham Corp. Retrieved November 27, 2007 from www.workshop.com/wssi/method.pdf

Greasley, S. and G. Stoker. 2008. Mayors and urban governance: developing a facilitative leadership style. *Public Administration Review,* 68(4): 722–730.

Greif, A. and D. D. Latin. 2004. A theory of endogenous institutional change. *American Political Science Review,* 98(4): 633–652.

Greiner, L. 1967. Patterns of organizational change. *Harvard Business Review,* 45 (3): 119–130.

GSA. 2007. GSA Historical Highlights. Washington, DC: US General Services Administration. Retrieved December 1, 2007 from http://gsa.gov/Portal/gsa/ep/contentView.dl?programId=9413&channelId=13262

Haeuser, J. L. 2007. Hurricane babies: the experience of a receiving hospital after Katrina. *Public Administration Review,* 67(December Supplement): 143–146.

Halachmi, A. 1986. Strategic planning and management? Not necessarily. *Public Productivity Review,* 10 (2): 35–50.

Hall, D. T., and Schneider, B. 1972. Correlates of organizational identification as a function of career pattern and organizational type. *Administrative Science Quarterly,* 17 (3): 340–350.

Hall, R. H. 1999. *Organizations.* 7th ed. Upper Saddle River, NJ: Prentice Hall.

Hamilton, S.. 2003. *Maximizing your ERP system.* New York: McGraw-Hill.

Hammer, M.. 1996. *Beyond reengineering.* New York: Harper-Collins.

Hammer, M. and J. Champy. 2003. *Reengineering the corporation,* 2nd ed. New York: HarperCollins

Hampton, H. 2003. *Public power: the fight for publicly owned electricity.* Toronto: Insomniac Press.

Haque, M. S. 2001. The diminishing publicness of public service under the current mode of governance. *Public Administration Review,* 61(1): 65–82.

Harrison, N. 1999. *How to design self-directed and distance learning.* New York: McGraw-Hill.

Harvey, D. and D. R. Brown, 2001. *An experiential approach to organization change.* 6th ed. Upper Saddle River, NJ: Prentice-Hall.

Hasen, R. L. 2005. Crisis of trust over voting difficulties must be addressed. *Roll Call,* (January 10, 2005). Retrieved January 9, 2007 from http://electionlawblog.org/archives/7718-1.html

Hatch, M. J. 1993. The dynamics of organizational culture. *Academy of Management Review,* 18 (4): 657–693.

Heinrich, C. J., C. J. Hill, and L. E. Lynn, Jr. 2004. Governance as an organizing theme for empirical research. In P. W. Ingraham and L. E. Lynn, Jr., eds. *The art of governance: analyzing management and administration.* Washington, DC: Georgetown University Press. 3–19.

Helmetsie, C. and K. Kapust. 2005. *Exploring the competitive sourcing environment.* Presentation at the Content Management Update, September 14, 2005. Washington, DC: Library of Congress. Retrieved December 3, 2007 from www.lic.gov/flicc/video/cmwg/update05/kw.ppt

Hemlin, S., C. M. Allwood and B. R. Martin. 2004. What is a creative knowledge Environment? In S. Hemlin, C. M. Allwood and B. R. Martin, eds, *Creative Knowledge Environments.* Cheltenham, UK: Edward Elgar: 9.

Hempel, D. J. and P. J. LaPlaca. 1975. Strategic planning in a period of transition. *Industrial Marketing Management,* 4 (6): 305–314.

Hill, C. W. L., and G. R. Jones. 2001. *Strategic management theory,* 5th ed. Boston: Houghton Mifflin.

Hillsborough County. 2008. *Hillsborough County Strategic Plan—March 6, 2008.* Retrieved June 29, 2008 from www.hillsboroughcounty.org/strategicmanagement

Hines, J. E. 2006. *U.S. Centcom history.* Retrieved December 9, 2006 from www.centcom.min/sites/uscentcom1/Shared%20Documents/History.aspx

Hitt, M. A., R. E. Freeman, and J. S. Harrison, eds. 2001. *The Blackwell handbook of strategic management.* Oxford: Blackwell.

HMSO. 2005. *Transformational government: enabled by technology.* Cabinet Office report to Parliament (November). London: Her Majesty"s Stationary Office. Retrieved October 25, 2007 from http://www.cio.gov.uk/transformational_government/strategy/

Ho, A. 2002. GPRA after a decade: lessons from the government performance and results act and related federal reforms: introduction. *Public Productivity and Management Review,* 30(3): 307–11.

Hodge, G. A. and C. Greve. 2007. Public-private partnerships: an international performance review. 2007. *Public Administration Review*, 67(3): 545–558.

Hoffman, S. 2006. For U.S. charities, a crisis of trust. *MSNBC,* (November 21, 2006). Retrieved January 9, 2006 from www.msnbc.msn.com/id/15753760/print/2/displaymode/1098/

Hofstede, G. 1995. Cultural constraints in management. Chapter 37 in J. Thomas Wren, ed., *The leader's companion: insights on leadership through the ages.* New York: The Free Press.

Holley, L., M. D. Dufner, and B. J. Reed. 2002. Got SISP? Strategic information systems planning in U.S. state governments. *Public Performance and Management Review,* 25 (4): 398–412.

Holmes, B. and J. Gardner. 2006. *E-learning: concepts and practice.* London: Sage.

Holsapple, C. W. and A. Lee-Post. 2006. Defining, assessing, and promoting e-learning success: an information systems perspective. *Decision Science Journal of Innovative Education.* 4 (1): 67–85.

Howard, A. 1995. Technology and the organization of work. In A. Howard, ed. *The changing nature of work.* 89–96. San Francisco: Jossey-Bass.

HUD 2002. Chapter 3: Meeting a National Objective. *State Community Development Block Grant Program.* Retrieved December 31, 2006 from www.hud.gov/offices/cpd/ communitydevelopment/library/stateguide/ch3.pdf

Hughes, O. E. 2003. *Public management & administration.* Houndmills, UK: Palgrave Macmillan.

Hunger, J. D. and T. L. Wheelen. 2000, *Strategic management.* Upper Saddle River, NJ: Prentice Hall.

Hurst, D. K. 1995. *Crisis and renewal.* Boston: Harvard Business School Press.

Hwang, A. and J. B. Arbaugh. 2006. Virtual and traditional feedback-seeking. In T. Kelley and N. Nanjiani, eds., *The business case for e-learning.* Indianapolis, IN: Cisco Press.

IBM. 2004. Enterprise transformation: three scenarios for choosing retooling over rebuild-ing. *The Mainstream,* 11 (November). Retrieved January 17, 2006 from www-306. ibm.com/software/swnews/swnews.nsf/n/lasn677ugy

ICMA. 2005. *Performance management: when results matter.* Washington, DC: International City/County Management Association. Retrieved June 22, 2008 from http://www. icma.org/upload/bc/attach/{EDFADAF9-80BB-4BY-A711-4D86A2812527} PerfMeas_small.pdf

Inamdar, S. N., R. S. Kaplan, M. L. Helfrich-Jones, and R. Menitoff. 2000. The balance scorecard: a strategic management system for multi-sector collaboration and strategic management. *Quality Management in Health Care*, 8 (4): 21–39.

Ingraham, P. W., S. C. Selden, and D. P. Moynihan. 2000. People and performance: chal-lenges for the future of public service—the report from the Wye River conference. *Public Administration Review,* 60 (1): 54–60.

Intel. 2005. *Digital community deployments.* Retrieved March 25, 2007 from http://down-load.intel.com/business/bss/industry/government/digital-community-deployments. pdf

IPMA-HR. 2006. *Human resources transformation in public sector organizations.* Alexandria, VA: International Personnel Management Association for Human Resources.

ISB. 2006. *ISB enterprise architecture committee: mission, objectives, and goals.* Olympia, WA: Information Services Board. Retrieved May 24, 2006 from http://isb.wa.gov/committees/enterprise/mission.aspx

James, L. R., L.A. James, and D. K. Ashe.1990. The meaning of organizations: the role of cognition and values. In B. Schneider, ed., *Organizational climate and culture.* San Francisco: Jossey-Bass. 40–84.

James, W. 1909/1996. *A pluralistic universe.* Lincoln, NE: University of Nebraska Press.

Jick, T. D. 1991. Implementing change. In T. Jick, ed., *Managing Change,* Boston: Irwin, 1993.

Johnston, J. and G. Callender. 2000. Multiple perspectives on economic rationalism and the new managerialism: power and public interest? *Administrative Theory & Praxis.* 22 (3): 585–604.

Joyce, P. 1999. *Strategic management for public services.* London: Open University Press.

Julnes, P. de L. and M. Holzer. 2001. Promoting the utilization of performance measures in public organizations: an empirical study of factors affecting adoption and implementation. *Public Administration Review,* 61(6): 693–708.

Jurkiewicz, C. L. 2007. Louisiana's ethical culture and its effect on the administrative failures following Katrina. *Public Administration Review,* 67(December Supplement): 57–63.

Kahler, M. and D. Lake. 2003. *Governance in a global economy.* Princeton, NJ: Princeton University Press.

Kahn, M. and R. Swanborough. 1999. Information management, IT and government transformation: innovative approaches in the new South Africa. *Institute for Development Policy and Management Working Paper Series. Paper No. 8.* University of Manchester. Retrieved January 4, 2007 from http://unpan1.un.org/intradoc/groups/public/documents/NISPAcee/UNPANB015481.pdf

Kamensky, J. M., T. J. Burlin, and M. A. Abramson. 2004. Networks and partnerships: collaborating to achieve results no one can achieve alone. In J. M. Kamensky, T. J. Burlin, and M. A. Abramson, eds. *Collaboration: Using Networks and Partners.* Lanham, MD: Rowman & Littlefield: 3–20.

Kampden, J. H. K., S. V. Walle and G. Bouckaert. 2006. Assessing the relation between satisfaction with public service delivery and trust in government: the impact of the predisposition of citizens toward government on evaluations of its performance. *Public Performance and Management Review,* 29(4): 387–404.

Kang, Y. C. 2005. Strategic management in the public sector: major publications. *Public Performance and Management Review,* 29 (1): 85–92.

Kanter, R., B. Stein, and T. Jick. 1992. *The challenge of organizational change: how companies experience it and leaders guide it.* New York: The Free Press.

Kaplan, R. S. and D. P. Norton. 1992. The Balanced Scorecard—measures that drive performance. *Harvard Business Review,* 73 (1): 75–85.

Kaplan, R. S. and D. P. Norton. 1995. Using the balance scorecard as a strategic management system. *Harvard Business Review,* 70 (1): 71–79.

Kaplan, R. S. and D. P. Norton. 2000. Having trouble with your strategy? Then map it. *Harvard Business Review,* 78 (5): 167–176.

Kearney, A. T. 2007. *Shared services in government.* Whitepaper retrieved December 2, 2007 from www.atkearney.com/shared_res/pdf/Govt_Share_Services-S.pdf

Kearney, R. C. and E. M. Berman. 1999. Introduction. In R. C. Kearney and E. M. Berman, eds, *Public Sector Performance.* Boulder, CO: Westview Press: 1–5.

Keeton, K.B. and B. Mengistu. 1992. The perception of organizational culture by management level: implications for training and development. *Public Productivity and Management Review* 16 (2): 205–213.

Keim, G. 2001. Business and public policy: competing in the political marketplace. In M. A. Hitt, R. E. Freeman and J. S. Harrison, eds., *Handbook of strategic management*. Malden, MA: Blackwell: 283–601.

Kelman, S. 2005. Unleashing change: A study of organizational renewal in government. Washington, DC: Brookings Institution Press.

Keneoane, R. O. and J. Nye. 2000. Governance. In R. O. Keohane and J. D. Donahue, eds., *Governance in a globalizing world*. Washington, DC: Brookings Institution Press. 12. Cited in D. F. Kettl. 2002. *The Transformation of Governance:*119.

Kennedy, S. S. 2006. Holding 'governance' accountable. *The Independent Review,* 11 (1): 67–77.

Kerka, S. 1997. Distance learning, the Internet, and the World Wide Web. *Eric Digest*. Retrieved January 28, 2006 from www.ericdigests.org/1997-1/distance.html

Kesner, I. F. 2001. The strategic management course: tools and techniques for successful teaching. In M. A. Hitt, R. E. Freeman, and J. S. Harrison, eds., *The Blackwell handbook of strategic management*. Malden, MA: Blackwell: 671–696.

Kets de Vries, M. F. R. and K. Balazs. 1999. Transforming the mind-set of the organization: a clinical perspective. *Administration and Society.* 30 (6): 640–675.

Kettl, D. F. 2006. Managing boundaries in American administration: the collaboration imperative. *Public Administration Review,* 66(December Supplement): 10–19.

Kettl, D. F. 2005. *The global public management revolution*. Washington, DC: Brookings Institution Press.

Kettl, D. F. 2002. *The Transformation of Governance*. Baltimore: Johns Hopkins University Press.

Keup, J. R., A. A. Walker, H. S. Astin, and J. A. Lindholm. 2001. Organizational culture and institutional transformation. Washington, DC: ERIC Clearinghouse on Higher Education. Report No. ED464521. Retrieved November 19, 2007, from www.ericdigests.org/2003-1/culture.htm

Kiel, L. D. 1994. *Managing chaos and complexity in government*. San Francisco: Jossey-Bass

Kim, S. 2002. Participative management and job satisfaction: lessons for management leadership. *Public Administration Review,* 62 (2): 231–241.

Kim, S. K. M., J. Halligan, N. Cho, C. H. Oh, and S. M. Eikenberry. 2005. Toward participatory and transparent governance: report on the sixth global form on reinventing government. *Public Administration Review,* 65(6): 646–654.

Kim, S. and H. Lee. 2006. The impact of organizational context and information technology on employee knowledge-sharing capabilities. *Public Administration Review,* 66(3): 370–385.

King, C. S., K. M. Feltey, and B. Susel. 1998. The question of participation: toward authentic public participation in public administration. *Public Administration Review,* 58(4): 317–326.

Koontz, T. M., T. A. Steelman, J. Carmin, K. S. Korfmacher, C. Moseley, and C. W. Thomas. 2004. *Collaborative environmental management: what roles for government?* Washington, DC: Resources for the Future.

Kotter, J. P. and L. A. Schesinger. 1979. Choosing strategies for change. *Harvard Business Review,* 57 (2): 106–114.

Kotter, J. P. 1996. *Leading change*. Cambridge, MA: Harvard Business School Press.

Kotter, J. P. 2007. Leading change: why transformation efforts fail. *Harvard Business Review,* 57 (1): 106–114.

Klickert, W. J. M., E. H. Klijn, and J. F. M. Koppenjan, eds. 1997. *Managing complex networks strategies for the public sector.* 1997. London: Sage.

KPMG. 2000. *Attitudes to e-learning: a national survey.* London: Campaign for Learning.

Lane, Jan-Erik. 2000. *New public management.* London: Routledge.

Lanvin, B. 2003. Transforming government through e-government projects. *I-Ways: Digest of Electronic Commerce Policy and Regulation,* 26 (2003): 23–37.

Lashgari, Malek. 2004. Corporate governance: theory and practice. *Journal of American Academy of Business.* 5 (September): 46–51.

Lau, C. M., L. M. Kilbourne, and R. M. Woodman. 2003. A shared schema approach to understanding organizational culture changes. In W. A. Pasmore and R. W. Woodman, eds,. *Research in organizational change and development,* Vol. 14. Amsterdam: JAI (Elsevier Science): 225–256.

Laudon, K. C. and J. P. Laudon. 2006. *Management information systems,* 9th ed. Upper Saddle River, NJ: Pearson Prentice Hall.

Lawler. E. E., D. A. Nadler, and C. Camman, 1980. *Organizational assessment.* New York: Wiley.

Lawther, W. C. 2002. *Subcontracting for the 21ˢᵗ century: a partnership model.* Washington, DC: IBM Endowment for the Business of Government.

Lee, G. and J. L. Perry. 2002. Are computers boosting productivity? A test of the paradox in state governments. *Journal of Public Administration Research and Theory,* 12(1): 77–102.

Lee, S. M. 1971. An empirical analysis of organizational identification. *Academy of Management Journal,* 14 (2): 213–226.

Leganza, G.. 2005. Making the case for enterprise architecture. *PublicCIO* (On-line version). November 8. Retrieved May 20, 2006 from www.public-cio.com/story.print.php?id=97210

Lenkowsky, L. and J. L. Perry. 2000. Reinventing government: the case of national service. *Public Administration Review,* 60(4): 298–307.

Lester, W. and D. Krejci. 2007. Business 'not' a usual: the national incident management system, federalism and leadership. *Public Administration Review,* 67(December Supplement): 84–93.

Levin, S. B. 2007. The 5 keys to successful shared services. Trenton: New Jersey State league of Municipalities. Article reprinted from February 2007 edition of *New Jersey Municipalities.* Retrieved December 2, 2007 from www.njslom.org.magart0207_p12.html

Levine, C. H. 1988. Police management in the 1980s: from decrementalism to strategic thinking. In K. S. Cameron, R. I. Suton and D. A. Whetten, eds., *Readings in Organizational Decline.* Cambridge, MA: Ballinger: 333–345.

Lewin, K. 1951. *Field theory in social science.* New York: Harper Brothers.

Lewis, P. S., S. H. Goodman, and P. M. Fandt. 2001. *Management challenges in the 21st century,* 3rd ed. Cincinnati, OH: South-Western.

Light, P. C. 2006. The tides of reform revisited: patterns in making government work. *Public Administration Review,* 66 (1): 6–18.

Litwin, G. H., and R. A. Stringer, Jr. 1968. *Motivation and Organizational Climate.* Boston: Harvard University.

Lutril, C. L. and A. K. Settle. 1992. *American public administration: concepts and cases,* 4th ed. St. Paul, MN: West Publishing Co.

Madden, J. 2000. All eyes on $1B outsourcing deal. *PC Week,* 16 (2): 14.

Mandell, M. P., ed. 2001. *Getting results through collaboration: networks and network structures for public policy and management.* Wesport, CT: Quorum Books.

Mandersheid, R. W. 2005. Information technology can drive transformation. *The Public Manager,* 33 (3): 3–6.

Manganelli, R. L. and M.M. Klein. 1994. *Handbook of implementing reengineering.* New York: AMACOM.

Martin, J. 2002. *Organizational culture: mapping the terrain.* Thousand Oaks, CA: Sage.

Marvel, M. K. and H. P. Marvel. 2007. 2007. Outsourcing oversight: a comparison of monitoring for in-house and contracted services. *Public Administration Review,* 67(3): 521–530.

Mathaisel, D. F. X. and C. L. Comm. 2004. Sustaining public sector enterprises: educating a lean transformation. Paper presented at the 2004 Hawaii International Conference on Business (June). Retrieved March 10, 2007 from http://faulty.babson.edu.mathaisel/ Pubs/LEA%20Sustaining&20Public%20Sector%30Hawaii%202004.pps

Mazouz, B. and B. Tremblay. 2006. Toward a postbureaucratic model of governance: how institutional commitment is challenging Quebec's administration. *Public Administration Review,* 66(2): 263–273.

McCue, C. P. and G. A. Gianakis. 1997. The relationship between job satisfaction and performance: the case of local government finance officers in Ohio. *Public Productivity and Management Review.* 21 (2): 170–191.

McElroy, M. W. 2003. *The new knowledge management.* Amsterdam: Butterworth-Heinemann.

McGrossan, T. 2007. Public sector revisits outsourcing hotbutton. *Government Procurement,* 15(1): 16–17.

McKinnon, C. 2005. Challenges facing the public sector. *KMWorld-Best Practices in Government Supplement,* 14(6): S3–S4.

McNabb, D. E. 2005. *Public utilities: management challenges for the 21st century.* Armonk, NY: Edward Elgar.

McNabb, D. E. 2007. Knowledge management in the public sector. Armonk, NY: M. E. Sharpe.

McNabb, D. E. and J. T. Barnowe. 2006. Integrating knowledge management into public administration: public sector enterprise architecture initiatives. Paper presented at the 5th Global Conference on Business & Economics, 6–10 July 2006, Cambridge University, Cambridge, UK.

McNabb, D. E., L. K. Gibson, and B. W. Finnie. 2006. The case of the vanishing workforce. *Public Performance and Management Review,* 29(3): 358–368.

McNabb, D. E. and F. T. Sepic. 1995. Culture, climate and total quality management: measuring readiness for change. *Public Productivity and Management Review,* 18 (4): 369–385.

McNabb, D. E. and F. T. Sepic. 2000. When bigger isn't necessarily better: how failure to address the human component results in organizational disequilibrium. Paper presented at the 29th annual Western Decision Sciences Institute Conference (April).

McNabb, D. E. and F. T. Sepic. 2001. Diagnosing disequilibrium in a public agency. Paper presented at the Second Latvian Scientific Congress, Riga, Latvia.

McNabb, D. E., F. T. Sepic, J. T. Barnowe, and M. Simpson. 1997. A re-evaluation of the effects of organizational climate upon productivity in public organizations. Paper presented at the 26th annual Western Decision Sciences Institute conference.

Melkers, J. and K. Willoughby. 2005. Models of performance-measurement use in local governments: understanding budgeting, communication, and lasting effects. *Public Administration Review,* 65 (2): 180–190.

Meyer, J. P. and Allen, N. J. 1997. *Commitment in the workplace: theory, research and application.* Thousand Oaks, CA: Sage.

Mihm, J. C. 2002. *Managing for results: next steps to improve the federal government's management and performance.* Testimony before the House Subcommittee on Government Efficiency, Financial Management, and Intergovernmental Relations. Document GAO-02-439T. Washington, DC: General Accounting Office.

Mihm, J. C. 2007. *Human capital: federal workforce challenges in the 21st century.* Testimony before the House Subcommittee on Financial Services and General Government, Committee on Appropriations, House of Representatives. Document GAO-07-556T. Washington, DC: General Accounting Office.

Miles, R. H. 1997. *Leading corporate transformation.* San Francisco: Jossey-Bass.

Millstone, E, and P. van Zwanenberg. 2000. A crisis of trust: for science, scientists, or institutions? *Nature Medicine* 6(12). Retrieved January 9 from www.nature.com/nm/journal/v6/n12/full/nm1200_1307.html

Moon, M. J. 2000. Organizational commitment revisited in new public management: motivation, organizational culture, and managerial level. *Public Performance and Management Review,* 24 (2): 177–194.

Moore, A. 2005. What makes government different? *KM World—Best Practices in Government Supplement,* 14 (6): S2.

Moore, M. H. 1995. *Creating public value: strategic management in government.* Cambridge, MA: Harvard University.

Morris, J. C., E. D. Morris, and D. M. Jones. 2007. Reaching for the philosopher's stone: contingent coordination and the military's response to Hurricane Katrina. *Public Administration Review,* 67(December Supplement): 94–106.

Mowday, R. T., R. M. Steers, and L. W. Porter. 1979. The measurement of organizational commitment. *Journal of Vocational Behavior,* 14: 224–247.

Moynihan, D. P. 2005. Goal-based learning and the future of performance management. *Public Administration Review,* 65 (2): 203–216.

Moynihan, D. P. 2006. Managing for results in state government: evaluating a decade of reform. *Public Administration Review,* 66(1): 77–89.

M3 Planning. 2006. *Mission statements: defining your mission.* Retrieved December 38, 2006 from http://mystrategicplan.com/strategic-planiing-topics/mission-statements.shtml

MTA. 2007. *Mission and vision statements.* Michigan Townships Association. Retrieved October 6, 2007 from www.michigantownships.org/mission.asp

Nadler, D. M., J. R. Hackman and E. E. Lawler III. 1979. *Managing organizational behavior.* Boston: Little, Brown.

Nadler, D. M., R. B. Shaw, and A. E. Walton. 1995. *Discontinuous change.* San Francisco: Jossey-Bass.

NASA. 1998. Office of the chief information officer internal memo: president's information technology advisory committee, amendments to executive order 13035. (February 11, 1997). Retrieved February 23, 2007 from http://nodis3.gsfc.nasa.gov/displayEO.cfm?id=13092

NASCIO. 2006a. Keys to collaboration: building effective public-private partnerships. Transforming government: role of information technology. Lexington, KY: National Association of State Chief Information Officers (May) Issue Brief. Retrieved March 30, 2007 from http://nascio.org/publications/documents/NASCIO-Key%20to%20Collaboration.pdf

NASCIO. 2006b. *2006 compendium of NASCIO recognition awards for outstanding achievement in the field of information technology.* Lexington, KY: National Association of State Chief Information Officers (December). Retrieved March 30, 2007 from http://nascio/org/publications/documents/NASCIO-2006RecognitionAwardsCompendium.pdf

NASCIO. 2006c. *IT consolidation and shared services: states seeking economies of scale.* Lexington, KY: National Association of State Chief Information Officers (March) Issue Brief. Retrieved December 2, 2007 from www.nascio.org/publications/documents/NASCIO-Con_and_SS_Issue_Brief_0303.pdf

NASCIO. 2006d. *NASCIO's survey on IT consolidation and shared services in the states.* Lexington, KY: National Association of State Chief Information Officers (May) Issue Brief. Retrieved December 3, 2007 from http://www.nascio.org/publications/documents/NASCIO-ITConsolidationMay2006.pdf

NASCIO. 2007a. *Transforming government through change management: the role of the State CIO.* Lexington, KY: *National Association of State Chief Information Officers.* Retrieved November 14, 2007 from http://nascio/org/publications/documents/NASCIO-Transforming%20Goft-Research%20Brief.pdf

NASCIO. 2007b. Harmony helps: a progress report on state government Internet presence. *Field of Information Technology.* Lexington, KY: *National Association of State Chief Information Officers* (December) *Issue Brief.* Retrieved March 30, 2007 from http://nascio/org/publications/documents/NASCIO-HarmonyHelps.pdf

NASCIO. 2007c. *Building better government through enterprise architecture.* Lexington, KY: *National Association of State Chief Information Officers.* Retrieved March 30, 2007 from http://nascio/org/publications/documents/NASCIO-EABrochure.pdf

Nathan, R. P. 1995. Reinventing government: what does it mean? *Public Administration Review,* 55 (2): 213–215.

National Research Council. 1999. *The changing nature of work.* Washington, DC: National Academy Press.

National Research Council. 2002. *Information technology research, innovation, and e-government.* Washington, DC: National Academy Press.

Nicolav, J. A. 2002. The wagging tail of technology. *Public Administration Quarterly.* 26(1): 65–88.

Nonaka, I. and H. Takenchi. 1995. *The knowledge creating company: how Japanese companies create the dynamics of innovation.* Oxford: Oxford University Press.

Norris, D. F. and M. J. Moon. 2005. Advancing e-government at the grassroots: tortoise or hare? *Public Administration Review,* 65(1): 64–75.

Nosmokingday.org.uk. 2006. *National objectives.* Retrieved December 31, 2006 from www.nosmokingday.org.uk/corporate/objectives.htm

NPRG. 1999. *Balancing measures: best practices in performance management.* Washington, DC: National Partnership for Reinventing Government (formerly the National Performance Review). Retrieved June 22, 2008 from http://govinfo.library.unt.edu/npr/library/papers/bkgrd/balmeasure.htm.

Nye, J. Jr. and J. Donahue, eds. 2000. *Governance in a globalizing world.* Washington, DC: Brookings Institution.

NZSSC. 2006. *Enabling transformation: a strategy for e-government.* Wellington, NZ: State Services Commission. Retrieved November 27, 2007 from http://www.e.gov.nz/about_egovt/strategy/strategy-nov-06.pdf

OGC. 2007. *Business process improvement: 10 exemplars from local government.* UK Office of Government Commerce, Office of the Treasury. Retrieved November 28, 2007 from www.ogc.gov.uk/documents/DCLG_Local_Authority_Exemplars.pdf

O'Keefe, S. 2007. Looking back, moving forward. 2007. *Public Administration Review,* 67(December Supplement): 5–21.

OMB. 1998. *Federal activities: inventory reform act of 1998.* Public Law 105-270. Washington, DC: Office of Management and Budget. Retrieved December 6, 2007 from www.whitehouse.gov/omb/procurement/fairact.html

OMB. 2002. *The president's management agenda.* Washington, DC: Office of Management and Budget. Retrieved May 20, 2005 from www.whitehouse.gov/omb/budget/fy2002/mgmt.pdf

OMB. 2003. *Circular No. A-76: revised.* May 29. Washington, DC: Office of Management and Budget. Retrieved December 3, 2007 from www.whitehouse.gov/omb/circulars/a076/a076-incl_tech_correction.html

OMB. 2004. *Expanding e-government: partnering for a results-oriented government,* (December). Washington, DC: Office of Management and Budget. Retrieved December 6, 2007 from http://www.whitehouse.gov/omb/budintegration/expanding_egov12-2004.pdf

OMB. 2005a. *Expanding e-government: improved service delivery for the American people using information technology.* Washington, DC: Office of Management and Budget (December). Retrieved May 18, 2005 from http://www.whitehouse.gov/omb/budintegration/expanding_egov_2005.pdf

OMB. 2005b. *Presidential initiatives: e-training.* Washington, DC: Office of Management and Budget (December). Retrieved May 24, 2005 from www.whitehouse.gov/omb/egov/c-4-1-eTraining.html

OMB. 2005c. *FY07 budget formulation FEA consolidated reference model document.* Washington, DC: Office of Management and Budget (May). Retrieved December 6, 2007 from http:// www.whitehouse.gov/omb/egov/documents/CRM.pdf

OMB. 2006a. *E-Gov: Federal enterprise architecture.* Washington, DC: Office of Management and Budget (December). Retrieved May 21, 2005 from www.whitehouse.gov/omb/egov/a-1-fea.html

OMB. 2007. *FY 2006 report to Congress on implementation of the e-government act of 2002* (March 1). Washington, DC: Office of Management and Budget Retrieved December 6, 2007 from http://www.whitehouse.gov/omb/inforeg/reports/2006_egov_report.pdf

OPM. 2005. *HCAAF practitioner's guide: forward* and *introduction.* Washington, DC: Office of Personnel Management. Retrieved November 17, 2007, from www.opm.gob/hcaaf_resource_center/assets/HCAAF_O_Forward.pdf and www.opm.gob/hcaaf_resource_center/assets/HCAAF_O_Introduction.pdf

OPM. 2006. *E-gov: e-learning overview.* Washington, DC: Office of Personnel Management. Retrieved May 24, 2006 from www.opm.gov/wgov/training_overview.asp

O'Reilly, C., and J. Chatman. 1986. Organizational commitment and psychological attachment: the effects of compliance, identification and internalization on prosocial behavior. *Journal of Applied Psychology,* 71 (3): 492–499.

Orilkowski, W. J. and S. R. Barley. 2001. Technology and institutions: what can research on information technology and research on organizations learn from each other? *MIS Quarterly,* 25 (2): 145–65.

Osborne D. and P. Plastrik. 1991. *Banishing bureaucracy.* Reading, MA: Addison-Wesley.

Osterweil, L. J., L. I. Millet, and J. D. Winston, eds. 2007. *Social security administration electronic service provision: a strategic assessment.* Washington, DC: Committee on the Social Security Administration's E-Government Strategy and Planning for the Future, National Research Council. Retrieved November 19, 2007 from www.nap.edu/catalog/11920.html

Page, S. 2004. Measuring accountability for results in interagency collaboratives. *Public Administration Review,* 64 (5): 591–606.

Page, S. 2005. What's new about the New Public Management? Administrative change in the human services. *Public Administration Review,* 65 (6): 713–727.

Painter, M. 2005. Transforming the administrative state: reform in Hong Kong and the future of the developmental state. *Public Administration Review,* 65 (3): 335–346.

Pattakos, A. N. 2004. The search for meaning in government service. *Public Administration Review,* 64 (1): 106–112.

Peaucelle, I. 2007. The hospital industry: the consequences of the reforms in Eastern Germany. *Journal of Economic Issues.* 16 (2): 443–450.

Perry, J. L. D., Mesch, and L. Paarlberg. 2006. Motivating employees in a new governance era: the performance paradigm revisited. *Public Administration Review,* 66(4): 505–514.

Peters, T. and R. Waterman. 1982. *In search of excellence.* New York: Harper and Row.

Pettigrew, A. M. 1990. Organizational climate: two constructs in search of a role. In B. Schneider, ed., *Organizational Climate and Culture.* San Francisco: Jossey-Bass: 413–423.

Pettigrew, A., H.Thomas, and R. Whittington, eds. 2002. *Handbook of strategy and management.* Thousand Oaks, CA: Sage.

Piccolo, R. and J. A. Colquitt. 2006. Transformational leadership and job behaviors: the mediating role of core job characteristics. *Academy of Management Journal,* 49 (2): 327–340.

PITAC. 1999. *Information technology research: investing in our future.* Arlington, VA: National Coordination Office for Computing, Information, and Communications.

Poister, T. H. and G. D. Streib. 1999. Strategic management in the public sector. *Public Productivity and Management Review,* 22 (3): 308–325

Poister, T. H. and G. D. Streib. 2005. Elements of strategic planning and management in municipal government: status after two decades. *Public Administration Review,* 65(1): 45–56.

Poister, T. H. and D.M. Van Slyke. 2002. Strategic innovations in state transportation departments. *Public Performance and Management Review,* 26 (1): 58–74.

Porter, L. W., W. J. Crampon, and F. J. Smith. 1976. Organizational commitment and managerial turnover: a longitudinal study. *Organizational Behavior and Human Performance.* 15 (February): 87–98.

PPS. 2005. *Federal brain drain. Partnership for public service brief PPS-05-08.* Retrieved February 24, 2007 from www.ourpublicservice.org/hsr_doc/PPS-05-08

Prigogine, I. 1989. The philosophy of instability. *Futures,* 21: 396–400.

Provan, K. G., M. A. Veazie, L. K. Staten, and N. I. Teufel-Shone. 2005. The use of network analysis to strengthen community partnerships. *Public Administration Review,* 65 (5): 603–613.

Pulliam, D. 2007. Administration calls for boost in technology spending. *Govexec.com Daily Briefing,* (February 7). Retrieved April 24, 2007 from www.govexec.com/story_page.c fm?articleid=30494&printfriendlyVers

Puran, A., and M. Ngoyi, M. 2000. How to achieve performance improvement: A symposium introduction. *Public Performance and Management Review,* 24 (2): 117–120.

Qiao, Y. and K. V.Thai. 2002, Reinventing government at the federal level: the implementations and the prospects. *Public Administration Quarterly,* 26 (1): 89–116

Quirk, M. 2004. Private military contractors. *Atlantic Monthly,* 294 (2): 39.

Rainey, H. G. and J. Thompson. 2006. Leadership and the transformation of a major institution: Charles Rossotti and the Internal Revenue Service. *Public Administration Review,* 66(4): 596–604.

Raphael, D. D. 1990. *Problems of political philosophy.* Atlantic Highlands, NJ: Humanities Press International.

REconsulting. 2006. *Ready to transform? A snapshot of local government business process improvement.* Retrieved November 28, 2007 from www.resconsulting.co.uk/PDF/BPI%20local%20government%20Survey%20results.pdf

Rhodes, R. A. W. 1997. *Understanding governance: policy networks, governance, reflexivity, and accountability.* Buckingham, UK: Open University Press.

Robb, K. 2004. Agency software systems face hurdles: ERP systems difficult to adopt. *Federal Times* (July 19). Retrieved April 19, 2007 from www.federaltimes.com/index.php?S=260839

Robbins, M. D., B. Simonsen and B. Feldman. 2008. Citizens and resource allocation: improving decision making with interactive Web-based citizen participation. *Public Administration Review*, 68(3): 564–575.

Robinson, K. 1999. *Work transformation: planning and implementing the new workplace.* New York: HNB Publishing.

Rosenberg, M. J. 2001. *E-learning: strategies for delivering knowledge in the digital age.* New York: McGraw-Hill.

Rosenberg, M. J. 2006. *Beyond e-learning: approaches and technologies to enhance organizational knowledge, learning and performance.* San Francisco: Pfeiffer/Wiley.

Rosenbleeth, M., C. DeCamp and S. Chen. 2007. The coming enterprise software shakeup. *Strategy+Business* (online). Retrieved March 13, 2007 from http://www.strategy-business.com/media/file/resilience=04-13-06.pdf

Ross, J. W., P. Weill, and D. C. Robertson. 2006. *Enterprise architecture as strategy.* Cambridge: Harvard Business School Press.

Rouse, W. B. 2005. A theory of enterprise transformation. *Systems Engineering*, 8 (4): 279–295.

Rouse, W. B., ed. 2006. *Enterprise transformation: understanding and enabling fundamental change.* Hoboken, NJ: John Wiley.

Rouse, W. B. and M. L. Baba. 2006. Enterprise transformation. *Communications of the ACM*, 49 (7): 67–72.

Ruby, D. 2004. Erecting the Framework, Part I. *FTP Online* (February 19). Retrieved May 21, 2006 from www.ftponline.com/ea/magazine/spring/online/druby/default_pf.aspx

Schank, R. C. 2002. *Designing world-class e-learning.* New York: McGraw-Hill.

Schein, E. H. 1990. *Organizational culture and leadership.* San Francisco: Jossey-Bass Publishers.

Schneider, S. K. 2005. Administrative breakdowns in the governmental response to hurricane Katrina. *Public Administration Review*, 65 (5): 515–516.

Scholz, J. T. and C. L. Wang. 2006. Cooption or transformation? Local policy networks and federal regulatory enforcement. *American Journal of Political Science*, 50(1): 81–97.

Seddon, C. 1999. Partnering: the UK experience. *International Law FORUM du droit international*, 1(2): 73–76.

Senge, P. 1995. *The fifth discipline: the art and practice of the learning organization.* New York: Doubleday.

Sepic, F. T. and D. E. McNabb. 2004. Revitalizing public service: transforming disequilibrium into a force for change. Paper presented at the 2005 International Association of Management and Business Conference (November), Las Vegas, NV.

Sepic, F. T., J. T Barnowe, M C. Simpson, and D E. McNabb, 1998. Assessment of organizational climate and commitment: first steps toward organizational transformation. Paper presented at the 27th annual meeting of the Western Decision Sciences Institute. Reno, NV.

Sharma, R. K. 2003. Understanding organizational learning through knowledge management. *Journal of Information and Knowledge Management*, 2 (4): 343–352.

Shea, R. 2005. The President's management agenda delivers. *The Public Manager,* 33 (2): 7–8.

Shin, S. J. and J. Zhou. 2003. Transformational leadership, conservation, and creativity: Evidence from Korea. *Academy of Management Journal,* 48 (6): 703–714.

Siggerud, K. 2007. *U.S. postal service: postal reform law provides opportunities to address postal challenges.* Testimony before the Subcommittee on Federal Workforce, Postal Service, and the District of Columbia, House of Representatives Committee on Oversight and Government Reform. GAO Report 07-684T. Washington, DC: General Accountability Office.

Simo, G. and A. L. Bies. 2007. The role of nonprofits in disaster response: an expanded model of cross-sector collaboration. *Public Administration Review,* 67(December Supplement): 125–142.

Skweyiya, Z. 1997. *White paper on transforming service delivery.* South Africa. Retrieved October 10, 2008 from http://unpan1.un.org/intradoc/groups/public/documents/un/unpan005184.pdf

Slavin, A. M. and J. B. Woodard. 2006. *Enterprise transformation: lessons learned, pathways to success.* Albuquerque, NM: Sandia National Laboratories report SAND2006-2228. Retrieved March 10, 2007 from www.prod.sandia.gov/cgi-bin/techlib/access-control.pl/2006/062228.pdf

Sloman, M. and J. Rolph. 2003. *The change agenda: e-learning.* London: Chartered Institute of Personnel and Development.

Smelzer, L. R. 1991. An analysis for announcing organization-wide change. *Group and Organization Studies,* 16 (1): 5–24.

Smith, K. B. and M. J. Licari. 2006. *Public administration: power and politics in the fourth branch of government.* Oxford: Oxford University Press.

Smith, L. D., J. F. Campbell, A. Subramanian, D. A. Bird, and A. C. Nelson. 2000. "Strategic planning for municipal information systems: some lessons from a large city." *American Review of Public Administration,* 31(2): 139–175.

Smith, P. A. C. 1998. Systematic knowledge management: managing organizational assets for competitive advantage. *Journal of Systematic Knowledge Management.* 1(4). Np. Retrieved November 3, 2007 from www.tlainc.com/article8.htm

Smith, S. R. and M. R. Sosin. 2001. The varieties of faith-related agencies. *Public Administration Review,* 61(6): 651–670.

Smith, S. R. 2003. Government and nonprofits in the modern age. *Society,* 4 (4): 36–45.

Smither, R. D., J. M. Houston, and S. D. McIntire. 1996. *Organization development: strategies for changing environments.* New York: Harper-Collins

SSI. 2007. *Shared services initiative.* Brisbane, AU: Shared Service Initiative Policy and Program Office. Retrieved November 30, 2007 from www.sharedservices.qld.gov.au

State of Illinois. 2007. *State of Illinois shared services program.* Retrieved November 30, 2007 from www.sharedservices.illinois.gov/currentefforts.htm

State of Washington. 2002. *Executive order 02-03: sustainable practices by state agencies.* Retrieved December 31, 2006 from www.governor.wa.gov/execorders/eoarcgive/eo_02-03.htm

State Services Commission of New Zealand. 2006. Enabling transformation: a strategy for e-government 2006. Retrieved November 27, 2008 from www.e-gov.nz/about_egovt/strategy/strategy-nov-06.pdf

Steinhaus, C. S. and J. L. Perry. 1996. Organizational commitment: does sector matter? *Public Productivity and Management Review,* 19 (3): 278–288.

Sternstein, H. 2006. *Designing and teaching an online course.* Boston: Allyn and Bacon.

Stewart, F. M and R. M. Ketcham. 1941. Intergovernmental contracts in California. *Public Administration Review,* 1(3): 242–248.

Stivers, C. 2007. 'So poor and so Black.' Hurricane Katrina, public administration, and the issue of race. *Public Administration Review,* 67(December Supplement): 48–56.

Streib, G. 1992. Applying strategic decision making in local government. *Public Productivity & Management Review,* 15 (3): 341–354.

Styles, A. B. 2003. Testimony before the committee on government reform, U.S. house of representatives. June 26. Office of Management and Budget. Retrieved December 3, 2007 from www.whitehouse.gov/omb/legislative/testimony/styles062603.html

Taffinder, P. 1998. *Big change.* Chichester, UK: John Wiley & Sons.

TBS. 2005. Shared services—frequently asked questions. Treasury Board of Canada Secretariat. Retrieved November 30, 2007 from www.tbs-sct.gc.ca/spsm-rgsp/qa-qr_e.asp

Thompson, J. R. 2000. The reinvention laboratories: strategic change by indirection. *American Review of Public Administration,* 30(1): 46–68.

Thompson, J. R. 2006. The federal civil service: the demise of an institution. *Public Administration Review,* 66(4): 496–504.

Thompson, K. R. and F. Luthans. 1990. Organizational culture: a behavioral perspective. In Benjamin Schneider, ed., *Organizational Climate and Culture,* San Francisco: Jossey-Bass. 319–344.

Teisman, G. R. and E. H. Klijn. 2002. Partnership arrangements: governmental rhetoric or governance scheme? *Public Administration Review,* 62(2): 197–205.

Timney, M. M. and T. P. Kelly. 2000. New public management and the demise of popular sovereignty. *Administrative Theory & Praxis.* 22 (3): 555–5691.

Tiwana, A. 2002. *The knowledge management toolkit,* 2nd ed. Upper Saddle River, NJ: Prentice Hall.

Tolbert, C. J., K. Mossberger, and R. McNeal. 2008. Institutions, policy innovation and e-government in the American states. *Public Administration Review,* 68(3): 549–563.

Tonichia, S. and A. Tramontano. 2004. *Process management for the extended enterprise.* Berlin: Springer.

Tsoukas, H. and R. Chia. 2002. On organizational becoming: rethinking organizational change. *Organizational Science,* 13 (5): 567–582.

UK Cabinet Office. 2005. *Transformational government.* London: UK Cabinet Office. Retrieved November 17, 2007 from http://cio.gov.uk/documents/pdf/transgov/transgov-strategy.pdf

USALearn 2005. *USALearning: about USALearning.* Retrieved May 21, 2006 from www.usalearning.gov/USALearning/index.cfm?room=about&roomaction=about

USCO. 2004 *Human capital management plan 2004-2008.* Washington, DC: United States Copyright Office, Library of Congress. Accessed November 18, 2007 from www.copyright.gov/reports/humancal2004-2008.pdf

Vasu, M. L., D. W. Stewart and G. D. Garson.1998. *Organizational behavior and public management.* New York: Marcel Becker.

Ventriss, C. 2000. New public management: an examination of its influence on contemporary public affairs and its impact on shaping the intellectual agenda of the field. *Administrative Theory & Praxis.* 22 (3): 500–518.

Vigoda, E. and R. T. Golembiewski. 2001. Citizen behavior and the spirit of new managerialsim: a theoretical framework and challenge for governance. *American Review of Public Administration,* 31(3): 273–295.

Von Heerden, I. L. 2007. The failure of the New Orleans levy system following hurricane Katrina and the pathway forward. *Public Administration Review,* 67(December Supplement): 24–35.

Walker, D. M. 2002. *Managing for results: using strategic human capital management to drive transformational change.* Testimony before the National Commission on the Public Service (July 15). Washington, DC: General Accounting Office. Retrieved November 15, 2007 from www.eric.ed.glv/ERICDocs/data/ericdocs2sql/content_storage_01/0000019b/1a/4b/a7/pdf

Walker, D. M. 2005. *Management reform: assessing the president's management agenda.* Testimony before the Senate Subcommittee on Federal Financial Management, Government Information, and International Security. (April 21). Washington, DC: General Accounting Office. Retrieved November 15, 2007 from www.gao.gov/new/items/d05574t.pdf

Walker, D. M. 2007a. *Long-term budget outlook: saving our future requires tough choices today.* Testimony before the U.S. Senate Committee on the Budget, January 11, 2007. Washington, DC: General Accountability Office (GAO).

Walker, D. M. 2007b. *21st century transformation challenges.* Speech at the April 5, 2007 Excellence in Government Conference. Washington, DC: General Accountability Office Document GAO-07-74GC.

Walters, L. C., J. Aydelotte and J. Miller. 2000. Putting more public in policy analysis. *Public Administration Review,* 60(4): 349–359.

Walters, J. and C. Thompson. 2005. *The transformation of the government accountability office: using human capital to drive change.* Washington, DC: IBM Center for the Business of Government.

Ward, C. J. 2006. ERP: integrating and extending the enterprise. *The Public Manager,* 35 (1): 30–33.

Watkins, M. 2004. Electronic government forges new partnerships. *The Public Manager,* 33 (1): 13–18.

Watson, H. J. and T. A. Carte. 2000. Executive information systems in government organizations. *Public Productivity and Management Review,* 23 (3): 371–382.

Waugh, W. L. Jr. 2007. EMAC, Katrina, and the governors of Louisiana and Mississippi. *Public Administration Review,* 67(December Supplement): 107–113.

WDOA. 2006. Wisconsin retirement board budget recommendations and agency description. Wisconsin department of administration. Retrieved December 31, 2006 from www.doa.state.wi.us/debf/doc_view2.asp?budid=34

Weber, M. 1947. *The theory of social and economic organization* (translated by A. M. Henderson and T. Parsons), T. Parsons, ed. New York: Free Press.

Wechsler, B. and B. Clary. 2000. Implementing performance government. *Public Productivity and Management Review,* 23(3): 264–266.

Weigelt, M. 2006. Congress blamed for poor e-government performance. *Federal Computer Week,* 20 (15): 54–55.

Weisberg, J. 1996. *In defense of government: the fall and rise of public trust.* New York: Scribner.

White House. 2002. Homeland security council executive order. (March 21). White House Office of the Press Secretary. Retrieved February 22, 2007 from www.whitehouse.gov/news/releases/2002/02/print/20020321-9.html

White House. 2007. E-gov: federal enterprise architecture, business reference model (BRM). Retrieved January 17, 2007 from www.whitehouse.gov/omb/e-gov/a-3-brm.html

Wilhelm, W. 1992. Changing your corporate culture--or corporate behavior? How to change your company. *Academy of Management Executive,* 6 (4): 72–77.

Wilson, C. 2005. Tech companies launch digital communities initiative. *Telephonyonline.com* (August 18). Retrieved March 24, 2007 from http://telehonyonline.com/broadband/news/Intel_WiFi_cities_081805

Wilson, J. Q. 1989. *Bureaucracy: what government agencies do and how they do it.* New York: Basic Books.

Wilson, T. D. 2002. The nonsense of 'knowledge management.' *Information Research*, 8(1). Retrieved December 17, 29=008 from http://InformationR.not/ir/8-1/paper144.html

Wise, C. R. and R. Nader. 2002. Organizing the federal system for homeland security: problems, issues and dilemmas. *Public Administration Review,* 62(Special Issue): 44–57.

Wollner, G. E. 1992. The law of producing quality. *Quality Progress.* 28 (January): 35–40.

Wonacott, M. E. 2002. Implications of distance education for CTE. *Eric Digest.* Retrieved January 28, 2006 from www.ericdigests.org/2002-1/cte.html

Worral, Les, Chris Collinge, and Tony Bill. 1998. Managing strategy in local governments. *International Journal of Public Management,* 11 (6): 472–485.

Yang, K. and Callahan, K. 2005. Assessing citizen involvement efforts by local governments. *Public Performance and Management Review,* 29(2): 191–216.

Yang, K. and M. Holzer. 2006. The performance-trust link: implications for performance measurement. *Public Administration Review,* 66(1): 114–126.

Yang, K. and J. U. Hsieh. 2007. Managerial effectiveness of government performance measurement: a middle-range model. *Public Administration Review,* 67(5): 861–879.

Yang, S.-B. and M. E. Guy. 2006. Genxers versus boomers: work motivators and management implications. *Public Performance and Management Review,* 29(3): 267–284.

Young, K. 2004. E-commerce faces a crisis of trust. *IT Week,*(November 17, 2004). Retrieved January 9, 2007 from www.vnunet.com/articles/print/2086277

Zachman, J. 1987. Viewing and communicating information infrastructure: enterprise architecture (EA). Retrieved May 21, 2006 from www.valuebasedmanagment.net/methods_zachmanenterprise_architecture.html

Zagans, M. D. 1997. The dilemma of the modern public manager: satisfying the virtues of scientific and innovative management. In A. A. Altshuler and R.D. Behn, eds., *Innovation in American Government.* Washington, DC: The Brookings Institution. 104–118.

Zander, A. 1994. *Making groups effective*, 2nd ed. San Francisco: Jossey-Bass.

Zanetti, L. A. and G. A. Adams. 2000. In service of the Leviathan: democracy, ethics and the potential for administrative evil in the new public management. *Administrative Theory & Praxis.* 22 (3): 534–55.

Appendix A: Organizational Assessment Instrument

Assessment of Organizational Climate (3rd ed.)[*]

David E. McNabb, F. Thomas Sepic,
and J. Thad Barnowe

Pacific Lutheran University, Tacoma, WA 98447

INSTRUCTIONS: This survey instrument has several different parts. All are designed to help you to say how you see things where you work. Everyone has exactly the same questions, and everyone's complete privacy is absolutely guaranteed; no one questionnaire will ever be singled out for any purpose. Only the opinions of the entire organization are important. To answer each question, simply fill in or check the space that reflects your response in the space provided on the answer sheet. **Thank you for your participation!**

---

[*] Some repetition of items will be found in some scales. This is intentional; do not delete the repeated items.

Section 1. [STRUC]

		Very Definitely Describes ∇						Does Not Describe ∇
1.	The jobs in this organization are clearly defined and logically structured.	[7]	[6]	[5]	[4]	[3]	[2]	[1]
2.	In this organization it is sometimes unclear who has the formal authority to make a decision.	[1]	[2]	[3]	[4]	[5]	[6]	[7]
3.	The policies and structure of the organization have been clearly explained to me.	[7]	[6]	[5]	[4]	[3]	[2]	[1]
4.	Red tape is kept to a minimum in this organization.	[7]	[6]	[5]	[4]	[3]	[2]	[1]
5.	Excessive rules, administrative details, and red tape make it difficult for new and original ideas to receive consideration here.	[1]	[2]	[3]	[4]	[5]	[6]	[7]
6.	Our productivity sometimes suffers from lack of organization and planning.	[1]	[2]	[3]	[4]	[5]	[6]	[7]
7.	Our management isn't so concerned about formal organization and authority, but concentrates instead on getting the right people together to do the job.	[7]	[6]	[5]	[4]	[3]	[2]	[1]
8.	In some of the projects I've worked on, I haven't been sure exactly who my boss was.	[1]	[2]	[3]	[4]	[5]	[6]	[7]
9.	The goals of this organization are clearly defined and regularly reviewed.	[7]	[6]	[5]	[4]	[3]	[2]	[1]

10.	All managers and supervisors here have the opportunity to participate in setting goals and objectives.	[7]	[6]	[5]	[4]	[3]	[2]	[1]

Section 2.   [RESP]

		Very Definitely Describes ∇						*Does Not Describe* ∇
11.	We don't rely too heavily on individual judgment in this organization; almost everything is double-checked.	[1]	[2]	[3]	[4]	[5]	[6]	[7]
12.	Around here, management resents your checking everything with them; if you think you've got the right approach, you just go ahead.	[7]	[6]	[5]	[4]	[3]	[2]	[1]
13.	People from different cultures are given equal treatment here.	[7]	[6]	[5]	[4]	[3]	[2]	[1]
14.	Supervision in this organization is mainly a matter of setting guidelines for subordinates — letting them take responsibility for the job.	[7]	[6]	[5]	[4]	[3]	[2]	[1]
15.	Our organizational philosophy emphasizes that people should solve their problems by themselves.	[1]	[2]	[3]	[4]	[5]	[6]	[7]
16.	Managers here respect our abilities and skills.	[7]	[6]	[5]	[4]	[3]	[2]	[1]
17.	People here are treated like children; we do what we are told.	[1]	[2]	[3]	[4]	[5]	[6]	[7]

Section 3.   [RISK]

		Very Definitely Describes ▽						Does Not Describe ▽
18.	The philosophy of our management is that, in the long run, we get ahead fastest by playing it slow, safe, and sure.	[1]	[2]	[3]	[4]	[5]	[6]	[7]
19.	You get rewarded for taking risks in this organization.	[7]	[6]	[5]	[4]	[3]	[2]	[1]
20.	Decision making in this organization is too cautious for maximum effectiveness.	[1]	[2]	[3]	[4]	[5]	[6]	[7]
21.	You won't get ahead in this organization unless you stick your neck out and take a chance now and then.	[7]	[6]	[5]	[4]	[3]	[2]	[1]
22.	We do things by the book around here.	[1]	[2]	[3]	[4]	[5]	[6]	[7]
23.	We have to take some pretty big risks occasionally to make sure the organization meets its objectives.	[7]	[6]	[5]	[4]	[3]	[2]	[1]
24.	Taking risks is strongly discouraged in this organization.	[1]	[2]	[3]	[4]	[5]	[6]	[7]

Section 4.   [RWRD]

		Very Definitely Describes ▽						Does Not Describe ▽
25.	We have a promotion system here that helps the best person to rise to the top.	[7]	[6]	[5]	[4]	[3]	[2]	[1]
26.	In this organization the rewards and encouragement you get usually outweigh the threats and criticism.	[7]	[6]	[5]	[4]	[3]	[2]	[1]

27.	You get quite a lot of support and encouragement for trying something new in this organization.	[7]	[6]	[5]	[4]	[3]	[2]	[1]
28.	In this organization people are rewarded in proportion to the excellence of their job performance.	[7]	[6]	[5]	[4]	[3]	[2]	[1]
29.	There is not enough reward and recognition given in this organization for doing good work.	[1]	[2]	[3]	[4]	[5]	[6]	[7]
30.	A person doesn't get the credit he or she deserves for accomplishments in this organization.	[1]	[2]	[3]	[4]	[5]	[6]	[7]

Section 5.   [W&S]

		Very Definitely Describes ∇					Does Not Describe ∇	
31.	Mistakes in this organization just aren't tolerated.	[1]	[2]	[3]	[4]	[5]	[6]	[7]
32.	My supervisor is genuinely interested in helping me get ahead in this organization.	[7]	[6]	[5]	[4]	[3]	[2]	[1]
33.	There is a great deal of criticism in this organization.	[1]	[2]	[3]	[4]	[5]	[6]	[7]
34.	A very friendly atmosphere prevails among the people in this organization.	[7]	[6]	[5]	[4]	[3]	[2]	[1]
35.	You wouldn't get much sympathy from higher-ups in this organization if you make a mistake.	[1]	[2]	[3]	[4]	[5]	[6]	[7]
36.	This organization is characterized by a relaxed, easy-going working climate.	[7]	[6]	[5]	[4]	[3]	[2]	[1]

37.	You get quite a lot of support and encouragement for trying something new in this organization.	[7]	[6]	[5]	[4]	[3]	[2]	[1]
38.	People in this organization tend to be cool and aloof toward each other.	[1]	[2]	[3]	[4]	[5]	[6]	[7]
39.	The philosophy of our management emphasizes the human factor (how people feel, etc.)	[7]	[6]	[5]	[4]	[3]	[2]	[1]

Section 6. [CONF]

		Very Definitely Describes ∇					Does Not Describe ∇	
40.	A very friendly atmosphere prevails among the people here.	[7]	[6]	[5]	[4]	[3]	[2]	[1]
41.	The attitude of our management is that some conflict between competing units and individuals can be very healthy.	[7]	[6]	[5]	[4]	[3]	[2]	[1]
42.	There is a good deal of disagreement, even some fighting, between various people in this organization.	[1]	[2]	[3]	[4]	[5]	[6]	[7]
43.	In this organization, cooperation and getting along well are very important.	[7]	[6]	[5]	[4]	[3]	[2]	[1]
44.	People here are encouraged to speak their own minds, even if it means disagreeing with supervisors.	[7]	[6]	[5]	[4]	[3]	[2]	[1]
45.	The best way to make a good impression around here is to steer clear of open arguments, disagreements, and fights.	[1]	[2]	[3]	[4]	[5]	[6]	[7]

| 46. | Hardly a day goes by here without somebody arguing about something. | [1] | [2] | [3] | [4] | [5] | [6] | [7] |

Section 7.   [ORID]

		Very Definitely Describes ∇				Does Not Describe ∇		
47.	People are proud of belonging to this organization.	[7]	[6]	[5]	[4]	[3]	[2]	[1]
48.	In this organization people pretty much put their own interests above the good of other employees.	[1]	[2]	[3]	[4]	[5]	[6]	[7]
49.	There is a feeling of belonging to a team here.	[7]	[6]	[5]	[4]	[3]	[2]	[1]
50.	Management goes out of its way to make us feel an important part of this organization.	[7]	[6]	[5]	[4]	[3]	[2]	[1]
51.	I feel good about telling people where I work.	[7]	[6]	[5]	[4]	[3]	[2]	[1]
52.	This organization has trouble keeping good people.	[1]	[2]	[3]	[4]	[5]	[6]	[7]
53.	I would encourage anyone to work for this organization.	[7]	[6]	[5]	[4]	[3]	[2]	[1]
54.	When I tell people abut me, I often do so by describing my job.	[7]	[6]	[5]	[4]	[3]	[2]	[1]
55.	I am embarrassed to tell people where I work.	[1]	[2]	[3]	[4]	[5]	[6]	[7]

Section 8.   [APRAC]

		Very Definitely Describes ∇				Does Not Describe ∇		
56.	People here show routine or unimaginative thinking.	[₁]	[₂]	[₃]	[₄]	[₅]	[₆]	[₇]
57.	People here avoid responsibility and get away with it.	[₁]	[₂]	[₃]	[₄]	[₅]	[₆]	[₇]
58.	Management here rewards workers who come up with excellent ideas for making improvements or solving problems.	[₇]	[₆]	[₅]	[₄]	[₃]	[₂]	[₁]
59.	People here are not punished for making risky decisions that turn out to be wrong.	[₇]	[₆]	[₅]	[₄]	[₃]	[₂]	[₁]
60.	Achieving the goals of your unit by taking advantage of others in the section is common here.	[₁]	[₂]	[₃]	[₄]	[₅]	[₆]	[₇]
61.	Keeping costs down to the minimum and striving to reduce all expenses is the primary objective of management here.	[₁]	[₂]	[₃]	[₄]	[₅]	[₆]	[₇]
62.	Our managers encourage workers to come up with new ideas or recommendations for changes.	[₇]	[₆]	[₅]	[₄]	[₃]	[₂]	[₁]
63.	Failing to follow through on a commitment is typical behavior here.	[₁]	[₂]	[₃]	[₄]	[₅]	[₆]	[₇]
64.	Having an inquisitive mind and constantly questioning the how and why of things describes the people working here.	[₇]	[₆]	[₅]	[₄]	[₃]	[₂]	[₁]

Section 9.   [VALUES]

		Very Definitely Describes ▽				Does Not Describe ▽		
65.	Everyone who works here knows about and fully understands the organization's code of ethical conduct.	[7]	[6]	[5]	[4]	[3]	[2]	[1]
66.	Top management is sincerely committed to upholding the organization's code of ethical conduct.	[7]	[6]	[5]	[4]	[3]	[2]	[1]
67.	People working here are expected to follow their own ethical beliefs.	[1]	[2]	[3]	[4]	[5]	[6]	[7]
68.	Our code of ethical conduct effectively tells how to handle just about every situation encountered on the job.	[7]	[6]	[5]	[4]	[3]	[2]	[1]
69.	People working here are expected to do whatever it takes to further the organization's best interests.	[1]	[2]	[3]	[4]	[5]	[6]	[7]
70.	Our professional ethics code is upheld in all decisions.	[7]	[6]	[5]	[4]	[3]	[2]	[1]
71.	It is all right for people who work for the public to accept small gifts as tokens of gratitude for a job well done.	[1]	[2]	[3]	[4]	[5]	[6]	[7]
72.	Sometimes, even when rules are clear, it is best to do what you know is right (follow your conscience).	[1]	[2]	[3]	[4]	[5]	[6]	[7]
73.	When faced with making a decision, the first consideration should be whether it violates any law.	[1]	[2]	[3]	[4]	[5]	[6]	[7]

74.	Everyone here shares in the values spelled out in our organization's mission statement.	[7]	[6]	[5]	[4]	[3]	[2]	[1]
75.	We all believe in the same vision of the future that management has for our organization.	[7]	[6]	[5]	[4]	[3]	[2]	[1]

Note: The items in the following Sections 10 and 11 have not been tested or standardized. They are included here only as examples of items that might be included in a readiness-for-change section. Readers are encouraged to test the items for themselves. The items are in two sections: The first (PERREAD) section contains items to test the attitudes of individuals toward change. The second (ORGREAD) section contains items to evaluate the beliefs of individuals regarding their perceptions of the readiness of the organization to accept a change.

Section 10.   [PERREAD]

		Very Definitely Describes ∇						Does Not Describe ∇
76.	I look forward to helping in the effort to change our organization.	[7]	[6]	[5]	[4]	[3]	[2]	[1]
77.	Other workers in my work group often ask for my advice on issues regarding changes in our work.	[7]	[6]	[5]	[4]	[3]	[2]	[1]
78.	I no longer enjoy coming to work.	[1]	[2]	[3]	[4]	[5]	[6]	[7]
79.	I know exactly what my manager expects of me.	[7]	[6]	[5]	[4]	[3]	[2]	[1]
80.	I do not look forward to changing the way I do my work in the agency.	[1]	[2]	[3]	[4]	[5]	[6]	[7]
81.	The people I work with are supportive when our managers explain why the agency is undergoing a change.	[7]	[6]	[5]	[4]	[3]	[2]	[1]

82.	I understand why our organization needs to change the way we work.	[7]	[6]	[5]	[4]	[3]	[2]	[1]
83.	I don't think that we need any changes in our organization.	[1]	[2]	[3]	[4]	[5]	[6]	[7]
73.	I am considered an innovative leader in my work group.	[1]	[2]	[3]	[4]	[5]	[6]	[7]
84.	I look forward to coming to work in the morning.	[7]	[6]	[5]	[4]	[3]	[2]	[1]
85.	If I could, I would make big changes in our organization.	[7]	[6]	[5]	[4]	[3]	[2]	[1]

Section 11.   [ORGREAD]

		Very Definitely Describes ∇						Does Not Describe ∇
86.	The people in this organization are willing to put up with lots of uncertainty during a time of change in the agency.	[7]	[6]	[5]	[4]	[3]	[2]	[1]
87.	Our leadership rewards our efforts to transform the organization.	[7]	[6]	[5]	[4]	[3]	[2]	[1]
88.	Our highest-level managers are barriers to change in the organization.	[1]	[2]	[3]	[4]	[5]	[6]	[7]
89.	We are doing a good job of transforming the way we do things around here.	[7]	[6]	[5]	[4]	[3]	[2]	[1]
90.	The people I work with often tend to sabotage any effort to change the way we do things around here.	[1]	[2]	[3]	[4]	[5]	[6]	[7]
91.	The people in this organization know that big changes in the agency are needed immediately.	[7]	[6]	[5]	[4]	[3]	[2]	[1]

92.	My immediate supervisor is a strong supporter of efforts to transform the organization.	[7]	[6]	[5]	[4]	[3]	[2]	[1]
93.	All of us know exactly what we want this organization to be in the next 5 to 10 years.	[7]	[6]	[5]	[4]	[3]	[2]	[1]
94.	Our top leaders have done a good job of forming a strong team to lead change in the organization.	[7]	[6]	[5]	[4]	[3]	[2]	[1]
95.	The people in this organization don't seem to care about the vision our leadership has for the agency.	[1]	[2]	[3]	[4]	[5]	[6]	[7]
96.	Our organization seems to float along rudderless, with no clear goal or direction.	[1]	[2]	[3]	[4]	[5]	[6]	[7]
97.	Our organization is a leader when it comes to adopting new ideas and practices.	[7]	[6]	[5]	[4]	[3]	[2]	[1]
98.	Top management encourages people in the organization to try new ideas.	[7]	[6]	[5]	[4]	[3]	[2]	[1]
99.	Anyone trying to change the way we do things here is quickly rebuffed by our managers.	[7]	[6]	[5]	[4]	[3]	[2]	[1]
100.	People here recognize the critical urgency of changing the organization to meet the challenges and threats facing our agency's very existence.	[7]	[6]	[5]	[4]	[3]	[2]	[1]

Section 12. CLASSIFICATION ITEMS

ABOUT YOU [Record your answers in the space provided]
(For statistical purposes only—your responses will NOT be used to identify you to anyone in your organization)

101.	Your gender:	Male [₁]	Female [₂]				
102.	Years with this organization:	1–5 [₅]	6–10 [₄]	11–15 [₃]	16–20 [₂]	20+ [₁]	
103.	Highest level of education you have attained:	Graduate work or degree [₆]	4-year college degree [₅]	2-year college degree [₄]	Some college [₃]	High school graduate [₂]	Not a HS graduate [₁]
104.	How many supervisory training classes have you taken during the last 5 years?	None [₁]	1–2 [₂]	3–4 [₃]	5+ [₄]		
105.	Please indicate to which age group you belong.	24 yrs or younger [₁]	25–34 yrs [₂]	35–44 yrs [₃]	45–54 yrs [₄]	55 yrs or older [₅]	
106.	Do you have supervisory responsibility now?	Yes [₁]	No [₂]				
107.	If you answered YES to Question 106, how many years have you held a supervisory position? [Leave blank if answer to 106 was NO]	1–5 [₁]	1–10 [₂]	11–15 [₃]	16 + [₄]		

Constructs and Indices:

1. **STRUCTURE** (Items 1–10):

    This is the feeling that employees have about structural constraints in the organization. It includes such aspects as: how many rules, regulations, and procedures there are; whether "red-tape" hinders functioning of the organization; and whether employees must always go through channels for decisions or if the organization is characterized by a free-flowing informality.

2. **RESPONSIBILITY** (Items 11–17):

    This construct measures employee's feelings of being "their own boss," and of not being forced to double-check all decisions with higher authority. It closely follows the ideas of empowerment. It is also the feeling that an employee gets when, given a job to do, he or she knows that it is his or her job; the employee is not told how to do it.

3. **RISK** (Items 18–24):

    This construct assesses the sense of risks and challenges encountered in the organization. Is there an emphasis on taking calculated risks, or is "playing it safe" the best way to operate? Scoring leans toward the idea that organizations that support some degree of risk-taking are more vibrant places in which to work, and in consequence, tend to be more effective at achieving growth objectives.

4. **REWARDS** (Items 25–30):

    This construct measures employees' perceptions that they are equitably rewarded for a job well done. The emphasis in the organization is on positive rewards for personnel rather than punishments. Employees perceive that recognition, pay, and promotion policies are handled fairly and equitably.

5. **WARMTH & SUPPORT** (Items 31–39):

    This is the feeling of good fellowship that prevails in the work group's environment. Employees feel they are well liked and that management respects their skills and abilities, and that managers and other work-group members are helpful and supportive. Employees perceive that friendly formal and informal social groups prevail. There is an emphasis on mutual support from above and below.

6. **CONFLICT** (Items 40–46):

    This construct is based on the idea that some conflict in organizations is positive, in that it is equated with healthy competition. There is a feeling that managers and other workers want to hear different opinions and that workers are not expected to just "toe the party line." Management is interested in getting problems out in the open rather than smoothing them over or ignoring them.

7. **ORGANIZATIONAL IDENTITY** (Items 47–55):

This is the extent to which members of the group identify with the organization, their fellow workers, and with the underlying mission and philosophy of their work groups, larger units within the organization, and the organization as a whole. It is synonymous with "organizational commitment."

8. **APPROVED PRACTICES** (Items 56–64):

This construct addresses the perceived importance of implicit and explicit goals and performance standards. Is there an emphasis on doing a good job, or is doing the least work possible the way things are done? It also addresses the challenge represented in personal and group goals.

9. **ETHICS AND VALUES** (Items 65–75):

This construct specifically addresses shared values in the culture of the organization. It measures the extent to which members of the group believe that ethical principles are important to them personally, and whether they believe that the organization's core values and codes of conduct can and should be upheld in all circumstances. Does everyone endorse ethical courses of action, or does expediency rule?

Readiness Scales:

10. **PERSONAL READINESS FOR CHANGE** (Items 76–85):

This construct has been designed to provide insight into the attitudes and opinions of the individual workers in the organization regarding their willingness to accept a change initiative. In addition, the scale provides some introductory insight into the need for social network analysis.

11. **ORGANIZATIONAL READINESS FOR CHANGE** (Items 86–100)

This experimental scale is an early attempt in the process of developing a scale that can provide a benchmark metric for determining whether the organization is open to a change initiative. Low group mean scores on this and Scale 10 indicate a need for greater efforts to be expended in modifying the organization's culture.

12. **CLASSIFICATION ITEMS** (Items 101–107)

This construct includes several examples of optional demographic measurements.

Note 1: Constructs 10 and 11 are untested experimental tools included here for possible use in developing benchmark data for assessing individual and/or organizational change. Neither construct was included in previous organizational assessment applications. Neither scale has been tested for reliability or validity.

Note 2: Construct 12 in the instrument includes several examples of demographic measurements that may be added or deleted to meet specific evaluation objectives. Some demographic data are useful for analyzing and reporting findings.

Appendix B: URLs for Various Federal E-Government Transformation Reports

The Office of Management and Budget (OMB) FY2006 annual report to congress on the progress of 14 federal departments and 11 independent agencies, offices, or bureaus in implementing provisions of the E-Government Act of 2002 (OMB 2007). Individual agency E-Government Act reports can be accessed at the following URLs:

Organization	URL
Dept. of Commerce	http://www.osec.doc.gov/cio/oipr/egov_report_fy06.html
Dept. of Education	http://www.ed.gov/about/reports/annual/egov/status06.html
Dept. of Health and Human Services	http://www.hhs.gov/reference/HHSeGovAnnualReport2006.doc
Dept. of Homeland Security	http://www.dhs.gov/xfoia/editorial_0424.shtm
Dept. of the Interior	http://www.doi.gov/e-government/
Dept. of Justice	http://www.usdoj.gov/jmd/ocio/egovactreport2006.pdf
Dept. of State	http://www.state.gov/m/irm/rls/74822.htm
Dept. of the Treasury	http://www.treas.gov/offices/cio/egov/

Dept. of Veterans Affairs	http://www.va.gov/oit/
Environmental Protection Agency	http://www.epa.gov/oei/policies.htm
General Services Administration	http://www.gsa.gov/egovreport
National Aeronautics and Space Administration	http://www.nasa.gov/offices/ocio/home/index.html
Nuclear Regulatory Commission	http://www.nrc.gov/reading-rm/doc-collections/e-gov/index.html
National Science Foundation	http://www.nsf.gov/oirm/dis/FY06EGovReport10-20-06FINAL.pdf
Office of Management and Budget	http://www.whitehouse.gov/omb/organization/fy2006_e-gov_act_rpt.pdf
Office of Personnel Management	http://www.opm.gov/about_opm/10_18TokEGov_Report_2006.pdf
Social Security Administration	http://www.ssa.gov/irm/
U.S. Agency for International Development	http://www.usaid.gov/policy/egov/

Index